D1604036

Romantic Turbulence

ROMANTIC TURBULENCE

Chaos, Ecology, and American Space

ERIC WILSON

St. Martin's Press
New York

ROMANTIC TURBULENCE

ISBN 0-312-22882-1

Library of Congress Cataloging-in-Publication Data
Wilson, Eric, 1967-
Romantic turbulence : chaos, ecology, and American
space / Eric Wilson.
p. cm.
Includes bibliographical references and index.
ISBN 0-312-22882-1
1. American literature—19th century—History and
criticism. 2. Science in literature. 3. Romanticism—
United States. 4. Literature and science—United
States—History—19th century. 5. Nature in litera-
ture. I. Title.

PS217.S34 W55 2000
810.9'356—dc21   00-020514

I'd like to thank HBJ for the permission to use Ovid
and Penguin, Inc. for the permission to use Walt
Whitman.

Book design by Adam B. Bohannon

First edition: March 2000

10 9 8 7 6 5 4 3 2 1 0

FOR MY PARENTS,
Linda and Glenn

Contents

Acknowledgments

I am thankful to many people who helped me complete this book over the past five years. I owe special thanks to Philip Kuberski and James Hans; without their conversation and friendship, this book would not exist. I am also especially thankful for the guidance of my mentors at the Graduate Center of the City University of New York, where this book began: Joan Richardson, William Kelly, Joseph Wittreich, and Angus Fletcher. Enthusiastic thanks go to Allen Mandelbaum and Robert D. Richardson Jr., who have generously supported my intellectual pursuits over the past few years. I would like to extend special thanks to Marilyn Gaull as well, who has helped and encouraged me in numerous ways since I have known her. I have also appreciated very much my talks with Philip Arnold, who reminds me always that the physical world is enough.

Other colleagues and friends have assisted me in important and countless ways. I would like to thank Granville Ganter, Ralph Black, Ken Cooper, Terry Price, Laura Dassow Walls, and Michael Lopez for their perceptive conversation and kind encouragement. While my current colleagues at Wake Forest University and my former ones at St. John's University were all supportive of my labors, I owe special thanks to Nancy Cotton, William Moss, Barry Maine, Mary DeShazer, Dillon Johnston, Steve Sicari, John Lowney, and Greg Maertz. I would also like to thank Kristi Long, my editor at St. Martin's Press, for her expert assistance.

My heartiest appreciation goes to my parents, Glenn and Linda Wilson; they have made possible everything I've ever achieved. I would also like to offer enthusiastic thanks to Bill and Helen Hamilton, whose benevolence has been boundless.

Finally, and most importantly, I would like to thank Sandi Hamilton, whose unselfish support and perpetual generosity have been as unmerited as they have been unbelievable.

Sections of this book were originally published in different forms and under different titles in various scholarly journals: parts of "Emerson's Paralogical

Currents" appeared in *Mosaic* 33:1 (2000); "Melville and the Ungraspable Phantom," in *Colby Quarterly* 34:3 (1998); "Thoreau Over the Deep," in *Concord Saunterer* 6 (1998); "Whitman's Atoms," in *Arizona Quarterly* 55:3 (1999). My thanks to the editors of these journals for permission to reprint.

ABBREVIATIONS

CW Ralph Waldo Emerson, *The Collected Works of Ralph Waldo Emerson*, 5 vols. to date, eds. Robert Spiller, Joseph Slater, et al. (Cambridge, Mass. and London: Belknap Press of Harvard Univ. Press, 1971-).

EL Ralph Waldo Emerson, *The Early Lectures of Ralph Waldo Emerson*, 3 vols., eds. Stephen E. Whicher, Robert E. Spiller, and Wallace E. Williams (Cambridge, Mass.: Harvard Univ. Press, 1959-72).

EW Ralph Waldo Emerson, *The Complete Works of Ralph Waldo Emerson*, 12 vols., ed. Edward Waldo Emerson (Boston: Houghton Mifflin, 1903-4).

LG Walt Whitman, *Leaves of Grass: A Textual Variorum of the Printed Poems*, 3 vols., eds. Sculley Bradley, et al., *The Collected Writings of Walt Whitman* (New York: New York Univ. Press, 1980).

J Henry David Thoreau, *Journal*, ed. John C. Broderick (vols. 1-3) and Robert Sattelmeyer (vols. 4-), *The Writings of Henry David Thoreau* (Princeton: Princeton Univ. Press, 1981-).

JMN Ralph Waldo Emerson, *The Journals and Miscellaneous Notebooks of Ralph Waldo Emerson*, 16 vols., eds. William H. Gilman and Ralph H. Orth, et al. (Cambridge, Mass. and London: Belknap Press of Harvard Univ. Press, 1960-82).

MD Herman Melville, *Moby-Dick, or, The Whale*, eds. Harrison Hayford, Hershel Parker, and G. Thomas Tanselle (Evanston: Northwestern Univ. Press; Chicago: Newberry Library, 1988).

N Ralph Waldo Emerson, *Nature: A Facsimile of the First Edition*, intro. Jaroslav Pelikan (Boston: Beacon Press, 1985).

SD Walt Whitman, *Specimen Days*, ed. Floyd Stovall, *Prose Works*, *The Collected Writings of Walt Whitman* (New York: New York Univ. Press, 1963).

SL Margaret Fuller, *Summer on the Lakes, in 1843*, intro. Susan Balasco Smith (Urbana and Chicago: Univ. of Illinois Press, 1991).

SM Walt Whitman, "Song of Myself," *Walt Whitman's Leaves of Grass: The First (1855) Edition*, ed. Malcolm Cowley (New York: Penguin, 1959).

SS Johann Wolfgang von Goethe, *Scientific Studies, Goethe: The Collected Works*, vol. 12, ed. and trans. Douglas Miller (Princeton: Princeton Univ. Press, 1988).

W Henry David Thoreau, *Walden*, ed. J. Lyndon Shanley, *The Writings of Henry David Thoreau*, (Princeton: Princeton Univ. Press, 1971).

WC Henry David Thoreau, *A Week on the Concord and Merrimack Rivers*, ed. Carl F. Hovde, *The Writings of Henry David Thoreau* (Princeton: Princeton Univ. Press, 1980).

WN Margaret Fuller, *Woman in the Nineteenth Century*, ed. Larry J. Reynolds (New York: Norton, 1998).

Preface

For the past thirty-three years, the body of James H. Bedford has lain frozen in liquid nitrogen at 321 degrees below Fahrenheit. Diagnosed with cancer from which he would die in 1967, Bedford decided to fight death by becoming the first "cryonaut." Resting in his icy coffin, he awaits an ingenious doctor of the future to liberate him from his de-animation, to restore him to life, perhaps to grant him physical immortality. Perhaps he lapsed into darkness hoping it nothing more than a cold, brief sleep.[1]

A huge, hideous corpse lies on a primitive operating table. Rusty wires reaching from a portal in the ceiling are attached to its deformed body. Standing above the lifeless shape is Victor Frankenstein, pallid and fevered. He pulls an iron lever. The grinding of metal echoes through the laboratory. A current crackles through the wires. Flesh convulses. An eye opens, yellow. Horrified, Frankenstein flees.

These corpses—place them side by side in your mind—are emblems pointing to two different ways of apprehending the cosmos. The first, the actual Mr. Bedford, cryonically frozen and awaiting resuscitation when science finally vanquishes death, symbolizes the enduring vision of modernity, which arose in the seventeenth century with dreams of subduing nature to fit human desires. The second, the fictional monster of Mary Shelley, signals the dangers of altering the rhythms of nature, especially its primary polarity between life and death. It thus represents a more ecological *Weltanschauung*—humans best thrive by moving with the whorls in nature's grain.

Cryonics is indeed a synecdoche for all that's wrong with modernity, while the tale of the monster betokens the Romantic challenge to such excessive modifications of nature's economy. Certainly cryonics is an extreme example of what Max Weber has called the "disenchantment" of modernity, the reduction of the mysteries of life and death to predictable, controllable systems. According to Weber, Western thinkers since the seventeenth century have steadily convinced themselves that "the process of intellectualization" is the most effective mode for relating to the world. This increasing "rationalization" results in the following situation:

[T]here are no mysterious incalculable forces that come into play, but rather one can, in principle, master all things by calculation. This means that the world is disenchanted. One need no longer have recourse to magical means in order to master or implore the spirits, as did the savage, for whom such mysterious powers existed. Technical means and calculations perform the service.[2]

This "disenchantment of the world"—of which cyronics is a result—is the "fate of our times," bequeathed to us by the Protestant Reformation, a bizarre blend, Weber suggests, of humility and hubris, asceticism and arrogance. Weber believes that the Puritans inaugurated and exemplified the "rational mastery of the world" and its consequent "disenchantment" by combining "the rejection of the world" to its opposite, an "eagerness to dominate the world."[3] For the Puritan, the physical world is not intrinsically valuable but merely a visible reflection of God's laws. To know God, then, he must rationally pursue natural laws; to please God, he must systematically conform his life to these laws. Part of this endeavor is the methodological fulfillment of his earthly "calling": the Puritan must seek monetary profit in an orderly fashion, carefully and consistently renewing his worldly wealth. He accrues money, however, not to enjoy it but to make more, hoping that his financial success is a sign of his spiritual merit in eternity.[4]

Thus is born, according to Weber, modernity, in which the spirit of capitalism is inextricably linked to Christian transcendence and empirical science. All three ostensibly disparate modes combine to reduce the living qualities of nature to dead quantities. The capitalist turns beings into commodities and values them according only to their price in the market. The Puritan conceives of temporal events as measurable signs of God's rational laws. The positivistic scientist attends only to those occurrences that fit within his equations. What can be measured is significant; the immeasurable is anathema. Matter is not mysterious matrix but numerable mass.

William Bradford's *History of Plymouth Plantation* (1630-51), Sir Isaac Newton's *Opticks* (1704), Adam Smith's *The Wealth of Nations* (1776): these three unlikely texts result in Mr. Bedford waiting to vanquish death. While cryonics may seem to suggest the ultimate enchantment—a magical revival from death—it on the contrary points to utter disenchantment: the idea that the body is a mere machine that eventually runs out of fuel but can one day be refilled. Indeed, cryonics signals the most disturbing strains of modern disenchantment. It presupposes that natural processes, even death, are predictable and controllable, if only we have enough data. Neither life nor death is a mystery ultimately beyond our rational ken; rather, each is a mechanism we have not quite yet mastered. Moreover, the cryonics industry is thoroughly anthropocentric, assuming that if humans wish to live forever, they should be allowed to, regardless of what effect immortal people would have on an already overpopulated global environment. Further, the cryonaut would remove a primary pole of biological and psychological existence—death—forgetting that death is required for life to thrive and that finitude is very likely necessary for one's sense of identity and purpose.

Taken together, these elements of cryonics—different components of modernity taken to logical extremes—would likely result in ecological death. If life is severed from death, if creation is divided from destruction, if negentropy is divorced from entropy, if order is separated from chaos—then the cosmos will surely stiffen into stone. Indeed, our current ecological crises are certainly a consequence of the cryonic view: the urge for anthropocentric control and satisfaction, regardless of global impact, has severely damaged the rhythms of the environment. Soon winter may recede entirely before global warming, biodiversity may eventually dissolve into a human monoculture.

We realize the prophetic power of Shelley's novel, the first consideration of cryonics. Long before Weber's analysis of disenchantment (and before, I might add, Martin Heidegger's indictment of "calculation" and "Sputnik," Herbert Marcuse's lament over the "one-dimensional man," Evelyn Fox Keller's attacks on violent "masculine science," Jean-Francois Lyotard's critique of "totalization," Ken Wilber's depiction of "flatland"[5]), Shelley presciently reveals the result of a non-polarized cosmos: an ice age. Her choice to end her tale in the North Pole suggests that when one antinomy vanquishes its necessary opposite—when life overcomes death, when order annihilates chaos—ice whitens the entire landscape, reducing difference to the same. The death of dying is the dying of life.

Mr. Bedford, frozen, dreams of Bacon, Newton, and Laplace liberating his bodily machine from the snares of biology; the monster fades into the North Pole while he yearns for living polarities—fire and ice, creation and destruction. The cryonaut is ostensibly a Romantic hungering for immortality but really a mechanist loving control over chance, system over chaos; the deformed wretch is seemingly a perversion of modern science but actually a Romantic hero, desiring to embrace the difficult conflicts of life: reason and emotion, female and male. The cryonic specimen constitutes a potential Lazarus of the cult of reason, a holy saint of rational control; the new Adam points to an innocence that is not Eden but biological rhythm, time unfolding in a dance of death and life, cosmos and chaos.

Romantic Turbulence is a tale of two corpses, a contrast between a specimen whose physical immortality is eternal death and an organism whose tragic death lives as an ecological parable. On the one hand, the book examines the destructive results of viewing the universe as a machine that excludes the immeasurable, the mysterious, and the chaotic in favor of measure, certainty, and system. On the other, it explores the idea that the cosmos is a living organ—a form of an abysmal, irreducible source of life, a polarized dance of limit and the sublime, of mystery and clarity, of law and chance.

I concretize this general contrast—not a novel one but certainly (still) a neglected one—by examining in new light some of Mary Shelley's Romantic contemporaries and successors. Traditionally, Romantic thinkers have been read as if they were early cryonauts: idealists who wish to transcend the pain and struggle of time to acheive a realm of infinity and immortality. Certainly, the great Romantics of Germany, England, and America often lament their wounds from the thorns of life and pine for what is not. However, they also realize that abrasions and dying evergreens are necessary for the biological rhythm of life. Indeed—and this is the primary and most revisionary argument of my book—frequently key Romantic figures embrace the turbulence of the temporal world, understanding that coherent patterns emerge only from turbid energies, that order arises from and is dependent upon chaos.

The Romantic figures that I study, then, often take a middle path. They do not reject science for poetry, reason for emotion, order for chaos. Rather, they attempt to poeticize science and scientize poetry—to study nature to discover organic forms and aesthetic patterns; to write poetry that reveals the undulations of the cosmos. They try to strike a balance between rational inquiry into the world outside of their skin, and emotional sympathy with the life that permeates and unifies inside and outside, subject and object. They search for stable laws but suspect that stability is always temporary—a fleeting wave on the turbulent matrix of life.

So—and this is another important argument of this book—certain Romantics don't reject science outright but rather employ it to re-enchant the cosmos, to feel the pulse of life. The Romantics I study are versed in the scientific information of their day, which they employ to gain a deeper understanding of the patterns of nature. However, they are not mere positivists: they generally relate to scientific data as Dante associated with Virgil—as helpful guides to the ultimate mystery that springs beyond empirical sight and discursive reason. For these Romantics, science divorced from gnosis is vapid; rational inquiry separated from ethics and poetry is worthless.

Attending to how these Romantics study the abyss of life and its polarized forms with the aid of science, I am inevitably concerned with ecology—in organic unity and diversity, in living wholes and parts. On one level, I study the ways in which certain Romantics struggle to overcome the anthropocentric strains of modernity and alternatively to celebrate their place as part of a larger whole. On another, I am interested in how this ecological tendency affects aesthetic endeavors, the *logos* (the word) of the *oikos* (home). In exploring this second, stylistic dimension, I offer novel readings of major Romantic texts, demonstrating how polarized words participate in the undulations of the woods.

Because of this ecological element of the book, I have found it fruitful to focus more on American Romantics than European ones. I have chosen this emphasis not because American Romantics are necessarily more ecological than their European predecessors. Rather, I have opted to stress Americans because of their landscape. Unlike European Romantics, American Romantics were forced to contend with an environment almost entirely devoid of Western culture—a bare habitat that perpetually challenged anthropocentrism, that threatened with annihilation. This cultural emptiness of the American wild (void of *European* culture; Native American culture was rich) did not enrage American Romantics into transforming unruly forests into stable cities—as it did their Puritan forebears. Instead, American space inspired Romantic writers to rethink traditional Western visions of nature, primarily Enlightenment ones, and to forge new, pragmatic ways of seeing, naming, and acting on the woods, plains, and rivers.

In sum, in *Romantic Turbulence*, I study a neglected tendency in Romantic thought and art: the embrace of an unruly abyss of life as the origin of living polarities—of turbid power and cogent form. I attempt to show how this vision of an agitated *kosmos*—achieved with the aid of scientific inquiry and information—is related to an ecological *ethos* and *logos*—an effort to participate in the pulses of nature in deed and word. More specifically, I argue that a primary source of this "chaosmic"[6] ecology is Goethe, who combines science and poetry in his soundings of the mystery of life. On an even more concrete level, I contend that while Goethe's vision of the living abyss and its visible polarities is an important current in European Romanticism, it finds especially powerful patterns in the wilds of America. I show how Emerson, Fuller, Melville, Thoreau, and Whitman—inspired by the insights of Goethe and other scientists—attempt to relinquish the Western rage for order and alternatively to sound the abysmal spaces of their habitat, hoping to channel its boundless forces into their turns and tropes.

Given the turbulent, heterogeneous nature of my content, my theoretical and methodological dispositions in this book are appropriately fluid and diverse. Following the important advice offered by Morse Peckham some thirty years ago, I do not offer a static theory of Romanticism—I do not try to decide what Romanticism *is* as a stable concept, a coherent *Weltanschau-*

ung. Rather, like Peckham, I study a Romantic *situation*—a set of concrete conditions and problems faced by intellectuals roughly during the first half of the nineteenth century.[7] Firmly focused on how certain Romantics labor to overcome metaphysical desire and instead to embrace physical turbulence, I must necessarily admit that Romanticism is many disparate things at once: Platonism, Christianity, idealism, empiricism, organicism, ecology, to name only a few (later we shall see that Romanticism is also a Gnosticism and perhaps a Western version of Zen Buddhism). A. O. Lovejoy was probably right back in 1924: it is impossible to reach a stable definition of Romanticism.[8] This is no reason to despair. Rather, we can see Romanticism as we would a thriving rain forest—as a complex, diverse ecosystem.

My study reflects this theoretical diversity. Though I focus primarily on the turbulent ecological current—basically ignored—in certain Romantics, I also draw indirectly from several of the more famous and lasting theories of European Romanticism. For instance, I am indebted to Jacques Barzun (Romanticism is a realism, an embrace of the immediate situation, a biological revolution); René Wellek (Romanticism is organicism); Mario Praz (Romanticism is a struggle with dejection, limitation, dark moods); Morse Peckham (Romanticism involves the recognition of an unbridgeable gap between the coherent patterns of the human mind and an inaccessible, chaotic environment); and M. H. Abrams (Romanticism is a naturalization of Christian concepts). In a more direct way, I have relied on the recent and important studies of Romantic ecology by Karl Kroeber and Jonathan Bate. Each of these studies is groundbreaking, forging rich and startling new paths into the landscapes of Wordsworth and Percy Bysshe Shelley.[9]

I have also found helpful certain theories of American Romanticism, even though they do not focus on relationships between turbulence and ecology. Obviously, I am indebted to F. O. Matthiessen's still important study of the American Renaissance, which reminds us that one of the deepest concerns of Emerson and his contemporaries was how to live in the open air. I have also been influenced by more recent studies that have challenged Matthiessen's new critical harmonies. John T. Irwin, for instance, has brought post-structuralist theory to bear on the American Renaissance in his study of Egyptian hieroglyphics, in which he reveals connections between writing and indeterminacy, primarily in Edgar Allan Poe. Richard Poirier and Stanley Cavell have also problematized Matthiessen. Poirier has demonstrated the pragmatic tendencies in Emerson (and indirectly in Emerson's circle), focusing on ways that Emerson embraces agitation and vagueness as inspirations for thinking and writing. Cavell has treated the American Romanticism of Emerson and Thoreau as a major philosophical current—one that responds to skepticism not by avoiding it in metaphysical flights but by placing it at the core of thought in order to keep meditation mobile, alive. Even more recently, Lawrence Buell's volume on Thoreau and the ecological imagination has established the central place of the environment in American literature; Laura Dassow Walls's study of Thoreau's science has suggested neglected empirical currents in other American Romantics; Lee Rust Brown's book on Emerson has defined American Romanticism as a practical, scientific pursuit of an inaccessible whole; and Michael Lopez's meditation on Emerson and power—in which he shows that Emerson shares fundamental affinities with Nietzsche and James—has opened up avenues for considering the embrace of physical power in Fuller, Melville, Thoreau, and Whitman.[10]

My inclusive, rather eclectic theory of Romanticism is matched by my interdisciplinary methods. My assumption is that it is reductive and perhaps impossible to read Emerson, Fuller, Melville, Thoreau, and Whitman only as poets: they are also philosophers and scientists. They are of course not professional, systematic philosophers or institutionalized, positivistic scientists. Rather, they are what might well be called cosmologists: thinkers who yearn to know immediately the universe—its laws scientifically, its meanings philosophically, and its aesthetic patterns poetically. Indeed, for these and other Romanic figures (primarily Goethe), science, philosophy, and poetry are inseparable, different aspects of the same holistic vision.

Given the eclecticism of these American Romantics, I explore them from several scientific and philosophical angles. For instance, I draw from the biology and physics of Goethe; the electrochemistry and electromagnetism of Humphry Davy and Michael Faraday; the cosmology of Alexander von Humboldt; the evolutionary theory of Charles Darwin. Likewise, I invoke the philosophical perspectives of Thales, Heraclitus, Plato, Lucretius, Goethe, Nietzsche, and Heidegger.

Considering relationships among poetry, science, philosophy, and ecology, I have also found it helpful to invoke the work of several recent interdisciplinary theorists. To elucidate connections between order and chaos, I have drawn from the work of Michel Serres, Ilya Prigogine and Isabelle Stengers, and David Bohm. In drawing distinctions between Platonic and ecological tendencies in the writers I study, I have found help in the nomadology of Gilles Deleuze and Felix Guattari, who distinguish between thinker as engineer yearning for stasis and thinker as nomad moving with the pulses of the landscape. Likewise, I have also used Richard Rorty's important division between the "systematic" philosopher who wishes to freeze the world in static concepts and the "edifying" thinker who participates in an open-ended universe by engaging in perpetual conversation.

As is the case with all books, some caveats are in order. First of all, I should be clearer about how I mean "Newtonianism," "Platonism," and "Christianty." Throughout, I basically follow Goethe, Blake, and Coleridge in focusing primarily on those aspects of Newton (and the Enlightenment) that inaugurate Weber's "modernity"—that is, on those elements of Newton's science that emphasize mechanism, predictability, and quantity. I realize, of course, as did Wordsworth, P. B. Shelley, and Emerson, that there is much more to Newton than these negative qualities. (For instance, one can easily find affinities between Newton and Boehme, Newton and Romantic pantheism, and Newton and hermetic alchemy.[11]) I don't mean to suggest that Newton and the Enlightenment are entirely negative forces—of course they are not; I simply mean to follow Romantic representations of Newton and eighteenth-century positivism. Likewise, I often use "Platonism" and "Christianity" in similarly reductive ways, invoking them as worldviews that value spirit over matter, eternity over time, and order over chaos. Again, I don't mean to claim that these two rich traditions are *merely* flights from temporal turbulence and that they are *always* pernicious to ecological thinking. In casting these two important modes in largely negative lights, I am simply adhering to the obvious fact that the Platonist and the Christian is necessarily interested in soul more than body, heaven more than earth.

I should also address the issue of God. While the Romantics that I consider persistently invoke a deity in their works, I rarely mention God in my analyses. The reason I exclude the concept of God is to avoid confusion. Since the mention of "God" in the West generally conjures the deity of the Judeo-Christian tradition and since the deity worshipped by the writers I consider is *not* Judeo-Christian, I thought it best to find alternative terminology about the sacred. As I suggest throughout, for the ecological Romantics I consider, "god" is not a divine lawgiver but rather an intelligent abyss—both lawful and random—that generates, sustains, and organizes the polarized forms of the cosmos. If I were to define the "religion" of these Romantics, I would have to say it's a blend of Gnosticism and pantheism—a belief in an unknowable, abysmal god that is continuous with nature. As is the case with most of the major ideas of this book, Goethe is the exemplar. As he writes in an 1828 letter, his "religion" has always tended toward a "pantheism," based on the "thought that what meets us in the world springs from an unfathomable, limitless, humorous, self-contradictory being" who proceeds by playing an earnest game (*SS* 6). Emerson's unruly deity is similar: it is a "light, unsystematic, indomitable," "young and joyful, million-orbed, million-colored" [that] will break into any cabin" just as it beamed "over the universe . . . on the first morning" (*CW* 2:45-6). As for Fuller's god: in *Sum-*

mer in the Lakes, in 1843, she suggests that nature is a work-in-progress produced by an endlessly scrawling sketch artist (*SL* 5). In *Moby-Dick*, Melville suggests that divinity is Leviathan—contradictory, ungraspable, unpredictable, paradoxical, vortical, alive. Thoreau's god in *Walden* is an "Artist" who plays in the mud in the springtime, randomly strewing the muck into new forms (*W* 306). Whitman's deity is a loving bedfellow who occasionally drops in for a nocturnal visit, erotic in tone, and leaves behind bulging baskets of bread; he lives in the aroma of armpits and morning glories (*SM* 3:51-3, 24:526-9; 24:551). In sum, while each of these Romantics, fundamentally shaped by his or her Judeo-Christian unbringing, still believes in some sort of spiritual power, this power is known only through nature and is as chaotic as it is ordered.

I should also account for exclusions. Why have I not included Hawthorne and Poe in this study of American Romanticism? Primarily because of the ecological emphasis of my book. Though Hawthorne is an astute critic of the excesses of modern science, he remains much more interested in the human heart—primarily its Calvinistic struggles with sin—than in relationships between humans and nature. Poe is a more difficult case. Certainly he, too, is a powerful critic of unfettered positivistic reason (*vide* the Dupin of the detective tales, the narrator of "MS Found in a Bottle"). Likewise, he is a sounder of abysses, notably suggesting in *The Narrative of Arthur Gordon Pym* (1838) that the origin and end of life may be a watery deep. Moreover, he is a poetic cosmologist, in *Eureka* (1848) synthesizing Kepler, Laplace, and Humboldt into a grand vision of an aesthetic universe. On the surface, it seems that he would be a prime exemplar of the ideas I explore in this study. However, Poe, it seems to me, is, like Hawthorne, more interested in psychic dispositions than in physical ones: his landscapes are almost entirely symbolic of unconscious and conscious aspects of a self. Moreover, as he himself claims in "The Philosophy of Composition" (1846) and "The Poetic Principle" (1848-9; 1850), he is more interested in poetic beauty than in scientific truth, more eager to transcend time to eternal harmony than to engage immanent temporal currents. Even his "scientific" cosmology, *Eureka*, is more committed to the harmony of beauty than the energy of matter: a "true" theory exhibits the "consistency" of a poem; the cosmos is the simplicity and unity of God diffusing itself into complexity and diversity only to return again to the first harmony.

One might further want to know why Emily Dickinson is not a part of this book. Certainly, Camille Paglia, Joanne Feit Diehl, and Margaret Homans have convincingly argued that Dickinson is a Romantic figure.[12] I agree. In fact, almost up until press time, I was going to include a chapter on

Dickinson. However, the more I thought about her verse, the more I realized that her major concerns were beyond the scope of this book. Though Dickinson is certainly interested in the abyss (usually figured as circumference) and has many interesting things to say about positivistic science (as Daniel Orsini, Richard B. Sewall, and I respectively have shown[13]), she, like Poe and Hawthorne, finally seems more interested in the interiors of the psyche than in the exteriors of nature. Though she persistently meditates on birds, insects, stones, storms, and flowers, she primarily uses these natural phenomena as symbols for mental or emotional states.

But there is another, perhaps deeper reason why I did not include my chapter on Dickinson—her extreme skepticism. While the Romantics I study in this book are skeptical toward absolute orders, they are quite optimistic, indeed idealistic, about the healing powers of the living abyss. I rarely find this optimism in Dickinson. When I add to this her powerful meditations on death, limitation, and pain, I wonder if she is more a Modernist poet with Romantic elements than a Romantic one with Modernist aspects, closer to T. S. Eliot and Wallace Stevens than to her nineteenth-century contemporaries.

Finally, some readers might argue that my book "totalizes" the five writers it considers, that it melds diverse writers into static unity. If valid, this would be a powerful critique indeed since this book is a statement in favor of heterogeneity over totalization. Certainly readers might question my comparisons. It has long been a commonplace of American studies that Melville diverged aggressively from Emerson, openly satirizing him *The Confidence Man* (1857).[14] Likewise, as Christina Zwarg has shown, Fuller's feminist struggles significantly separate her from the "Emersonian," male canon of the "American Renaissance."[15] Other divisions have largely been agreed upon: Whitman breaks from Emerson in his emphasis on the body and *eros*; Thoreau diverges from the abstract theorizing of the Concord sage in his strict observations of nature.[16]

Facing these undeniable differences, how, then, someone might ask, can one argue that these five writers share a common cosmology, ethic, and poetics? I can make such an argument for at least three reasons. One, the "Emersonian" tendencies that I locate in these other four writers are not necessarily their defining traits—these tendencies are important trends, drifts, and currents that have been largely neglected. The differences, in other words, between and among these figures are valid; they simply do not tell the entire story. Two, the recurring elements I reveal do not take the same form in each writer. While certain motifs recur in all five figures, these themes take different patterns in each, based on divergent inflections and distinct contexts—electricity and physics in Emerson becomes water and biology in Thoreau becomes the rhizome and Lucretian atomism in Whitman. Put another way, I focus as much on diversity as unity, as much on heterogeneity as homogeneity. The book is polarized like its subject matter. Three, though I explore similar themes in each chapter, the study is not merely synchronic. It features a diachronic element as well: as the American nineteenth century unfolds, its Romantic writers become increasingly turbulent. Emerson, Fuller, and Melville struggle mightily between the poles of Plato and Nietzsche, laboring to relinquish metaphysical desire and to embrace the pulses of *physis*. Thoreau the practicing biologist struggles less, is better adapted to the sun fish than the Neoplatonic Sun. Whitman—the lover of unfettered motion, glistening bodies, and erotic hum—is even less troubled by a yearning to transcend temporality, happier in mud time. In other words, while I continually return to similar themes, I am also aware of historical differences.

In the introduction, "Houses Founded on the Sea," I lay out the primary themes of this book, invoking Goethe as a rich exemplar and illustrating how his persistent ideas inform key currents in European Romanticism. I suggest that while Goethe's presence in American Romanticism is considerable, American Romantics differ from their German predecessor in degree. While they share with Goethe a belief that life emerges from a turbulent abyss, that this abyss thrives in polarized forms, and that one apprehends this abyss and its patterns through a scientific gnosis, they diverge from him in their struggle to achieve this ecological vision in a landscape largely devoid of cultural comforts, a wilderness constantly threatening anthropocentric desire.

In the first chapter, "Emerson's Paralogical Currents," I revise traditional readings of Emerson as a representative of the transcendentalist sublime by showing how his attention to the science of Davy and Faraday revealed to him a physical sublime. The world picture offered by these scientists suggested to Emerson that nature resists unity, that it is paralogical: both stable matter and polarized energy. I demonstrate how Emerson struggles between the transcendental and paralogical sublime in *Nature*. While Emerson in theory extols a transcendental harmony, in stylistic practice he perpetually dissolves order into chaos. I employ the work of several recent philosophers of science, including Serres, Prigogine, Lyotard, and Bohm, to illuminate Emerson's polarities.

In "Fuller's Metamorphoses," I show how Fuller struggles in *Woman in the Nineteenth Century* between the stable orders of Plato and the disturbing transformations of Ovid. Fuller sometimes views the changes in nature as temporal unfoldings of a static, ideal form, and other times sees natural metamorphoses as unsystematic, agitated, and polarized processes. While the former paradigm precludes real change, the latter—which shares important affinities with Goethe's cosmology—ensures that actual revolution can occur and thus vouchsafes a potential overturn of patriarchy. I argue that Fuller in *Summer on the Lakes* resolves this *agon* by leaving Plato behind for Ovid. On the vast prairies of the Midwest, Fuller becomes a wilderness philosopher, a poet of waterfalls and whirlpools.

"Melville and the Ungraspable Phantom" draws from philosophers—Heraclitus, Nietzsche, Heidegger, and Deleuze and Guattari—and scientists—Goethe and Darwin—to examine the primary antagonism in *Moby-Dick*: between nomad and pilgrim. I treat this antagonism as an essential structuring device. "Ishmael: nomad" and "Ahab: pilgrim" organize several oppositions that produce meanings on cosmological, philosophical, mythological, imagistic, and narrative levels. These pattern tensions between the following: organ and machine, evolution and essentialism, Heraclitus and Plato, spiral and line, recursivity and discursivity. Throughout his novel, Melville referees this battle between nomad and pilgrim, in the apocalyptic finale celebrating the victory of Ishmael.

In "Thoreau Over the Deep," I focus on Thoreau's Thalesian cosmology, in which life is aqueous, physical, and agitated. Unearthing this neglected tendency in Thoreau, I show how *A Week on the Concord and Merrimack Rivers* and *Walden* are frequently overwhelmed by water, in both form and content. Both texts often assert that liquid—rivers, ponds, mud—is the labile source of life and embody these aqueous currents in slippery language. These books, I argue, point to Thoreau's late essay "Walking," in which he claims that the mucky swamp is the source of wilderness, the origin of life.

"Whitman's Atoms" shows how Whitman revolts against essentialist philosophies in his 1855 "Song of Myself" by subscribing to the atomism of Lucretius. Whitman in this poem inflects Lucretius's philosophy through his love of motion, energy, and potential to uproot the radicle symbols of idealist thought—plant, leaf, tree, parts controlled by a whole—and to replace them with Deleuze and Guattari's radical rhizomes: heterogeneous, shifting, unstable gatherings—fields of grass. I further illuminate Whitman's unsettling vision by invoking the fluxional psychology of William James.

Finally, in a brief epilogue, "Clouds Over the Ocean" I meditate on how Romantic turbulence flourishes in C. S. Peirce's clouds and clocks and William James's streams and currents.

Introduction
Houses Found on the Sea

Hurrying over these Abysses

On October 5, 1847, Emerson shipped on the *Washington Irving*, bound for Liverpool, where he would begin a lecture tour in England, including a series entitled "Representative Men." This was only his second voyage beyond the sight of land, his inaugural one taking place in 1832-3, when he sailed to Europe as a young man on a Romantic *Bildungsreise*. Now wiser and sadder than in those days of pure possibility, Emerson still felt the excitement of the waves. A few days from the ports of Boston, he mused in his journal on the contradictory feelings inspired by the deeps: "There is at least this pleasure in hurrying over these abysses that whatever dangers we are running into, we are certainly running out of risks of hundreds of miles every day which have their own chances of squall, collision, sea-stroke, piracy; cold, thunder, & the rest" (*JMN* 10:204). While one may be anxious about the perils of the sea, one is also exhilarated by the abyss, feeling in every well-turned rise and plunge the joy of escaping injury, the pleasure of living. Perhaps this sense that insecurity inspires vigor led Emerson a short time later (while still under sail) to mediate on relationships between opposites: "For great power, great body also. You must draw on the extremes. Before concentration, there must be sleep" (*JMN* 10:204). With waves rising and falling all around him, Emerson no doubt saw the virtue in polarized rhythms—the strife between opposing tendencies is creative, making turbulent yet beautiful patterns. As the sea, so the man: intellectual force is dependent upon bodily health. Extremes are not separate and at war but complementary, and interdependent.

Perhaps these ostensibly inconsequential reflections on the abyss, power, and polarity took on profound significance some months later, in April, when Emerson, now on British soil and enjoying literary success, went to hear Michael Faraday lecture. Emerson had admired Faraday for years, often praising the scientist's discovery of electromagnetic induction and his corollary theory that matter is not solid and discrete but rather a polarized field of force. Indeed, Emerson in 1833 even wondered if Faraday's discovery of the "identity of electricity & magnetism" had opened "a door to the secret

mechanism of life & sensation" (*JMN* 4:94).[1] Sitting before Faraday, a noto-
riously galvanizing speaker, Emerson was no doubt struck again—perhaps
more deeply than before—by Faraday's primary discovery, which Emerson
recorded in his journal around the time he heard Faraday lecture: "there [is]
no ultimate atom, only forces" (*JMN* 10:225). The universe, as Faraday again
revealed to Emerson from the podium, is a plenitude of boundless electrical
force cohering into polarized bundles of energy. These bundles combine to
make things and organs, each of which is discrete and distributed, turbulent
power and cogent form. Perhaps, as Faraday described this cosmos, Emerson's mind wandered back to the sea where he himself had pondered some
months before a fathomless abundance of water, a source of life shaping
itself into undulating swells.

With these profound thoughts no doubt troubling his sleep but vivifying
his dreams, Emerson was himself electrifying British audiences with his
utterances on Plato, Swedenborg, Montaigne, Shakespeare, Napoleon, and
Goethe. In a striking passage from his lecture on Montaigne, published in
essay form two years later, Emerson brings to light what must have been his
unconscious depths.

> The philosophy we want is one of fluxions and mobility. The Spartan
> and Stoic schemes are too stark and stiff for our occasion. A theory of
> Saint John, and of nonresistence, seems, on the other hand, too thin
> and aerial. We want some coat woven of elastic steel, stout as the first,
> and limber as the second. We want a *ship* in these billows we inhabit.
> An angular, dogmatic house would be rent to chips and splinters, in
> this storm of many elements. No, it must be tight, and fit to the form
> of man, to live at all; as a shell is the architecture of a house founded
> on the sea. The soul of man must be the type of our scheme, just as
> the body of man is the type after which a dwelling-house is built.
> Adaptiveness is the peculiarity of human nature. We are golden aver-
> ages, volitant stabilities, compensated or periodic errors, houses
> founded on the sea. (*CW* 4:91)

Emerson translates Faraday's science into a philosophy of the sea. Life, he
realizes, is not a matter of stable order; nor is it to be found in heaven. It is
here, careening through our veins, comprised of potent currents. It is a "billows," a "storm of many elements," a "sea." Philosophies that believe otherwise are not only wrong, they also alienate the fluxes of life and are therefore
on the side of death. Stoics, for example, hold that the cosmos is rational and
that conformity to this universe leads to truth and goodness. However, our

"occasion" in the world is too tumultuous for such well-appointed schemes. Christians like St. John also espouse harmony, discovered not on earth but only in heaven. They would have us transcend the tides of time to an ethereal realm. Yet, to reject the pulses of nature is to be anemic. To *live*—to thrive *with* the whorled grains of the world (not *against* them or *above* them)—is to take the middle way between the stiff laws of the rationalist and the ghostly shapes of the saint.

Emerson has clearly experienced a *gnosis*, a flash of immediate knowing. Whether while on the waves or in the lecture hall or over a dream, he has recognized an unsettling fact that most thinkers have ignored or repressed: *chaos is the muse of life.* While most philosophers in the West have held to the mechanisms of the Stoics, based on logical theories, or latched onto the heavens of the apostles, grounded on faith, Emerson calls us to circulate with the labile energies of the earth, to *experience* its oscillating patterns in our bellies and brains. He revives, in other words, the watery abyss of Genesis—the "deep" "void," the "earth without form"—and restores it to its rightful place as the origin of the living universe. The Bible would have us believe that Yahweh in the beginning conquers this boundless deep, dividing it into superior light and inferior darkness, noble order and evil chaos, pristine heaven and muddy earth. However, Emerson counters: Yahweh is lying, for the original chaos persists in its turbulence, thriving in bipolar rhythms—pulsating between day and night, cacophony and harmony, thought and action. Emerson would have us break through Yahweh's deceptions and to return to the deep to embrace its living orders: ripples, billows, foam; shells, roses, zebras.

To experience these currents, the thinker must find a median between alienating modes of thought, between the Stoical science that would control the billows and the saintly religion that would transcend them. Merging the activity of the Stoic and the passivity of the saint, this middle way draws from the integrity of "steel" and the pliability of "elastic." It enables one to move through the waters of life like a "ship," directing and yielding to the flows. It is like a "shell," a convoluted form, a tension of centripetal and centrifugal directions. To follow this course—to participate consciously in the nature that animates unconscious processes anyway—one must embody the ocean, move with the breakers. That is, one must gather antagonistic forces, become a living coil: a "golden" average, a "volitant" stability, a "compensated or periodic" error, a house "founded on the sea."

Emerson's revision of Genesis—also a rewriting of Newton's cosmology (the universe is comprised of atoms moving mechanically in a void)—was likely missed by his British listeners and overlooked by his American readers. Certainly, the "Sage of Concord," the great Neoplatonic optimist, could not really mean that order without chaos is dead, that life thumps and thwacks in waves and lightning. Indeed, wasn't this Emerson, the arch transcendentalist, who persistently intoned that the universe quenches our idealist yearnings? Perhaps so, but here was also a vigorous Emerson, disturbing force that most of his readers and auditors failed (and have failed) to register. Call it Emerson's alter ego, his unconscious, his *anima*. However it is named, this agitated Emersonian current always runs under his more comforting deliberations, a deep physical power from which his ethereal harmonies arise.

Accordingly, Emerson's "mobile," "fluxional" strain—his embrace of physical turbulence as the source of life, his rejection of abstract stability as a condition of death—is the primary subject of this book. I attempt to sound this largely neglected current not only in Emerson but also in his American Romantic contemporaries: Fuller, Melville, Thoreau, and Whitman. Each of these writers follows Emerson in viewing traditional modes of thought (characterized by Stoic rationalism and saintly transcendence) as alienating institutions, perversions of life. Struggling to reject the life-denying conventions of Western thought, each yearns for an alternative gnosis, an immediate insight into the *fullness* of life, its coherent patterns *and* its unruly energies. Gaining such a vision—often with the help of scientific facts—each of these thinkers essays to participate in the abyss of life by creating his or her own turbulent forms: perturbed turns, torqued tropes—*ecological* compositions.

Exploring these American Romantics from this angle, I have these goals. I hope to deepen our understanding of these writers by bringing to light overlooked levels of meaning, related to turbulence. I also wish to shed light on largely ignored elements of Romanticism—both American and European—such as the embrace of chaos as the necessary other of order and the use of science to sound a living abyss. Moreover, I hope to unveil important connections among conventionally disparate modes of thought, for instance, among Romantic philosophy, late eighteenth- and early nineteenth-century science, and Gnostic modes of vision. Further, I desire to explore organicism from fresh angles, swerving it from Neoplatonic harmonies and pantheistic unities and toward agitated processes. Finally, I want to reveal the virtues of Emerson's philosophy of "fluxions and mobility" for ecological modes of thinking, acting, and writing.

But before I turn to these American matters, I should return to the abyss to clarify and contextualize this apostate thinking.

Pascal's Exile

Taking the middle path between Stoic and saint, between turbulence and pattern, Emerson also strikes a median between heretical theology and positivistic science—that is, between the Gnostic, for whom salvation lies in the unknowable abyss, and the scientist of complexity, who believes that life emerges from chaos. Let's pause on these curious conjunctions.

According to Hans Jonas in *The Gnostic Religion* (1958), Gnosticism is a response to alienation from life, that is, from freedom and spontaneity. For Jonas, the Gnostic of the second and third centuries rebelled against the laws of Yahweh—an ignorant, tyrannical demiurge in Gnostic tradition—for the same reason that the Romantic railed against Newton: because this god, like Newton, had placed him in a cold universe in which men and mountains and waves are ultimately insignificant, only atomic bits held together and moved by unalterable, indifferent laws. As Pascal—a latter-day Gnostic and proto-Romantic—laments in his *Pensees* (1670), Newton's cosmos (like Yahweh's) is an icy void where laws blindly push brute matter, rendering human endeavors inconsequential and arbitrary. Lost and superfluous, men and women no longer enjoy a natural home but rather suffer solitary confinement in a "little prison-cell."[2]

Coincidentally, a Nobel laureate scientist writing in the late twentieth-century also draws from Pascal to detail the alienating factors of Newtonian (classical) science. While the physicist Ilya Prigogine, with his philosopher-colleague Isabelle Stengers, certainly is not a Gnostic anti-materialist or a Pascalian visionary, he feels that Newton's mechanistic cosmology divorces humans from the pulses of nature. In *Order Out of Chaos* (1984), he and Stengers wonder how humans can find meaning in a "random world of the atoms." For them, as for Pascal, classical science leads inevitably to a fundamental and depressing separation between human and cosmos: humans are strange ghosts in a grinding machine.[3]

The Gnostics (and Pascal) accept this rift between humans and nature as an inescapable cosmic fact, a situation that cannot be healed but that must be transcended—to a true home beyond matter organized by an *agnostos theos*. So claims the *Secret Book According to John* (ca. 180 C. E.), "one of the most classic narrations of the gnostic myth," an account of creation basically shared by Gnostics as various as Thomas, Valentinus, and Mani.[4] For the unknown author of this text, the origin of everything is not Yahweh but a radically transcendent power, an "immeasurable," "unfathomable," "unlimited," "invisible" void—a vast nothing. This "monad" cannot be conceived of in rational concepts or described in discursive language: "It is not corporeal, it is not *incorporeal*, it is not large, it is not small, it is *not* quantifiable, nor *is it* a *creature*.

Indeed, no one can *think of it.*" Out of this original mystery emanates several thoughts, or androgynous *aeons*, each of which is a unique manifestation of its source.[5] This source and its polarized outflows comprise the *pleroma*, the first fullness, an origin assumed by most every Gnostic myth.[6]

The second primary Gnostic assumption is that one of these *aeons*—generally Sophia—disrupts the eternal harmony, causing division, discord, and descent.[7] According to the *Secret Book*, this primal disruption—caused by some thoughtless error—produces an ignorant being (generally known as Ialtobaoth, the Gnostic name for Yahweh) who is exiled to an inferior material realm outside of the *pleroma*. Wallowing in matter, he stupidly believes he is the first and only god and proceeds to produce a cosmos, poorly modeled on the *pleroma*, of which he possesses a dim memory.[8] This universe is our own: grossly material instead of transcendently spiritual, divided and hierarchical instead of differentiated and polarized, ruled by an arrogant, stiff dictator instead of a supple, springing power.

Yet, there is hope. The eternals plant a divine spark (*pneuma*) in the humans suffering under the weight of matter. If this spark is ignited in a moment of vision, then its bearer becomes a Gnostic, realizing his true origin in the *pleroma* and his present exile in the world. Consequently, he rejects the rigid laws and oppressive hierarchies of the physical world, liberating his soul to the lithe abyss.[9] This third major Gnostic motif is rendered in John's *Secret Book* as a matter of enslavement and deliverance: while the descendants of Adam are imprisoned by the demiurge, the abyss perpetually sends emancipators to awaken people to freedom.[10]

Prigogine and Stengers, of course, disagree: human souls are not forever separated from dead nature, saved only by a transcendent, living abyss. Rather, recent studies of organic and inorganic complexity have shown that humans, nature, and life are continuous, joined by an *immanent* abyss, a vigorous chaos. Seeing through the illusory and divisive mechanisms of Newton (the scientific Ialtobaoth), scientists have proven that anxious, unpredictable humans are not separated from an indifferent, rigid machine. Rather, accident and turbulence generate a cosmos that includes humans: in open systems in far-from-equilibrium conditions—a category including most natural and human processes—chaos is *pervasive* and *creative,* originating novel orders, new lives.[11]

Prigogine and Stengers evidence this fact through their revision of traditional (fallen) interpretations of time. Like Gnostics opposing the cosmology of Genesis, they counter both classical reversible time—which is static and predictable—and thermodynamic dissipative time—which is running down toward total entropy, heat death. While Prigogine and Stengers maintain that time is irreversible, they suppose that entropy is *productive*, originating greater complexity and differentiation. Of course, post-Darwinian evolutionists have always maintained that chance mutations are primary catalysts of differentiation, change, and increasing complexity. But what about micro-processes? Are they also generated by random fluctuations? Yes. Any system in a state far from equilibrium—which is any system open to outside influences, existing outside the closed laboratory—eventually reaches a point at which entropy threatens the stability of the entire system. At this juncture, a "bifurcation point," the system leaps into a new form, organizing itself out of chaos in an entirely unpredictable fashion: minute changes can produce unpredictably large transformations. This novel organization, of course, often returns to a state of relative stability but, as it is open to flows from outside, it will again be threatened and possibly renewed by entropy. So, for Prigogine and Stengers, inorganic matter, living organisms, and human cultures are "dissipative structures," open systems dependent upon entropic flows from the outside for their existence.[12]

While Prigogine and Stengers admit that these insights are unsettling, they also submit that the chaotic universe is redemptive. Similar to the *pleroma*, chaos is the content of a scientific insight that reconnects alienated humans to a living world—that "re-enchants" human perspectives of the cosmos. While classical physics separates man and matter and while nineteenth-century thermodynamics envisions a dying universe, the science of dissipative structures discovers that humans and nature are connected. This insight into the polarized relationships between chaos and order not only reconciles humans and nature; it also encourages men and women to create their own fluctuations that may transform the world into a better place.[13]

In spite of obvious and uninteresting differences between Gnostic visionaries and scientists of complexity, one rich similarity remains: an unbounded, ultimately unknowable power is the source of life—the "abyss" and "chaos" are homologous. Indeed, etymologically, "abyss" and "chaos" are analogous. "Abyss" derives from the Greek *abyssos*, adjectivally "bottomless," substantively "the deep." The word's primary signification in English is "the primal chaos." Originating from the Greek *kao*, "chaos" in English betokens "a gaping void, yawning gulf, chasm, or abyss."[14] These verbal affinities are confirmed: just as the *pleroma* is beyond logic, reason, order, representation, so the complex processes that organize matter in open systems are unpredictable (illogical), spontaneous (arational), turbulent (disordered), and non-linear ("represented" only by non-linear equations that cannot be solved). In addition, for the Gnostic and the chaos theorist, an embrace of the abyss/chaos overcomes alienation from life. While each struggles against a different source of alienation—the Gnostic fights against the unjust laws and corrupt matter of an inferior God; Prigogine and Stengers labor against the mechanistic laws and blind atoms of Newton—each nonetheless engages a common human dilemma: life in death. This condition occurs when a person is only half alive, emphasizing one polarity at the expense of its opposite. For instance, while trapped in matter, the Gnostic must perpetually try to conquer his material parts with his spiritual forces. Likewise, the classical scientist severs order and chaos, valuing only predictability and stability, ignoring random factors and creative turbulence. In both cases, perverse hierarchies hold sway; separate powers are at perpetual odds. Redemption in each instance lies in differentiated polarity. The saved Gnostic returns to a *pleroma*, a hidden abyss that springs in contrary forms. The scientist thrives only when he renounces false divisions and realizes that cosmos arises from chaos.

Gnostic Ecology

The ancient Gnostics and recent chaos scientists occupy extreme ends of a spectrum of apostate thinking that values the abyss as much as its coherent patterns, that embraces imbrications of chaos and order. The Gnostics dwell on the immaterialist, intuitive end of the continuum: the abyss is anti-cosmic and immeasurable, understood only through revelation. Chaos scientists live on the materialist, positivistic side: the chaotic pulse of life is immanent, realized through scientific inquiry, calculable through probability mathematics. Lying between these two extremes are several other dissenting traditions and thinkers. Very close to the Gnostics, one would find the Hermeticists and Kabbalists. Closer to the middle, but still on the immaterialist portion, one would see the Renaissance *magi* (Paracelsus and Bruno) and Jacob Boehme. At the other end, close to Prigogine and Stengers, one would certainly find Werner Heisenberg and Niehls Bohr. More toward the middle, but still on the materialist side, one would also recognize Charles Darwin, Friedrich Nietzsche, and Carl Jung.

Almost exactly in the middle of this spectrum—in the center of this canon of perennial philosophers—one would certainly find Emerson and some of his European predecessors and American contemporaries. Taking a middle path between the Gnostics and the chaos scientists, the Romantics I have in mind attempt to marry transcendence and immanence, idealism and empiricism, gnosis and evidence, myth and science. Throbbing between Boehme and Nietzsche, these Romantics (like Goethe, Schelling, F. Schlegel, and Novalis in Germany; like Coleridge and Wordsworth in England; like the five Americans already mentioned) are Janus-faced.

One the one hand, they look back to Boehme, the purveyor of the "Pansophia," the universal science of the void, blending philosophy, theology, astrology, and alchemy. In the *Aurora* (1612), *Signatura Rerum* (1619-20), and *Mysterium Magnum* (1623), Boehme stares into the conflicts of nature and uncovers—in a moment of intuitive perception—a springing spiritual *Ungrund*. From this unconscious, capricious, dark abyss emerges a bipolar cosmos, opposing forces sporting all things into existence: free will and limiting desire, contraction and expansion, nothing and something, fire and light, male and female. These palpable polarities (always related by a third term: spirit) are the language, the music of the first nothing, distributing it through a cosmic epic, a symphonic universe. Everything is an Eolian Harp, sounding the origin with each new quiver.[15]

But, on the other hand, these Romantics look forward to Nietzsche, who in *Thus Spoke Zarathustra* (1883-5), *Ecce Homo* (1888-9; 1908), and *Will to Power* (1901), trades Boehme's immaterial *Ungrund* for physical chaos, the Dionysian force of life. This force is not blind but plays like an innocent child, perpetually creating and destroying forms, organizing itself into Apollinian appearances, dissolving again into evanescent flows. Yet, as Nietzsche learns in a flash of insight (reported in *Ecce Homo*), certain recurring patterns emerge from this flux: things eternally recur—the cosmos is a coincidence of being and becoming, law and chance. This interpretation of the universe in turn becomes Nietzsche's artistic inspiration: the Dionysian thinker participates in earthly energies by creating oscillatory texts—controlled accidents, organized fragments.[16]

Undulatory themselves, the Romantics I have in mind follow Boehme in locating life in an abyss that unfolds through strife; yet, they move toward Nietzsche in discovering this source in the physical world and in conjecturing that this source itself is comprised of material energies. Moreover, similar to Boehme, these Romantics don't think that this font can be registered through scientific method: it is apprehended through an intuitive vision. Yet, favoring Nietzsche, they maintain that this intuition comes only to the observer of phenomena who stares honestly at physical events. Finally, like Boehme, these Romantics look to nature for artistic inspiration, wishing to mimic the language of nature in their works. However, they point to the stylistic techniques of Nietzsche, channeling the billows of nature into unsettled compositions.

Gathering these poles, these Romantic writers practice what I would call *gnostic ecology*, ostensibly an oxymoron. "Gnostic" brings to mind visionaries who loathe matter; "ecology" elicits nature lovers. However, for the European Romantics I discuss in this introduction and in the American ones I examine in the chapters, the phrase is an important descriptor. The Romantics I consider are gnostics (I use lowercase to distinguish from the ancient Gnostic tradition) in their inflections of the primary elements of the apostate tradition I have described: embrace of the abyss over predictable order, emphasis on polarity over hierarchy, belief that life is flux and permanence is death. They are ecologists in their efforts to inhabit nature not as knowing subjects opposed to inert objects but as parts of a larger whole, as members thriving symbiotically in an organic system. As gnostic ecologists, they blend these two modes: they study nature to understand the abyss of life—its unfathomable being, its turbulent processes—hoping that this knowledge will foster local and global health.

The gnostic ecologist explores nature with a hunger for gnosis, an insight into the power and form of life. Extinguishing his anthropocentric desire to register and control nature as an object separate from his subjectivity, he apprehends an ungraspable origin—*nothing* to reason, logic, and language; *everything* to the wiggling universe—flowing through the stones and starlings, his breath and being. He realizes that this whole is not blind but adaptive, purposeful, and intelligent with organic rhythm. Enlivening parts and particles, this holistic energy—likely electromagnetic power or biological vitalism—unifies opposites, connecting human and nature, subject and object, life and death. To understand these relationships between abyss and its eddies more deeply, he studies it from several angles, tending toward interdisciplinary thought. He employs science to comprehend how nature functions; philosophy to meditate on relationships between human and non-human nature; religion to hold the cosmos holy. Moreover, this scientist of the abyss understands that ecology is also the *logos* (word) of the *oikos* (house, habitat, nature)—the poetics of time and space. He does not stop at seeing nature; he inscribes it in his works—which are not only *about* bipolar flows but also attempts to be *to be* these forces, *to be* ecosystems, *to be* re-enchanting compositions.

Let me clarify the ecological side of this hypothetical gnostic of matter. Obviously, the Romantics I shall consider here could not call themselves ecologists, for the word "ecology" was not yet in existence when they were thriving. Nor could they express outrage at extreme technological damage to the environment, for the Industrial Revolution—though destructive (as Wordsworth and Thoreau knew)—had not yet exploded into an earth-killing machine. Also, these Romantics (with the possible exceptions of Goethe and Thoreau) were unable to practice ecology in a strict scientific sense—not able, for instance, to study industrial damage to the Everglades—because they did not possess the requisite scientific skills.

These Romantics did, however, espouse an "ecological" way of seeing, acting, and writing. Doing so, they embodied one of two distinct strands of "ecologism" that, according to Anna Bramwell, arose in the late nineteenth century: "an anti-mechanistic, holistic approach" to life (4). This strand—the other is "energy economics"—is biological and normative. Studying symbiotic relationships between parts and wholes, the biological ecologist concludes that man is no longer the predominant species: the earth is not just raw material to be used by man but rather alive, with "its own serene ecological balance, its own will to live." An ethic corresponds to these facts: to disturb or harm this balance is wrong, to find one's place as an essential part of a living whole is noble.[17]

This holistic science was first codified by Ernst Haeckel, who in his Darwin-influenced *Generalle Morphologie* (1866) first coined "ecology." *Oekologie* was for him a descriptive (not normative) term, used to detail "the science of relations between organisms and their environment."[18] However, as several scholars have pointed out, Haeckel's holistic biology had its roots in the Romantic age, in the philosophy of organicism, detailed philosophically by Schelling and Coleridge, described scientifically by Goethe and Humboldt.[19] Indeed, as recent critics like Karl Kroeber, Jonathan Bate, Lawrence Buell, and Laura Dassow Walls have argued, various "green" tendencies in Romanticism—on both sides of the Atlantic—are definitively ecological and have been profoundly influential on environmentalist thinking.[20] As these scholars have shown, Romantic writers like Wordsworth and Thoreau blend descriptive and prescriptive tendencies in their thought and art: they see the cosmos as a living, and therefore sacred, organism; they engage in and espouse activities that flow with instead of against the currents of life; they create texts that embody the patterns of nature and instruct readers to do the same.

The five elements of gnostic ecology that I have sketched (life is an abyss, life functions in polarized forms, gnosis vouchsafes vision of life, various perspectives reveal life more fully than a single discipline, certain linguistic forms can gesture toward life) help deepen and extend this work on ecological Romanticism. Taken together, these motifs comprise a deeply ecological *Weltanschauung*, one that is as ambitious—combining cosmology, ethics, and poetics—as it is simple: desiring merely to live and let live. Yet, the pursuit of this simple desideratum is extremely complex, involving several levels of difficulty.

First of all, for the gnostic ecologist (for *any* ecologist), the pervasive institutions of the West are on the side of death, taking the forms of classical (positivistic, Newtonian) science and Christian/Platonic idealism. Attending only to phenomena that fit within his grids, the Newtonian scientist (Emerson's "stark and stiff" Stoic) dwells in a dead world, ignoring forces of life (chaos and turbulence), seeing only order and necessity. The Christian (Emerson's "St. John") likewise inhabits a morbid environment, caring only about spirit, devaluing material bodies as polluted. Against these deathly views—persistently identified and attacked by Goethe and Emerson—the gnostic ecologist envisions and inhabits a *living* universe: free, unpredictable, and creative, not an atomic machine or a sinful waste. Recognizing that life is as contingent as it is ordered, he escapes the "either/or" logics of the "Stoic" and the "saint" and is instead invigorated by "both/and" forms.

Yet, this holistic vision has its own problems, like the dilemma of organic determinism. Spinoza had suggested such a difficulty with his pantheistic organicism (described in his *Ethics* [1673; 1677]): nature is one with God; therefore, God is the strict cause of each event. (Coleridge, of course, struggled endlessly with this conclusion.) In such a universe, is there any place for freedom, and therefore, for ethics or creativity or evil? Yes, if the animating principle of nature is an unfettered abyss instead of a true, good, and just God. If a Christian God (or some analogous force, like the Neoplatonic One) is continuous with the universe, then its creatures are constrained to His will—even though He is free and inscrutable, the cosmos proceeds with a plan from which He swerves only in rare moments of revelation or miracle. However, if life is playful—as Nietzsche suggests it is—then most anything can happen at most any level (not just on the invisible, divine level). Like an ocean, the living abyss perpetually sports, whirling new waves and fresh eddies, spewing out novel beings and unpredictable laws. Because each of these patterns is a unique mode of life, it participates itself in this playful process: an unconscious flick from a plant, a semi-conscious dog leap, a willed action by a poet—each affects the composition of the whole, changing it in immeasurable ways. The thinkers in the gnostic ecological tradition are clear about this: the whole alters the parts, the parts swerve the whole; the free play of the abyss affects the games of the parts, the sport of the parts alters the mayhem of the whole. Schelling, for instance, believes that freedom in an organic cosmos emerges from the original abyss persistently injecting chaos into its systems.[21] Goethe agrees: nature emerges "from an unfathomable, limitless, humorous, self-contradictory being"—both spontaneous and measured (*SS* 6). In the same way, Emerson believes that life is "unsystematic," endlessly upsetting stable orders (*CW* 2:45-6).

But does this mean that the universe is anarchy? If life is as much chaos as order, are there no laws, no stable structures? No, for the abyss—again— *plays*; that is, manifests itself as necessity as well as chance, follows rules as well as breaks them. The cosmic game proceeds by way of bipolar processes, which are required to keep everything moving along. Mere order and necessity would stiffen into rock; simple chaos and chance would dissolve into a formless mass. Imbricated, these forces generate tumultuously coherent organisms participating in a cogently turbid planet. A woman, for instance, is a vortex, a self-interfering pattern, a coincidence of centrifugal (chaotic) and centripetal (cosmic) forces. On a physical level, her atoms are spheres of electromagnetic force, tensions between positive and negative energy, stable periodicity and sudden leaps to new orbits, particles and waves. On a biological level, her cells—made of atoms—are likewise polarized, fairly durable spheroids through which unpredictable energies constantly flow, motivated by chance irritations as much as necessary motions. On a psychic scale, her mental compositions—comprised (most likely) by atoms and cells—are a mix of habit and novelty, identity and difference, consciousness and unconsciousness. Romantic thinkers would agree. For Schelling, Goethe, and Emerson, life functions through torsion: casual causalities, predictable disruptions.[22]

However, if all things are polarized patterns of a playful abyss, is everything in the universe the same—a mere cipher of the whole? No. In any ecosystem—in any living whole—parts fulfill *different* functions and occupy different places on the evolving symbiotic (non-hierarchical) web, distinct chambers in the changing hive of being. If we treat the woman described above as a microcosm, we can see that she functions on several different levels, none of which is separate from or better than the other, each of which is dependent on the other. Her inorganic, physical processes are unconscious, "wavicles" wiggling in fields of energy; her organic, biological functions, dependent on her physical ones, are unconscious and conscious, usually more the former (involuntary) than the latter (voluntary); her psychic processes, contingent upon inorganic and organic ones, are also conscious and unconscious, generally more conscious (based on self-aware willing) than unconscious (connected to unknown instincts). As the woman, so the cosmos: a web of differentiated beings, some more conscious and complex than others. This idea is present, in varying guises, in the cases of Schelling, Goethe, and Emerson, primarily in their theories of imagination. While nature is largely an unconscious, "objective" manifestation of the abyss, humans are conscious, "subjective" modes, distinguished by their ability to imagine and create novel forms.[23]

The Case of Goethe

To render "gnostic ecology" more specifically and to set a richer stage for American inflections of it, I should now like to consider the case of Goethe, a vibrant exemplar of this mode of thinking.

While Goethe himself once claimed that Romanticism was sickly, the *magus* who created *Faust* (1790-1832) nonetheless exerted a profound influence on Romantic philosophies of nature and poetry.[24] In his scientific works are the seeds of Schelling's *Naturphilosophie*, Coleridge's bipolar organicism, Emerson's philosophy of nature; in his meditations on poetry are glimpses of the poetics of symbol, later found in Schelling's "Relation of the Plastic Arts to Nature" (1807), Coleridge's *Biographia Literaria* (1817), Emerson's "The Poet" (1844). But in Goethe's work as a whole is perhaps his most influential idea: science and poetry are not different in kind but in degree, each a way of perceiving, participating in, and perpetuating the grand organism of nature.

Aptly, Mitchell Feigenbaum, a noted chaos scientist, was drawn to Goethe's theories of nature and art in the 1960s, finding in *Color Theory* (1810) and *Faust* holistic challenges to the reductions of Newton.[25] Feigenbaum is not alone in sensing affinities between Goethe and complex processes: Albert Libchaber was supposedly deep in Goethe's *Metamorphosis of Plants* (1790) while experimenting on non-linear flows; likewise, two precursors to chaos theory, D'Arcy Wentworth Thompson and Theodor Schwenk, were also students of Goethe.[26] Recently, a handful of literary critics, most notably Herbert Rowland and Nicholas Vaszsonyi, have explored these connections. As Rowland has observed, Goethe's meditations on organicism share with "chaos theory" the idea that nature is a field of energy in which the activity of each part affects other parts and the whole. Vazsonyi reads *Faust* as such a system, as a turbid field beyond the calculations of reason.[27]

While these connections are provocative—perhaps seminal—one need not look solely to recent science to illuminate Goethe's theories of the universe. One can just as easily look to the Hermetic thinkers of the Renaissance, such as Paracelsus, Bruno, and Boehme, who interested Goethe from beginning to end.[28] In these thinkers, Goethe found the ideas that would permanently occupy him: life emerges from an unknowable power, life functions through strife, life is understood through imaginative gnosis, life is best studied from many angles, life can be channeled into artistic forms (alembics, symbols). With these past and present connections in mind, let us turn to Goethe's gnostic ecology.

Goethe's primary contribution to the scientific world was his "transcendental anatomy," an important source of the great Romantic "sciences"—*Naturphilosophie* and organicism—as well as of more "legitimate" biological undertakings, like those of Etienne Geoffrey Saint-Hilaire and Sir Richard Owen. As developed by Goethe, this sort of anatomy was distinguished by four assumptions: an ideal plan organizes the diverse functions of flora and fauna; this archetype is the force behind anatomical unity; scientists can discover this plan, even though it may not be purely physical; homologous forms in diverse species evidence this ideal type.[29] Goethe brought such presuppositions to bear not only on his studies of leaves and spines but also on his more ambitious quest: to understand the origin and function of everything.

Goethe first discovered an archetype, the botanical one, in the Public Gardens at Palermo in 1787. As he reports in his *Italian Journey* (1786-8), this scientific finding was a gnosis, overwhelming him in the flora:

> While walking in the Public Gardens of Palermo, it came to me in a flash that in the organ of plant which we are accustomed to call leaf lies the true Proteus who can hide or reveal himself in all vegetable forms. From the first to the last, the plant is nothing but leaf, which is so inseparable from the future germ that one cannot think of it without the other.

Cooling down after his vision, Goethe conjectures that this experience will give him a better insight into the cosmos, its life and metamorphosis.[30]

Returning to Weimar, Goethe developed his botanical theory (the individual plant is the unfolding of the primal leaf over time) in *The Metamorphosis of Plants* while in his journal *On Morphology* (1817-24), he ranged widely over the universe, setting down, for instance, the following speculation:

> Natural system: a contradictory expression.
> Nature has no system: she has—she is—life and development from an unknown center toward an unknowable periphery. Thus observation of nature is limitless, whether we make distinctions among the least particles or pursue the whole by following the trail far and wide. (*SS* 43)

Goethe's nature here is a vexed pattern of a hidden source, beyond logic and language; it is, in the words of Karl Vietor, "an immeasurable abyss, deep as the ocean, and monstrous her concealed interior."[31] Indeed, Goethe claims that a new "symbolism" would be required even to begin to describe this power (*SS* 43).

This dim center and ungraspable circumference, however, *partially* reveals itself in the forms of its beings—in, as Goethe writes in an 1832 letter, contrary processes: "constant creation and destruction."[32] As Goethe continues in his journal:

The idea of metamorphosis deserves great reverence, but it is also a most dangerous gift from above. It leads to formlessness; it destroys knowledge, dissolves it. It is like the *vis centrifuga*, and would be lost in the infinite if it had no counterweight; here I mean the drive for specific character, the stubborn persistence of things which have finally attained reality. This is the *vis centripeta* which remains basically untouched by any external factor. (*SS* 43)

While these forces—operating as they do at the same time—elude theoretical or mathematical exposition, they are nonetheless discernible to the immediate gaze, revealing the "unknown" center as waves unveil the ocean.

These two elements—life as an "unground" and manifestations of it as self-interfering patterns—occur throughout Goethe's scientific texts. Of course they appear in the Palermo vision, in which the leaf, the *Urtyp*, is the centripetal force, holding the centrifugal tendencies in a coherent pattern. These theories also inform Goethe's zoological work, in which he assumes that the vertebra is the principle of coherence for animal life (*SS* 111-6). But Goethe also finds these principles in inorganic processes, most notably in color, the spectrum of which is comprised of light and dark in different combinations (267-70). Goethe goes so far as to say that the entire cosmos, including organic and inorganic beings, is alive, springing from—as we have seen—"an unfathomable, limitless, humorous, self-contradictory being"— an intelligent, playful principle ensuring that nothing is blind or dead (6). The "driving forces" of this unsounded "being," he explicitly states, are "polarity" and "intensification." The former is a visible property, the constant "attraction and repulsion" of all matter; the latter, an invisible (spiritual) energy, pushes nature forward in an "ever-striving ascent," making it more complex, more flexible. But of course matter needs spirit; spirit, matter: these two forces are polarities themselves, dependent on one another for their existence (6).

The problem of beholding the whole in the part and the part in the whole inevitably led Goethe to another concern: scientific method. For Goethe—as Frederick Burwick and Rudolph Magnus have shown—there are true and false ways of knowing: the true method is based on sensory perception, the immediate gaze, while the false one is grounded on mathematical theory and philosophical abstraction.[33] Goethe calls this true sight an *Anschauung*, an "intuitive perception," an ecological gnosis into vibrant relationships. In *Theory of Color*, Goethe describes this ideal.

In general, events we become aware of through experience are simply those we can categorize empirically after some observation. These empirical categories may be further subsumed under scientific categories leading to higher levels. In the process we become familiar with certain requisite traditions for what is manifesting itself. From this point everything gradually falls into place under higher principles and laws revealed not to our reason through words and hypotheses, but to our intuitive perception [*Anschauung*] through phenomenon. We call these phenomena archetypal phenomena because nothing higher manifests itself in the world. (*SS* 195)

This progression reveals Goethe's desire, in the words of Dennis L. Sepper, to study things not in "isolation but within a larger context," a context "always capable of further enlargement, in the direction of the totality of phenomenal nature."[34] The scientist is first to study a phenomenon sensually, to examine visible qualities (the leaves and stalks of a plant). This attention leads the scientist to make connections with other scientific categories, other observations (the structural elements of this plant share affinities with those of another). Discerning these unities in diverse events, he realizes the "requisite conditions for what is manifesting itself" (the visible plant is dependent upon the primal leaf). At this point, still with palpable being steadily before his gaze, the insight occurs—gnosis—beyond the visible to the invisible (each plant is a convoluted form of an abysmal power). Indeed, Goethe ends his description of the path to "intuitive perception" by recording its results, in this case, in relation to his optics: the oppositions between colors (arising from a polarity between dark and light) lead "directly back to a common unity" (*SS* 195).

In other places Goethe develops "intuitive perception" more fully, meditating on its requirements and difficulties. This gnosis requires that one behold nature selflessly, without anthropocentric intentions. Observing nature only from a human standpoint—in terms of its utility or beauty— can lead to a "thousand errors," is the source of "humiliation and bitterness" (*SS* 11). However, if the scientist can relinquish his egotistical urges, he can explore "nature's objects in their own right and in relation to one another" (11). While the arrogant scientist imposes anthropocentric hierarchies onto nature, in reality, "nothing is higher or lower" in nature: "everything has equal rights to a common center which manifests its hidden existence precisely though [a] harmonic relationship between every part and itself" (45). While Goethe acknowledges the attraction of Kant's epistemology—the mind can never know nature in itself—he nonetheless believes that the selfless observer can achieve a gnosis into this cosmic ecology, "an intuitive perception of eternally creative nature" that might make him "worthy of participating spiritually in its creative process" (31). While uniting experi-

ence—sense of the particular—and idea—a theory of the whole—is a difficult task, this reconciliation can be reached in a vision of the archetype (31-2;
33-4). Overcoming the ego and Kantian doubt, refusing objectivity and
abstraction, bringing all of his faculties into play, Goethe would preserve, as
Arthur G. Zajonc has observed, "the full value and content of the phenomenal world," would hold things as intrinsically valuable parts of the ecological
web. Indeed, this way of seeing is, according to Nigel Hoffman, a "phenome-
nological ecology," an effort to understand how parts—both living and
artistic—"belong" in the whole.[35]

Goethe opposes this *Anschauung* to traditional scientific methods as
practiced by Newton. As Goethe argues in *Color Theory*, Newton's methods
in his *Opticks* (1704) were faulty from the start, for Newton did not rely
enough on his intuitive perception and depended too much on his theoretical one (*SS* 159). Newton grounded his optical theory, Goethe contends, on
only one laboratory experiment that was immediately reduced to mathematical equations. Ruled by prejudice, leaping precipitously from particular
to general, from practice to theory, from thing to number, Newton ignored
key physical phenomena and thus built his entire scientific edifice on sand
(272). He turned a brief perception into a concept, transformed the concept
into numbers, and then treated the numbers as if they were real things (270-
3). Seen this way, Newton commits what A. N. Whitehead has called the "fal-
lacy of misplaced concreteness": a way of knowing that ignores the
particular, perverts the processes of nature into anthropocentric, hierarchical grids, and envisions the universe as a mechanism—predictable, dead.[36]

Opposing Newton and employing his intuitive perception, Goethe ultimately desires to overcome dualism—between mind and matter, human
and nature. While Newton, following Descartes, would maintain that the
beholding mind is separate from the nature it observes, Goethe would have
us believe otherwise: the mind and nature are part of the same continuum,
symbiotic organs of a common matrix. We can readily apply to Goethe's
non-dualistic mode of seeing the Zen Buddhist terms that John G. Rudy has
connected to Wordsworth. Goethe, like Wordsworth, aspires to "obliterate
the felt presence of a separate organizing or opposing self in favor of a pre-
judgmental, prereflective consciousness so deeply aligned with a perceived
matrix of creative forces that it is impossible to say where the world's energies leave off and those of the poet begin." This recognition of an "inclusive
consciousness utterly continuous with the universe"—a deep force that
organizes the similar rhythms of mind and nature—is called by the Zennists
a *satori* (gnosis) of *sunyata* (the void). During this moment of gnosis, the
Zen Buddhist realizes that all things—including his body and mind—are

fleeting forms of the great emptiness: not a "mere vacuity" or "nihilistic vortex" but rather a groundless ground, similar to the Tao, from which all grows.[37] Not to be confused with traditional Western monism, this Zen unity is a non-dualistic oneness. That is, unlike monotheistic unity, which "does not include the element of self-negation and is substantial," non-dualistic oneness "includes self-negation and is insubstantial."[38] In other words, to experience the creative void, one must—as Goethe knows—negate the notion of self as a separate ego and realize that the real "self" is the abyss.

As these glimpses into the science of Goethe indicate, his sense of nature is much more "poetic" and "meditative"—emphasizing the ecological identity of self and nature—than "factual" and "objective"—a cataloging of discrete facts as they unfold before the discursive mind. Indeed, Goethe believed that true science was a subset of poetry: most people forget that "science arose from poetry, and [do] not see that when times change the two can meet again on a higher level as friends."[39] According to Peter Salm, Goethe's poetics reflects this merging of disciplines: the bipolar structures of *Faust* arise from his effort to channel nature's turns into his tropes.[40] Aptly, Goethe's definition of the literary symbol reveals his desire to elevate words into living creatures: the symbol places the "general in the particular," with the particular embodying the general "not as a dream or shadow, but as a living momentary revelation of the Inscrutable."[41] Here the symbol resembles the natural archetype, the composition that flashes the illegible whole. Recall that Goethe claimed that denotative language was entirely inadequate to limn the teeming energies of life. Symbol is an alternative: a linguistic form that simultaneously names and doesn't name, that gestures toward the living powers of abyss while revealing its own inability to describe these unnameable forces.

Goethe's definition of symbol thus blurs the traditional distinction between words and things. This important Romantic poetic ideal— espoused by Schelling, Coleridge, Emerson, and others—is indispensable to ecological writing: the *logos* of the *oikos*. Attempting to *write* nature—not to imitate it as a model but to participate in its processes (as a bird sings, as electricity sparks)—the symbolic writer aspires to create linguistic whorls of centrifugal and centripetal forces. These vexed works do not attempt to teach (didactically) the virtues of ecological seeing or to represent (mimetically) the powers of nature. Rather, they essay to inspire an experience of ecological seeing, to *be* the currents of nature.

Obviously, this is a difficult, perhaps impossible, undertaking, for this reason: words more often than not block gnosis because language divides the cosmos into discrete categories and arranges these categories into linear chains. Depending too heavily on language, one can come to think that the world itself is comprised of isolated units that function strictly in causal processes (subject causes a verb that affects an object). How, then, can one use words to reveal the insights that the cosmos is both undifferentiated *and* differentiated and that things are not links in a casual chain but events of simultaneously occurring forces (subjects and objects are modes of the same verb)? As we shall see, the gnostic ecologist generally contends with this question by deploying self-destructing forms—words that briefly signify only to dissolve into emptiness. While gnostic ecological texts feature centripetal structures—cogent forms, recursive elements—they endlessly upset these stabilizing components with centrifugal forces—illogical swerves, unpredictable *aporias*. The symbols of the gnostic ecologist, in other words, signify and de-signify simultaneously, like ripples on a pond or waves in an ocean. The attentive reader, ready for gnosis, will undulate on the currents, then sink to the depths.

Goethe's eclectic, poetic, and edifying science encourages heterogeneous ways of knowing. The unknowable center and periphery of life can never be exhausted by one mode of inquiry or by a single discipline. Goethe knew this: in his explorations of the abyss, he drew (of course) on poetry, botany, zoology, physics, geology, epistemology, ontology, and ethics—not to mention alchemy and hermetic philosophy. While each practice leads to the same conclusion—life is power churning struggling forms—each also offers a distinct angle of vision, a different way of apprehending and thus relating to the abyss. Goethe's interdisciplinary method is not a universal system subsuming all discursive knowledge; rather, it is a kaleidoscope of perspectives, each new array of stained glass a new refraction of the colorless nothing beyond.

Romantic Turbulence

As the case of Goethe reveals, gnostic ecology is not merely a synthesis of Gnostic cosmology and biological vitalism. It is also—and perhaps more importantly—an effort to merge scientific facts and poetic practice. In this endeavor, Goethe was not alone. Indeed, one of the primary trends of the Romantic Age—still often overlooked—was the attempt to blend a science of life with a vigorous poetry.

Goethe's age, of course, was a time before the "two cultures" of C. P. Snow had yet divided. Polymaths abounded, each searching for the secret of life with any means available. In Goethe's Germany, Schelling attempted to merge physics, biology, psychology, and philosophy; Novalis was a practicing engineer; J. W. Ritter wrote an essay entitled "Physics as Art"; F. Schlegel laid down the following imperative: "all art should become science and all science art; poetry and philosophy should be made one."[42] In England, the situation was similar: Coleridge mastered the chemistry of his friend Humphry Davy to improve his stock of metaphors; Davy, who discovered chemical affinity, wrote verse admired by Coleridge as well as an essay entitled "Parallels between Art and Science."

This blurring of science, philosophy, and poetry grew no doubt from the fact that early nineteenth-century science was not yet as specialized, technical, or mathematical as it came to be. However, there is perhaps a deeper reason for the artists developing an interest in science. At the turn of the nineteenth century, the Newtonian cosmology gave way to what I have elsewhere called a "science of the sublime"—a study of the source of life in turbulent, intractable forces.[43] During this time, an array of scientists were beginning to realize that the cosmos is formed and animated by huge, timeless, enigmatic energies. For instance, the astronomer John Herschel claimed in 1789 that the heavens are like an unruly garden perpetually agitated into death and life by an immense central force, perhaps gravity.[44] Around the same time James Hutton the geologist conjectured that the earth is far from stable; it is undergoing perpetual change, consistently and inexorably driven by gigantic pressures that reveal "no vestige" of a beginning or an end.[45] Just after the turn of the nineteenth century, Davy the chemist described how the elements of matter are held together by electrical forces.[46] In 1831, Michael Faraday, Davy's protégé, went further: his discovery of electromagnetic induction demonstrated, as we have seen, that all matter is electric. The discrete things of the universe are in reality fields of immense galvanic energies.[47] And, of course, developing alongside Goethe's search for archetypes (analogies in space) were nascent theories of evolution (changes through time), based on the idea—found in Lamarck's zoology—that all species emerge from and are driven through time by a common surge of life, one sap humming through the tangled branches.[48] This great shift from Newton's atoms, void, and gravity to fields of abysmal force could not help but lead poets like Goethe, Coleridge, and Emerson to a sense that—in the words of Marilyn Gaull—"scientific speculation about the infinite, the awesome, huge dimensions, durations, trauma, catastrophe, power . . . had more validity than the symmetrical, picturesque, orderly, finite taste of previous generations of scientists."[49]

What Gaull describes is a key element of Romantic organicism that is often overlooked: the emphasis on abysmal turbulent powers—not harmonious spirits—as the keys to life. Indeed, as A. N. Whitehead has argued, Romantic organicism helped to move science away from discrete matter and toward holistic force. In focusing on pervasive powers and their discrete bundles, this form of organicism was paramount to the four major ideas that emerged during the nineteenth century: electromagnetic waves, atomicity, evolution, and the conversation of energy. Taken together, these ideas and their organic analogues precipitated a major shift in the history of science, proven mathematically by Einstein in the twentieth century: mass is not "one final permanent quality" but rather "a quantity of energy considered in relation to some of its dynamical effects." Matter is energy.[50]

The scientific and poetic embrace of turbulence may well be the hidden current of the Romantic Age, the neglected "unground" of organicism. Karl Menges—directly following Dietrich Mathy's *Poesie und Chaos* (1984) and indirectly reviving Morse Peckham's *Man's Rage for Chaos* (1965)—is one of the few to discern this trend when he observes that "chaos is one of the central concepts in Romantic thought."[51] Surveying the fragments of F. Schlegel and Novalis, he has good reason to say so. Deep in Boehme and Goethe as well as the science of his age, Schlegel claimed in one of his "Critical Fragments" (1797) that "[t]he stance of nature toward chaos is reverence . . . and poetry is the stance of nature." This is not an isolated insight. Similar aphorisms abound: chaos is the origin of nature, art, and science; chaos is the ground of mythology; it is the origin of poetry. Novalis agrees in his own fragments (1797): the ground (or unground) of being is chaos; the discernible world is an organized chaos; true poetry is synonymous with chaos. Listing these fragments, Menges observes that Schlegel and Novalis abandoned "transcendentalism" and established an "anti-foundational" position, believing that "[w]hatever occurs, springs from disorder, lawlessness, anarchy, freedom, and takes shape in an evolutionary process of identity-formation that always follows the undecipherable blueprint of life."[52] Others agree: Lori Wagner finds in Schlegel an "aestheticized form of modern 'chaos theory'"; Joyce S. Walker discerns in Novalis a preference for "nonlinear, aperiodic, and organic models."[53]

Another assiduous student of Boehme, Goethe, and sublime science was Schelling, who, as I have already noted, also espouses a chaotic origin of life. Always a proponent of organicism, primarily in *Ideas for a Philosophy of Nature* (1797), Schelling spent his career countering mechanistic cosmologies in favor of one in which life is an endless strife between ideal and real, freedom and necessity, positive and negative. In *Of Human Freedom* (1809), Schelling, as we have seen, argues that these cosmic polarities emerge from a primary "unground" that ensures the free becoming of nature—a position developed powerfully in a recent study by Slavoj Zizek.[54]

Other German Romantic thinkers, of course, resemble Schelling in connecting the abyss of life to freedom—among them would be G. W. F. Hegel,

Jean Paul, or Ludwig Tieck. But we can also turn to England to find similar embraces of an unruly origin. Certainly Blake comes readily to mind. For him, as for Boehme (whom he studied and admired), the origin of life is an eternal font of energy that springs and dives in polarized, contrary patterns. Each living creature, rightly seen, is a form of this turbulent energy, a pattern, as Christine Gallant has shown, of chaos and order.[55] (Of course, given Blake's degradations of natural religion and Wordworth's organicism, one cannot push connections between Blake and Goethe too far.) Likewise, Coleridge—even though he struggled to remain orthodox in his fear of pantheism—sometimes stared into the turbulent abyss, especially around 1816 to 1818, as I have suggested elsewhere.[56] During these years, fresh from ardent study of Boehme and Schelling, he wrote in his "Theory of Life" that life is a mysterious "power" perpetually churning twisted forms; and he conjectured in a letter to C. A. Tulk that "chaos" is the "prothesis" from which all later dialectical beings emerge.[57] Wordsworth also sometimes practices the science of the abyss. Sharing important affinities with Boehme and Schelling— as N. P. Stallknecht and E. D. Hirsch have respectively shown—Wordsworth memorably embraces an "abyss" as the origin of mind—both his own and that of the universe—in book six of his *Prelude*. Also, his "sense sublime" of something "far more deeply interfused" in "Tintern Abbey" is not necessarily a "natural supernaturalism" but could well be a gnosis of the "unground."[58]

These various avatars of Goethe's gnostic ecology—sublime scientists, turbulent organicists—not only endorse at certain times a cosmology of the eddy and the abyss, but they also frequently favor gnosis (in the forms of ironic apprehension or imaginative intuition), eclecticism (blending science, philosophy, religion), and a turbulent poetics (the fragment, the symbol). Freeing the abyss from the laws of Yahweh and the equations of Newton, these figures may comprise a corporation of the void as much as a visionary company.

American Bareness

How does the American corps of the void relate to the European one? How do Emerson, Fuller, Melville, Thoreau, and Whitman find the roiling abyss on American soil? It has been customary for the American to distinguish his nation from Europe by declaiming the virtues of wilderness. From Jefferson's *Notes on the State of Virginia* (1782) to Whitman's preface to his 1855 *Leaves of Grass* to Theodore Roosevelt's "Wilderness Reserves: Yellowstone Park" (1905), the American difference has been developed as a natural one. America is a unique, perhaps superior, nation because its "purple mountain's majesties" and "fruited plans" are unparalleled in beauty, abundance, and power. Ironically enough, however, this praise of the natural resources of America has rarely led to an "ecological" sensibility. On the contrary, celebration of the fecundity of the American wilderness is usually of a piece with environmental exploitation: the bounteous land is matched by the strong will of its human inhabitants, who turn the teeming spaces of the country into lucrative commodities that translate to political superiority.

Aptly, the fertility of the American land, its resources for human use, is probably *not* what distinguishes American Romantics from their European forebears. In fact, what likely differentiates Emerson, Fuller, Melville, Thoreau, and Whitman from Goethe and Coleridge is precisely the opposite of American richness. It is American *bareness.* While Goethe and Coleridge walked through European landscapes fraught with cultural memories, Americans moved through scenes almost completely devoid of Western institutions. While European Romantics had to delve through layers of human history before reaching non-human nature, Emerson and his successors had to contend with the opposite dilemma: how to imbue an aggressively inhuman landscape with human significance. While certainly the American Romantics, like their European predecessors, felt the anxiety of influence from a European literary past, they also felt, in ways their forebears likely did not, an anxiety of insignificance, of having their works totally ignored by the vast and silent spaces engulfing them.

Of course, this difference has become something of a critical commonplace in its own way. As Henry James observed in his 1879 study of Hawthorne, one is struck at "the coldness, the thinness, the blankness" of Hawthorne's circumstances in America, which in Hawthorne's day had no state, no castles, no great universities, no literature, no museums—in short, no rich *human* culture. This bareness, James adds, would probably have been "appalling" to the "English or French imagination."[59] While James the ex-patriot does not find much imaginative merit in such a situation, Perry Miller on the contrary believes that "the vastness of the continent, its very emptiness, instead of meaning that [Americans] are blank and formless, make [them] deeply interesting amid [their] solitudes."[60] Along the same lines, Richard Poirier claims that this bareness—which may not be a "special plight of American writers"—is "very often salutary, something to be sought after," for "with nothing to depend on, nothing to lean on or rely on, the naked self and truth" might emerge. Poirier goes on to argue that American writers like Emerson, William James, Frost, and Stevens indeed turn bareness into a virtue by viewing it as an opportunity to rely not on cultural conventions but rather on one's own dynamic actions and tropes—on one's own pragmatic deeds.[61]

From a quick glance at some "bare spots" in the canons of American Romanticism, we can see Poirier's linking of paucity and pragmatism in clear relief. Emerson, remember, undergoes his famous "eye-ball" epiphany while *walking* across a *bare* common. Thoreau's Goethean gnosis of the primal form of life occurs while he is earning his living and gazing at unadorned mud. Engaging in what for him is a strenuous activity—"loafing"—Whitman observes a stark "spear" of summer grass, an experience of the void of life soon blooms. Melville's Ishmael finds his place in the whole while working on a whale ship, squeezing whale sperm with uneducated sailors. Fuller travels to the sparse prairies, gaining her insight into the abyss on unpeopled plains.

While it might be problematic to claim that each of these writers is a pragmatist, it is certainly the case that each faces an American landscape largely empty of human traces and must *work*—act, do—to find a way to connect to this environment. Now, of course, there is more than one way for a person to connect to a non-human environment. One can relate to nature as raw material to be subdued into commodities. Or, one can counter this typical American response by being a pastoralist; that is, by trying to find in nature a ground for human virtues. Or, a person can belong to nature in another way entirely: by viewing it ecologically, as a necessary pattern of life, a whole of which humans are a mere part. At the risk of oversimplification, one could say that these have been the three primary responses to the wilds of America: the will to conquer the "howling wilderness"; the desire to dwell in nature like Adam in Eden; the wish to live with nature, a strand in the web.

Of these three basic ways to relate to and act in the wild, the first two are anthropocentric, anti-ecological. While the first is obviously so, the second is an anthropocentrism as well—as Leo Marx has pointed out[62]—viewing nature as significant only in relation to human values. Now, obviously, several of the American Romantics I am considering in this book sometimes relate to nature in a pastoral fashion, as Marx and R. W. B. Lewis have shown.[63] However, each of them at other times reacts to nature in the third way, seeing the wilderness as both sacred other and holy identity—different as a unique and necessary part of the living abyss, the same as the abyss itself, the whole.

When American Romantics engage the wild in this latter way, they become gnostic ecologists, inflecting the ideas and practices of their European forebears in the empty spaces of America, working to connect ecologically to an intractable, inhuman environment. This curious American coincidence of bareness, pragmatism, and ecology requires additional explanation. While cultural bareness can be an invitation to humanize, it can also be a challenge to anthropocentrism, revealing the fragility and artificiality of many human institutions, forcing men and women to meditate freshly on the healthiest ways to relate to the land. If emptiness is conceived in the latter way, it is a call to action, to pragmatic deeds. Why? First of all, because this culturally vapid landscape is intransigent to human organizing systems, one must work to relate to it, must walk or sail or plant out in the green world in order to find points of affinity. Second, because the rules of culture do not function well in nature, one must come up with new codes of behavior, acceptable only if they mesh (pragmatically) with the lay of the land: convention is nothing, practicality all.

Now, if one wishes to forge a *living* (ecological) relationship to nature—as opposed to a deathly (exploitative or pastoral) one—then one will engage in practices that vouchsafe two results: *participation* in the processes of life and *purveyance* of these processes for the edification of others. For the American Romantics I shall consider, participation takes the form of moving with nature's transient, dynamic processes—walking, traveling, sailing, growing, circulating, playing—and purveyance comes in the shape of writing—turning (troping) the powers of nature into perturbed yet edifying texts.

So, while these American Romantics are similar in kind to their European predecessors—believing at times that life is an abyss, life functions in polarized forms, life is apprehended through gnosis, life should be studied from several angles, and certain linguistic forms embody life—they differ in degree, for they must struggle to connect to a culturally sparse environment with diligent action. Achieving this connection is not easy, for it is perpetually thwarted not only by the indifference of nature but also by the anti-ecological ideas pervading the nineteenth-century American intellectual scene. Indeed, as I show in each chapter, Emerson, Fuller, Melville, Thoreau, and Whitman must contend against their own Christian/ Platonic influences, must labor to relinquish these transcendentalist philosophies, to embrace the rough waves of the physical world. Throbbing between life and death, ecological gnosis and egotistical misprision, each in the end—as my chapters show—resolves this *agon*. Realizing that longing for stability breeds despair or death, each overcomes the rage for order and participates in the troubling flows of the earth, moving with the undulations of the palpable. This peripatetic mode keeps philosophy on the go—turning and troping with every new fresh bend in the road, each new curl in the current. On this philosophical *periplous*, traversing terrain new and shocking every minute, each of these figures achieves *life*, incarnating and making waves—houses founded on the sea.

Emerson's Paralogical Currents

Metaphysical Poverty, Practical Power

The death of his little boy Waldo, who succumbed to scarlet fever in January of 1842, unmoored Emerson. Suddenly, his familiar world—the village of Concord, his comfortable house, his wife and friends—appeared cryptic, and alien. As Emerson painfully recorded in his journal a day after his son's death, "Sorrow makes us all children again . . . . The wisest knows nothing" (*JMN* 8:165). His hospitable nooks had metamorphosed into Dante's dark wood, Spenser's cave of despair, Hamlet's "stale, flat and unprofitable" terrain. Lost, he groped for his old Platonic temples of wisdom—all is well *sub specie aeternitatis*—but found only the labyrinths of time. Nothing made sense.

Two years later—after much dark meditation, still much unsettled—Emerson tried to put his metaphysical crisis into words in the opening of his essay "Experience" (1844):

> Where do we find ourselves? In a series of which we do not know the extremes, and believe it has none. . . . Sleep lingers all our lifetime about our eyes, as night hovers all day in the boughs of the fir-tree. All things swim and glitter. Our life is not so much threatened as our perception. Ghostlike we glide through nature, and should not know our place again. (*CW* 3:27)

This nature is labile, radically ephemeral. To the man suffering from extreme doubt, who quests for stability, security, and certainty, it is "unhandsome" in its "evanescence and lubricity" (3:29). How can can one find a still point in such a turning world, a calm place in which to recover and rebound? Emerson labors to find such ontological and epistemological tranquillity for much of the essay, yet he is thwarted in every line of thought, always upset by his inability to know anything for sure, perpetually overwhelmed by the spews of nature.

Then, midway through the essay, out of nowhere, a flash: Emerson *knows*. The flitting forms, the whirling fragments, are not unrelated, isolated, alienated. They are not mere chaos, simple anarchy. Rather, behind them, periodically revealing itself in brief sparks, is "the Power" that "like a bird . . . alights nowhere, but hops perpetually from bough to bough," abiding "in no man and in no woman, but for a moment" speaking "from this one, and for another moment from that one" (*CW* 3:34). This perturbed power, Emerson realizes, generates the swimming and glittering shapes, the whispy fogs and slippery rocks. The fluxional world is not an illusion of some inaccessible heaven or a corrupt copy of unreachable and stable forms. Rather, this turbulent nature is the only life: "a mixture of power and form" (3:35). What was before an occasion for despair—ungraspable energy—is now a joyous event, an apprehension of an invigorating sublime: things are not ghosts of eternity but rather evolving forms of the power of life, discrete and distributed, separate and unified. Metaphysical poverty is practical power.

Transcendental Sublime and Physical Sublime

For the first part of "Experience," Emerson quests for what we might call the traditional sublime, a mode of transcendence: the transport from finitude to the infinite, from physical to spiritual. This transcendental sublime has generally been associated with Romanticism, especially with the visionary moments of Wordsworth and Coleridge.[1] Issuing from Edmund Burke and Immanuel Kant, this traditional sublime details a moment of metaphysical vision occurring when the mind is simultaneously pained and pleased: overtaxed by indeterminacy, it is stimulated toward the spiritual; threatened with annihilation, it is reassured by God.[2]

Jean-Francois Lyotard, however, has recently challenged these traditional, transcendental framings of the sublime. In *The Postmodern Condition* (1984), Lyotard claims that the sublime, as *he* understands it from Kant, can work *against* stable, eternal principles and alternatively be employed to describe emancipating forces *incommensurable* with totalizing concepts, ranging from postmodern art (Malevitch's squares, the works of Picasso) to recent developments in science (fractal geometry, catastrophe theory, quantum mechanics). These sublime energies are "paralogical"—beyond (*para*) logic, reason, and word (*logos*)—and thus liberating. They counter the "master" values of the West—unity, homogeneity, and predictability—with difference, heterogeneity, creativity: the muses of the agitated poet and the iconoclastic scientist.[3]

While Emerson conventionally has been read as an exemplar of the transcendental sublime,[4] he clearly moves toward the more turbulent, physical sublime of Lyotard (and Kant "de-transcendentalized") in the course of

"Experience." For good reason: some ten years before he wrote "Experience," he was becoming aware of developments in nineteenth-century science that challenged the Western narratives out of which transcendental aesthetics emerged. Attending to the electrochemistry of Humphry Davy and the electromagnetism of Michael Faraday in the 1830s, Emerson was faced with the possibility that matter is not a physical part of a spiritual whole but rather a vigorous field of force, a pattern of electrical energy. The galvanized of these emerging sciences suggested to Emerson that nature resists stable unity, that it is paradoxical, paralogical: it is simultaneously discernible matter and polarized energy, static and dynamic, substantive and transitive—"power and form." Beyond logic and representation, this volatile universe is indeed sublime, but not in the transcendental sense. Rather than inspiring a vision of a spiritual whole, it challenges the mind to represent unpresentable *physical* forces: evanescent currents, fluxional patterns, polarized strife.

Emerson's struggle between the transcendental and paralogical sublime not only agitates "Experience" but also appears much earlier, as a primary tension in his first book *Nature* (1836). This work, of course, has generally been read as a transcendental manifesto, some sort of Neoplatonic meandering. This is justified, for Emerson throughout this essay theorizes blithely about the possibility of spiritual harmony, of metaphysical certainty. Yet, seething underneath these optimistic dreams is a deeper, more disturbing, more exhilarating gnosis: the powers coursing through the cosmos are not heaven-sent but electrical charges, galvanic fluxes. The "currents of Universal Being" into which Emerson dissolves in his "transparent eye-ball" vision could be electromagnetic waves as easily as Neoplatonic spirits. While Emerson in *Nature* may reach toward the latter possibility in many of his overt claims, he suggests the former option in his stylistic practices. With unsettling tropes and agitated figures, he persistently dissolves order into chaos, liberating readers from unity, introducing them to the muses of paradox, discontinuity, and dissension.

Both transcendental theory and turbulent practice, *Nature* is at odds with itself, a poetic *agon*. While some might claim that this is a weakness in the text, a troubling inconsistency, I would say that this duplicity is a great potency, for it reveals *Nature* as a form of vigorous power—a paralogical figure—that is both being *and* becoming, cosmos *and* chaos. Attending to this tension in Emerson's earliest text, we can see the young Emerson in a fresh light. He is not merely a typical transcendentalist pining for spiritual regions. He is also an incipient gnostic ecologist, a Connoisseur of Chaos as much as a Concord Sage.[5]

Transparent Design

In the first chapter of *Nature*, Emerson announces a transcendental theory of the sublime: "[I]f a man would be alone, let him look at the stars. The rays that come from these heavenly worlds will separate him and vulgar things. One might think the atmosphere was made transparent with this design, to give man, in the heavenly bodies, the perpetual presence of the sublime" (*N* 9). Here the sublime is equated with the overwhelming vastness of space—the infinite fires of the heavens—but also with "design"—law, order, harmony. Though the skies are ostensibly boundless, they are nonetheless dictated by a ubiquitous ordering principle. In two other places in *Nature*, Emerson invokes the sublime in similar contexts. The ant becomes "sublime" when "a ray of relation is seen to extend from it to man" (36)—in other words, when the insect is understood from an anthropocentric angle, as a part of the same design of which man is a superior portion. Likewise, the following remark of Leonhard Euler is "sublime," no doubt because it suggests that the physical world is transcended and dictated by spirit. Speaking of his law of arches, the eighteenth-century mathematician remarks, "This will be found contrary to all experience, yet is true" (70). Emerson interprets Euler thus: his claim transfers "nature into mind" and leaves "matter like an outcast corpse" (70).

Emerson's implied theory of the sublime draws on two primary transcendental paradigms, Platonism and Kantian idealism. Emerson's epigraph to the 1836 edition of *Nature* from the *Enneads* of Plotinus establishes a key idea of the essay: "Nature is but an image or imitation of wisdom, that last thing of the soul." Emerson reiterates this thesis several times, recalling his avid reading of Plato, Plotinus, Proclus, and Iamblichus throughout the 1830s: a "Fact is the end or last issue of spirit" (*N* 44); spirit or soul is the "Unity in Variety" (54); "universal Spirit," or "Unity," "lies under the undermost garment of nature" (56). Emerson often translates this Platonic (and Neoplatonic) vocabulary into Kantian terminology: phenomena are mere patterns of inaccessible, spiritual *noumena*. He values, he claims, the "idealist hypothesis"—the theory that "matter is a phenomenon, not a substance"—because it "apprize[s] [him] of the eternal distinction between soul and world" (78-9). Both Platonic and idealist paradigms provide hospitable environments for the transcendental sublime: the moment when one ascends from the corrupt body to a harmonious spirit, from fleeting phenomena to stable *noumena*.

(Notably, however, Emerson reminds himself that "idealism" is but a "hypothesis," and perhaps one with problems, for it "makes nature foreign to [him], and does not account for the consanguinity which [he] acknowledge[s] to it" [*N* 78]. Indeed, a few sentences later, he claims that while a

"[S]pirit" or "Supreme Being"—God, one would suspect—is the source of life, one understands this principle as a *physical* process that "does not build up nature around us but puts it forth through us, as the life of the tree puts forth new branches and leaves through the pores of the old" [79-80]. In these passages, we see revealed the primary tension of the essay, between transcendence and *physis*.)

Currents

I have not yet examined, however, what is usually read as the *locus classicus* of the transcendental sublime, Emerson's notorious "transparent eye-ball" sequence. As James B. Twitchell has said, "[t]here is no better description of the Romantic sublime than Emerson's famous passage on the world beyond the slush."[6] Most readers of this sequence, like Twitchell, follow the interpretation of Harold Bloom: in becoming a "transparent-eyeball" Emerson transcends matter and—Gnostically—returns to the first spiritual abyss, "the place of original fullness, *before* the Creation."[7] While on the surface it appears that Emerson on the common is Valentinus *redivivus*, ascending from *hyle* to the *pleroma*, on a deeper level, one might find Emerson metamorphosing into Goethe, who in the Public Gardens of Palermo saw the living abyss coalesce into the primal plant. With this possibility in mind, let's take another look at this much discussed sequence.

> Crossing a bare common, in snow puddles, at twilight, under a clouded sky, without having in my thoughts any occurrence of special good fortune, I have enjoyed a perfect exhilaration. Almost I fear to think how glad I am. In the woods too, a man casts off his years, as the snake his slough, and at what period soever of life, is always a child. In the woods, is perpetual youth. Within these plantations of God, a decorum and sanctity reign, a perennial festival is dressed, and the guest sees not how he should tire of them in a thousand years. In the woods, we return to reason and faith. There I feel that nothing can befal me in life,—no disgrace, no calamity, (leaving me my eyes,) which nature cannot repair. Standing on the bare ground,—my head bathed by the blithe air, and uplifted into infinite space,—all mean egotism vanishes. I become a transparent eye-ball; I am nothing; I see all; the currents of the Universal Being circulate through me; I am part or particle of God. (*N* 12-3)

As I have argued elsewhere, this passage need not be read as a transcendental vision at all.[8] Rather, it can indeed be interpreted as Emerson's equivalent of Goethe's gnosis in Palermo, in which the primal *physis* flashes before the "intuitive perception." Notice that Emerson carefully attends to his physical environment: the snow puddles, the twilight, the clouded sky. Moreover, he is also aware of his psychic disposition: he has no thoughts of "special good fortune," enjoys "perfect exhilaration," "fears" to think how glad he is. Experiencing these palpable realities directly, Emerson recognizes a common pattern: each event, whether physical or psychical, is polar. Snow puddles are ice and water; the crepuscular moment is dark and light; clouds are formal and nebulous. Special good fortune suggests definite purpose (an event of good luck *appropriate* to a unique situation) and sheer chance (fortune by definition is a matter of *random* occurrence). Likewise, "perfect" intimates completeness and stasis, while "exhilaration" connotes agitated energy. Given these polarized conditions, it is no wonder that Emerson is fearful and glad, anxious and joyful. It is also no surprise that his thoughts, expressed as he continues to walk through the New England twilight, should take on a bipolar form. In the woods, he discerns both spontaneity (figured in the snake, the child, and "perpetual youth") and discipline ("decorum," "sanctity"); both reason (the faculty of rationality) and faith (an irrational mode).

Like Goethe in Palermo, Emerson progresses to increasingly larger contexts—from his immediate physical surroundings, to his psychic dispositions, to the woods—at each level discerning an antagonistic pattern. He realizes that the processes that spring within his skin also thrive without. This insight, based on close observation, suddenly explodes into a vision of the power generating these pulsations. Suddenly stopping—"standing on bare ground"—Emerson finds his place in the whole. He is not a separate ego against an alien world (what his "mean egotism" would lead him to think); rather, he is a point of infinity, a discrete yet distributed bundle of the "currents of Universal Being." There are several things to notice about Emerson's *Anschauung*, his *satori* of *sunyata*. First, again, it is the result of immediate experience. Second, it is simultaneous with his ecological (antianthropocentric) realization that he is an organ of a larger organism, part of a vast whole. Third, this whole is an unbounded ("infinite") current, which could be air, water, and/or electricity—a physical energy—as much as a spiritual force. Fourth, this whole is unknowable to rational inquiry: it is "nothing," an *Ungrund*, a *Nicht*—an abyss. Yet, it can be apprehended through a gnosis (seeing "all"), in which one understands that he is a unique circulation of these immense forces. Finally, this personal vision yields a cosmology: everything, from Emerson to the liminal sky to the melting puddles, is a convolution of the universal currents, a "house founded on the sea."

The visionary science that Emerson exhibits here finds a median between the anti-materialism of idealist thought (the unearthly visions of St. John, of the Christians and Platonists) and the reductive materialism of the scientific tradition (issuing from Bacon and Newton, reducing, like the Stoics, the universe to rational principles). To use Emerson's own terminology, borrowed from Kant's *Critique of Pure Reason* (1781) and Coleridge's *Aids to Reflection* (1825), Emerson negotiates in his vision and in *Nature* as a whole between Reason (the intuitive faculty, able to see through discrete things to the holistic, invisible "causes and spirits" animating them [*N* 62]) and the Understanding (the empirical faculty, which "adds, divides, combines, measures" the data of palpable experience [45]). Using both faculties simultaneously, Emerson discovers the inexhaustible matrix *in* the physical world: he sees, like Blake, infinity in a grain of sand. His Understanding keeps him from separating the holistic abyss from matter, refuses him the seductions of religious faith, holds him hard to the concrete: he *experiences* the energy generating the beings around him. His Reason preserves his skepticism toward scientific reductions, denies him the comforts of abstract theory. The billowing origin of life cannot be contained in the equations of the laboratory or corralled into smooth systems. Skeptical (like Montaigne) of rational reductions and heavenly cities, Emerson revises strict idealism and empiricism in his quest for a "*metaphysics* of conchology" (83)—an experience of the first currents coiling into luminous shells.[9]

This metaphysics of conchology is a gnostic ecology: a study of the "relation between things and thoughts," of "sympathy" among the "most unwieldy and eccentric forms of beast, fish, and insect," and of the connection each of these discrete shapes has to the abysmal "unity" (*N* 84). Even though Emerson, again, exhibits his transcendentalism by following his description of this method with a favorable citation of George Herbert's anthropocentric poem "Man," his ecological sensibility remains. Regardless of his youthful forays into Plato, Emerson nonetheless shows a keen desire to love the physical world as it is, to embrace its spiraling flows as the powers of life and to find his place in the evolving web of being. Even though he does not stroll, like Goethe, through a European garden, even though he instead must slog through a bare, muddy field in the dreary twilight, he still wants to hold hard to phenomena, waiting for their therapeutic shocks. As Michael Lopez has remarked in his study of Emerson and power, this Emerson of the bleak rocks "never turned away from brute fact," trying always—though at times he faltered—to embrace the sea-wave "world of risk, incompleteness, and conflict" as the only grounds, though groundless, of significant toil.[10]

Spherules of Force

So, even though Emerson was deep in abstruse transcendentalist research while writing *Nature*, he was also interested in shells, puddles, and clouds. These ecological concerns likely grew out of Emerson's other great love of the 1830s: recent scientific developments that suggested a theory of the sublime based solely on the physical world.

As I have shown elsewhere, in 1828 Emerson began reading Davy's *Elements of Chemical Philosophy* (1812), where he found exciting hypotheses on the electrical nature of matter.[11] Davy wonders "[w]hether matter consists of individual corpuscles, or physical points endowed with attraction and repulsion." Likewise, he conjectures that the "sublime idea" of the "ancient Philosophers"—that "there is only one species of matter"—might be rendered through attention to the physical world; specifically, by observing the arrangements of chemical and mechanical forms through electrical and magnetic affinities.[12] Attracted by Davy, Emerson refers to him in his 1836 lecture "The Humanity of Science." After remarking that recent scientists have shown the laws of heat and light to be analogous to those of magnetism and electricity, Emerson celebrates the work of Davy for demonstrating that "Magnetism and Electricity" are "identical" and for suggesting that "the primary cause of electrical effects and of chemical effects is one and the same" (*EL* 2:29). For Emerson, these "sublime conjectures" provide material for a *physics*—not a speculative philosophy—of the sublime, a study of "the central unity, the common law that pervades nature from the deep centre to the unknown circumference" (29). Although Emerson here uses the vocabulary of the transcendental sublime—"law" and "unity"—he breaks ground for a new, physical sublime in two ways. He bases his sublime speculation on phenomena; and he proposes that this physical "unity" and "law" is paralogical, beyond *logos*, emerging from an unfathomable ("deep") source and moving toward an unpresentable ("unknown") destination. (Notice that Emerson here rephrases—in the context of electricity—Goethe's passage from *On Morphology*: nature is "life and development from an unknown center to an unknowable periphery" [*SS* 43].)

Emerson was also aware in the '30s of the groundbreaking work of Faraday, Davy's famous student.[13] As Faraday reports in his *Experimental Researches in Electricity* (1839-55), in 1831 he discovered electromagnetic induction, which provided convincing evidence for the hypothesis that matter is inseparable from electrical energy, suggesting that there is no matter but only fields of force, no solid atoms but bundles of energy.[14] By 1844, after a series of further experiments, Faraday articulated a field theory of matter in "A Speculation Touching Electrical Conduction and the Nature of Matter":

[M]atter fills all space, or, at least, all space to which gravitation extends . . . for gravitation is a property of matter dependent on a certain force, and it is this force which constitutes matter. In that view matter is not merely mutually penetrable, but each atom extends, so to say, throughout the whole of the solar system, yet always retaining its own centre of force.[15]

Faraday's work helped to abolish the idea of mass, renaming it, as Alfred North Whitehead observes, a "quantity of energy considered in relation . . . to dynamical effects."[16] This revolution of Faraday and his mathematical successor James Clerk Maxwell was, in the words of Sir Karl Popper, "just as great as that of Copernicus, possibly greater."[17] Indeed, Albert Einstein and Werner Heisenberg, in spite of their differences, both credited Faraday with providing a new vision of reality that would lead to their iconoclastic work.[18]

For Emerson, Faraday's work translated into a sublime universe in which things are patterns of immense, dynamic, unpresentable, paralogical, *physical* forces: phenomena, ranging from the ant to the Andes, are polar, simultaneously discrete and continuous, stable and unstable, local and global, attractive and repulsive. As early as 1833, Emerson—as we have seen—praised Faraday for the "great long expected discovery of the identity of electricity & magnetism" that opens "almost a door to the secret mechanism of life & sensation" (*JMN* 4:94). Electricity, not spirit, generates the universe. Aware in 1836 of the "wonders opened" by Faraday and other electromagnetists (*EL* 2:38), by 1854 Emerson could deliver this accurate description of Faraday's cosmos in the lecture "Poetry and English Literature," which later became "Poetry and Imagination" (1876):

Nature . . . is on wheels, in transit, always passing into something else, streaming into something higher; . . . matter is not what it appears; . . . chemistry can blow it all into gas. Faraday . . . taught that when we should arrive at the monads, or primordial elements . . . we should not find cubes, or prisms, or atoms, at all, but spherules of force. (*EW* 8:4)

Emerson was already writing passages like this in the late 1830s and early 1840s, just after the publication of *Nature*. In the 1841 lecture "The Method of Nature," he exclaims that nature's

smoothness is the smoothness of the pitch of the cataract. Its permanence is perpetual inchoation. Every natural fact is an emanation, and that from which it emanates is an emanation also, and from every emanation is a new emanation. If anything could stand still, it would be crushed and dissipated by the torrent it resisted. (*CW* 1:124-5)

Likewise, in the essay "Circles," published the same year, Emerson intones, "There are no fixtures in nature. The universe is fluid and volatile"; "[n]othing is secure but life, transition, the energizing spirit" (2:179, 189). Nature's parts are both still and moving, static and dynamic, substantive and transitive—or, as Emerson observes in the 1844 essay "Nominalist and Realist," "*nature is one thing and the other thing*, in the same moment" (3:139).

Describing a Design

Emerson's own *Nature*, in struggling between Plato's harmonious cosmos and Faraday's agitated fields, is one thing and the other thing, in the same moment. While the essay is about the transcendental sublime, it tries *to be* the sublime physical universe (discovered by Faraday and articulated later by Lyotard): a paralogical figure that resists totalizing concepts and stable representations, a living field in which parts and the whole mutually affect one another.[19] Playing on the etymology of "essay"—the French *essayer*, "to attempt, to try"; from the Latin *exagere*, "to drive out"—*Nature* tries to be nature by trying (putting on trial) transcendentalism.

Emerson opens the essay in a revolutionary tone, urging readers to resist the past (biographies, histories, criticism) and embrace the present. The sentiment is gnostic: avoid textual authority and go straight to nature to experience "life."

Embosomed for a season in nature, whose floods of life stream around and through us, and invite us by the powers they supply, to action proportioned to nature, why should we grope among the dry bones of the past, or put the living generation into masquerade out of its faded wardrobe? The sun shines to-day also. There is more wool and flax in the fields. There are new lands, new men, new thoughts. Let us demand our own works and laws and worship. (*N* 5)

While one could read these "floods of life" as shadows of spirit, one could—as we now know—also see them as currents of electricity, animating a paralogical universe and inspiring coiled poetics. While these "floods" may be nourishing, they are also unruly and deadly. Unpredictable and excessive, floods overflow boundaries and often overwhelm entire systems of order, frequently drowning those who wish to control them. Ironically, these dis-

ruptive floods become the standard for a poetics and an ethics. Faded tex-
tiles (wardrobes), sepulchral texts (biographies, histories, criticism), and
retrospective figures (those who grope among dry bones) cannot participate
in and embody this dynamic world. Drawing from "wool and flax" in the
fields today, one should weave and construct texts and cut figures appropriate to nature; that is, one should turn (trope, evolve) with the whorls of the
flood.

In the next paragraph, Emerson further considers relationships among
nature, humans, and writing. On the surface, he seems to draw from a Platonic paradigm: "Every man's condition is a solution in hieroglyphic to
those inquiries he would put. He acts it as life, before he apprehends it as
truth. In like manner, nature is already, in its forms and tendencies, describing its own design" (6). Is this a tired rehearsal of the Platonic/transcenden-
talist notion that phenomena—humans and nature—are images or shadows
of divine things, hieroglyphs decipherable from the perspective of eternity?
As I have shown in another context, close attention to Emerson's words tells
us otherwise.[20]

A hieroglyph is a form of sacred writing (*hieros*, "sacred," and *gluphe*,
"carving"). The human condition, then, is a written form, a holy carving;
more specifically, it is a dialogue, for "condition" derives from the Latin
condicere, to talk together. This dialogic, antagonistic text is a "solution" to
inquiries, an answer to the great riddles. But is the answer clear and comforting? Perhaps not, for a solution is also a heterogeneous mixture of two or
more substances as well as a loosening (Latin: *solvere*, "to loosen").

Attending closely to this sentence, we discover that it *loosens*. A person's
condition does not offer a limpid solution in transparent writing—it is not a
particular symbol allowing access to universal significance. Rather, a condition is, again, a dialogue, an interaction of opposing forces, a conversation
perpetually turning (troping, converting) ideas into fresh directions. The
solution to this dynamic condition cannot be an incontrovertible, static
answer, as eight is the solution of four plus four. Instead, this solution must
be a loosening, a dissolution that transforms homogenous units into heterogeneous mixtures. Likewise, the hieroglyph that forms the solution to this
condition cannot be written in stone. It must be supple and plural, a written
answer to the riddle and a dissolution of the answer, simultaneously an
inscription and an erasure.

Nature is analogous to the human condition; it too acts out its condition
while at the same time incarnating a script: "In like manner, nature is
already, in its forms and tendencies, describing its own design." Nature
describes, or writes down, its own design, or pattern. Yet the prefix "de"

means the reverse of, or to remove from, as in to "de-throne." To de-scribe, then, also means "not to write," or to remove from writing, just as de-sign also signifies the undercutting or removal of a sign. The prefix "de" also derives from the Latin "from," or "out of," suggesting that the signs and scripts of nature are constantly moving outside of themselves, in transit, metamorphosing. Like human hieroglyphs, nature's patterns are double, still and still moving; they are *sous rature*, writing and erasing at the same time.

Emerson's own *Nature* is a solution in writing to the riddles of man and nature, a hieroglyph, a visible rendering of invisible laws, a book of nature. If its words are wild, what about the world it signifies? If it is a labyrinth, can it reflect heavenly temples?

The ancient idea that nature is a book is a theory of the relationship between the visible and the invisible, presence and absence. Emerson learned this idea and its corollary theories primarily from Emmanuel Swedenborg, the eighteenth-century scientist and mystic, whom he quotes in *Nature*: the "visible world and the relations of its parts, is the dial plate of the invisible one" (*N* 41). The physical world is a text whose meaning is the spiritual world; present signs reflect absent signifiers; matter and spirit *correspond*. As Emerson again quotes the Swedish visionary in an 1850 essay:

In our doctrine of Representations and Correspondences, we shall treat of both these symbolical and typical resemblances and of the astonishing things which occur . . . throughout nature, and which correspond so entirely to supreme and spiritual things, that one would swear that the physical world was purely symbolical of the spiritual world. (*CW* 4:65)

In this later essay, Emerson praises Swedenborg for applying his doctrine of correspondence to scientific studies: each natural being is a sign for the forces that comprise it. The mystic's desire to read the symbols of God becomes the scientist's impulse to read the language of the force of life (4:66-7).

While Swedenborg believes that each particular sign can be related to one and only one spiritual and scientific signified, Emerson maintains that natural phenomena are too restless to refer to only one sense. Criticizing Swedenborg, whose book of nature is univocal and pellucid, Emerson details a polysemous, nebulous natural text. Because the meaning of the world is a "never quite expressed fact" that avoids transparent representation, the symbols of nature are protean: they play "innumerable parts, as each particle of matter circulates in turn through any system." Nature rebels against any language or system—any "hard pedantry"—"that would chain her waves." "No literalist," nature is an inchoate figure (*CW* 4:68). As Emerson proclaims in "The Poet" (1844), every "sensuous fact" bears double, triple, quadruple, centuple, "or much more manifold meaning" (3:3-4).

In making these claims about the relationship between visible and invisible, Emerson was likely recalling a transforming epiphany he experienced in 1833 while strolling through the Jardin des Plantes in Paris. There, he beheld flora and fauna arranged according to formal affinities, visible structures referring to invisible relationships.

> The universe is a more amazing puzzle than ever as you glance along this bewildering scene of animated forms,—the hazy butterfly, the carved shells, the birds, beasts, fishes, insects, snakes,—& the upheaving principle of life everywhere incipient in the very rock . . . Not a form so grotesque, so savage, nor so beautiful but is an expression of some property inherent in man the observer,—an occult relation between the very scorpions and man. I feel the centipede in me—cayman, carp, eagle, & fox. I am moved by strange sympathies, I say continually, "I will be a naturalist." (*JMN* 4:199-200)

In this vision, poetics and science merge. As Emerson later commented on his experience: "Moving along these pleasant walks [in the Jardin], you come to the botanical cabinet, an inclosed garden plot, where grows a grammar of botany—where the plants rise, each in its class, its order, the genus" (*EL* 1:8). In the heat of his epiphany, however, Emerson does not find this "grammar" to be well-regulated or systematically arranged. Rather, it strikes him as an "amazing puzzle," a "bewildering scene" that reflects an "upheaving" principle of life. This principle is clearly not the totalizing spirit of Plato, the *noumena* of Kant—it is the elusive, polarized field of force detailed by Faraday, a physical current generating a tempestuous text—as Emerson himself reminds us in *Nature*, "*Spirit* primarily means *wind*" (*N* 32).

Entropic Negentropy

An essay on Emerson must respect circles: a stone thrown into a pond emanates expanding circles; so Emerson's sentences throw his readers into widening spheres.

Emerson's famous "transparent-eyeball" passage early in *Nature* is, as I suggested earlier, often taken to be an exemplary statement of the transcendental sublime. Yet, if we read it as a restatement of his vision in the Jardin des Plantes, we realize, from yet another angle, that it is perhaps a moment of the physical sublime—of ecological gnosis—revealing Emerson as a sign in nature's text, a hieroglyph describing his own design, dissolving his own solution. In looking at parts of this passage yet again, we shall see that its form is as vexed as its content.

Here is Emerson (once more), soon after his meditations on the human condition as a hieroglyph, detailing the fiery core of his primary gnosis: "Standing on the bare ground,—my head bathed by the blithe air, and uplifted into infinite space,—all mean egotism vanishes. I become a transparent eye-ball. I am nothing. I see all. The currents of the Universal Being circulate through me; I am part or particle of God" (13). Emerson's speaker (whom I shall call Emerson for the sake of convenience) here becomes an "amazing puzzle," a "bewildered" form animated by an "upheaving" principle of life. In the first sentence, he dissolves into formlessness, his individual being distributed throughout infinity. His discrete being literally disappears: employing a dangling modifier, Emerson does not provide the subject, "I," that the phrase "Standing on bare ground" clearly modifies. His "egotism" vanishing, Emerson becomes diffused through infinite space: his autonomous self becomes "nothing." Yet, in the next sentence, he coheres into a form, a transparent eyeball through which the "currents" of the "Universal Being" "circulate." This form is a torsion, dependent for its very existence on the forces circling through it. Apprehending himself thus, Emerson "sees" all, knows (gnostically) that he is a paralogical figure—centrifugal and centripetal, something and nothing—of an unrepresentable force. He is both a "part" of God, a coherent unit, and a "particle" in the current, a random speck or fragment. Simultaneously ordered and disordered, solved and dissolved, Emerson's condition is a solution in hieroglyphic.

Michel Serres claims that great literary artists often reveal scientific truths before scientists do.[21] Lucretius's *De Rerum de Natura* (ca. 94-55 B.C.E.), for example, "is a treatise on physics," on minimal angles, laminar flows, and turbulence.[22] So then is Emerson's *Nature*, a text whose complex relationships between matter and energy, word and meaning, foreshadow recent mergings of thermodynamics and information theory.

The second law of thermodynamics states that the universe moves toward increasing states of disorder, or entropy. While turn-of-the-century scientists like Sir William Thomson (Lord Kelvin) believed that entropy causes a "universal tendency toward dissipation" that eventually leads to "heat death," or utter stasis, more recent scientists like Ilya Prigogine (as we know) and Arthur Winfree maintain that entropy is creative, churning the world toward increasing complexity. Disorder stimulates new orders to organize themselves—cosmos requires chaos as the reservoir of energy out of which its patterns spontaneously form themselves.[23] Just as thermodynamicists study how coherent shapes organize themselves out of the flux of entropy, so information theorists attend to how meaningful messages emerge out of noise. For the information theorists, the world is a random flow of quantifiable bits of information out of which self-organizing patterns arise to constitute significant signs. In both thermodynamics and information theory, the intensity of entropy is proportional to possibilities for complexity: the more disorder, the more potential for richness and variation in order. It is not surprising that scientists have recently begun to apply these models to biological systems, asking: Can an organism's ability to adapt be measured by its level of organizational complexity and its aptitude for discerning meaningful patterns in the noise of its environment?[24]

Considering these homologies, Serres claims that the flow of entropy and noise is ironically a stable source of life. For an organism to thrive in a perpetually dissipating environment, it must open itself to these disordered, noisy energies—like food, sunlight, oxygen—and convert or translate them into nourishment or meaningful messages. In these vast seas, the successful organism is a temporary island of negentropy, organizing global chaos into its local cosmos. Serres describes such an organism:

> It is a river that flows and yet remains stable in the continual collapse of its banks and the irreversible erosion of the mountains around it. One always swims in the same river, one never sits down on the same bank. The fluvial basin is stable in its flux and the passage of its chreodes; as a system open to evaporation, rain, and clouds, it always—but stochastically—brings back the same water. What is slowly destroyed is the solid basin. The fluid is stable; the solid which wears away is unstable—Heraclitus and Parmenides were both right. Hence the notion of homeorrhesis. The living system is homeorrhetic.[25]

A living system—from cell to woman to ecosystem—is not homeostatic, in equilibrium, standing still (*stasis*), the same (*homos*). Rather, it is the same and not the same, still and flowing (*rhysis*, "to flow"), an example of Heraclitus (all changes) and Parmenides (nothing changes). Like a river, an organism is an interplay between flux and stasis, the perpetual currents of entropy and information and the negentropic habits that convert these global forces into local life. Ironically, Heraclitus's fluxional river is stable, a constant source of complexity and creativity; Parmenides stable banks are unstable, temporary patterns shaping the flow. This is a major reversal: Platonic spirit and idealist *noumena* are chaos; matter and form, cosmos. In the beginning was para-*logos*.

Serres has (unconsciously?) rewritten Emerson's transparent eyeball passage, in which Emerson becomes homeorrhetic, a current and a pattern of the current. In that passage, the transparent eyeball is a fluxional river—the Universal Being, the persistent source of life—and a temporary form circulating (turning and troping) the flow into nourishment on several levels: biological, emotional, poetical. Turning this agitated energy into his own forms, Emerson realizes his place in the system of nature, practicing his version of photosynthesis. Interpreting meaningful messages in the floods of life—air and light—streaming around and through him, he translates them through several analogous acts: respiration, digestion, naming. As Emerson proclaims later, in a piece aptly entitled "Perpetual Forces" (1876), humans, like alembics, transform the unsettling yet stable forces of nature into the coherent yet dissolving structures of their own lives:

> [M]an. . . . is able to subdue these terrible forces. . . . His whole frame is responsive to the world, part for part, every sense, every pore to a new element. . . . No force is but his force. He does not possess them, he is a pipe through which their currents flow. If a straw be held still in the direction of the ocean current, the sea will pour through it as through Gibraltar. (*EW* 10:62-3)

Serres's homeorrhetic river and Emerson's terrible forces are tropes for what Gregory Bateson calls the metapattern that connects all patterns.[26] The most powerful patterns—organisms, essays—acknowledge their connection to the metapattern and allow its energy to organize them. This connection, however, is as risky and unstable as it is enlivening and creative. The metapattern is not harmonious or spiritual. Rather, it is fluxional and boundless: a huge flood, a fast river, an infinite void. Emerson the poet opens himself to these energies, wishing them to be the muses of his vigorous words. Here is Emerson, summing his poetic process in 1876.

> There is one animal, one planet, one matter, and one force. The laws of light and of heat translate into each other;—so do the laws of sound and color; and so galvanism, electricity, and magnetism are varied forms of the selfsame energy. While the student ponders this immense unity, he observes that all things in Nature, the animals, the mountain, the river, the seasons, wood, iron, stone, vapor, have a mys-

terious relation to his thoughts and his life; their growths, decays, quality and use so curiously resemble himself, in parts and wholes, that he is compelled to speak by means of them. (*EW* 8:8-9)

Emerson's interweaving of nature, humans, and language points to David Bohm's poetics of quantum theory and relativity theory. According to Bohm, "both [theories] imply the need to look on the world as an undivided whole, in which all parts of the universe, including the observer and his instruments, merge and unite into one totality." This totality, of course, is not an orderly master narrative but a metapattern that manifests itself in paralogical "quanta" that are simultaneously particles and waves and that flow discontinuously and unpredictably. Echoing Emerson, Bohm believes that one efficient way to "merge and unite" with this metapattern is to use a language that does not chop the world into discrete, logical units, but rather patterns itself on the fluxional cosmos, emerging in "forms . . . [that] have as their content a series of actions that flow and merge into each other without separation and breaks. . . . [words] in harmony with the unbroken flow of existence as a whole."[27]

Exploding Cabinets

The famous Butterfly Effect assumes that a butterfly "stirring the air today in Peking can transform storm systems next month in New York."[28] Emerson's sentences, like the butterfly, sent pulses throughout this essay. Now to return to the track of the butterfly.

What does Emerson say of words in *Nature*? Does he treat them as actions, circulations, or living, paralogical hieroglyphs—rocks, trees, eagles? In his "Language" chapter, he provides the following definitions.

1. Words are signs of natural facts.
2. Particular natural facts are symbols of particular spiritual facts.
3. Nature is a symbol of spirits. (32)

In explaining this, Emerson claims that each word's etymology uncovers a root in material energy. For example, as we have seen, the origin of "spirit" is "wind." The origins of words, then, are natural facts. Adhering to Emerson's emphasis on etymology, we remember that "fact" derives from the Latin *facere*, "to do or make." Words are signs of deeds, actions, and process—not static conditions. In turn, natural facts symbolize spiritual facts; visible events relate to invisible ones. This relationship is dynamic: the root of "symbol" is *symballein*, Greek for "to throw together." Facts do not indicate metaphysical spirit. Rather, they throw or propel the drafts of the breeze, breath, *spiritus*. A relationship among words, nature, and spirit emerges: words pattern physical actions, which themselves are vehicles of wind, the metapattern. Hence, words are forms and bearers of the current of life. Emerson enunciates these connections overtly later in "The Poet": all symbols, seen in relation to *pneuma, physis,* "are fluxional; all language is vehicular and transitive, and is good, as ferries and horses are, for conveyance, not as farms and houses are, for homestead" (*CW* 3:20).

Both words and facts have etymologies, origins, in the metapattern. Just as the etymology of "spirit" is wind, so the etymology of Emerson on the bare common is the universal current, so the origin of a water bubble is the entire atmosphere of electricity—the "whirling bubbles on the surface of a brook, admit us to the secret of the mechanics of the sky" (*CW* 3:105). Attending to Emerson's words as if they are physical and biological specimens, we come to understand the original and sustaining forces criss-crossing the world. His words merge with the motions of creation.

In a further meditation on words in *Nature*, Emerson reveals that etymology unearths paralogy, order and chaos paradoxically joined.

> The moment our discourse rises above the ground line of familiar facts, and is inflamed with passion or exalted by thought, it clothes itself in images. A man conversing in earnest, if he watch his intellectual processes, will find that a material image, more or less luminous, arises in his mind, cotemporaneous with every thought. Hence, good writing and brilliant discourse are perpetual allegories. This imagery is spontaneous . . . It is proper creation. It is the working of the Original Cause through the instruments he has already made. (*N* 39)

Out of the chaotic flames of agitated thought and passion arise self-organizing orders: images, tropes, figures, metaphors. These spontaneous orders are products of conversion ("conversing"), the transformation of entropic energies into negentropic patterns, detailed earlier in *Nature* as the alchemical process by which raw materials are transmuted into fine gold (30). This process is natural, the working of "Original Cause," the metapattern, through the patterns it has created. Their etymology in powerful invisible forces—enflamed passions, expanding thoughts, the primal cause—these linguistic patterns remain polarized, dynamic, unsettled. According to Emerson's metaphor, words are clothes, which would of course be burnt or torn by fire and expansion, both signifying and de-signifying at the same time, *de*-scribing their own *de*-sign. Like homeorrhetic organs, they are stable and unstable. They are indeed "perpetual allegories," persistently speaking (*agoreuein*, "to speak") other (*allos*, "other").

The etymology of Emerson's own essay, his own images, was his experience in the Jardin des Plantes, where, beholding the upheaving principle of life manifested in cabinets of natural history, he vowed to be a naturalist. Emerson suggests that *Nature* is a linguistic version of these botanical and zoological cabinets, a sign of nature's laws. As he observes in his essay, "In a cabinet of natural history, we become sensible of a certain occult recognition and sympathy in regard to the most unwieldy and eccentric forms of beast, fish, and insect" (84). The cabinets in the Jardin organized specimens to show relationships among class, order, genus, species. In a similar fashion, Emerson's linguistic organisms are arranged into chapter headings, subheadings, paragraphs, and sentences to reveal relationships among nature, human, and language. Yet, Emerson's cabinets—unlike those at the Jardin— are not fixed. If they were made of wood and glass, they would splinter and break, cracked by the throbs of Emerson's words. His cabinets are made of more pliable materials, ready to yield to aleatory surges, recalling the *cabine*, Old Northern French for "gambling house."

Endless Inquiry of the Intellect

Nature appears to be a harmonious garden, a clean, bright cabinet, a well-appointed philosophical treatise. After the introduction, the essay is divided into the chapters "Nature," "Commodity," "Beauty," "Language," "Discipline," "Idealism," "Spirit," and "Prospects," most which are further separated into three or four numbered sub-sections. The essay seems to develop from matter to spirit, detailing first nature's material uses and then moving to its spiritual functions. However, Emerson uproots his garden, explodes his cabinet, deconstructs his treatise. His essay is about the impossibility of classification. Not a Jardin des Plantes, it is a field of force.

As I have shown in another context, Emerson contradicts himself often: *Nature* is one thing and the other thing, in the same moment, dissolving the law of non-contradiction, the sine qua non of classification.[29] For example, early in the essay "Nature" is marked off from the "ME" of the human self as the "NOT ME" (7). Later, though, Emerson claims that "Nature is so pervaded with human life, that there is something of humanity in all" (78). Still later, Emerson suggests that humans created nature: "Out from him sprang the sun and moon; from man, the sun; from woman, the moon" (88). In fact, Emerson contradicts himself in the same paragraph. He ends the chapter "Beauty" by claiming that the "world . . . exists to the soul to satisfy the desire of beauty. This element I call an ultimate end" (30). But three sentences later, he asserts that "beauty in nature is not ultimate. . . . not as yet the last or highest expression of the final cause of Nature" (31).

Perhaps Emerson cannot rest on a fixed structure for *Nature* because his subject is illimitable. Certainly, Emerson sets out to find the end—the purpose and limit—of nature. He opens his essay with a query: "to what end is nature?" (*N* 6), referring not only to sky, tree, and ocean but also to his own essay. At the beginning of "Commodity," his second chapter, he thinks about this *telos*: "Whoever considers the final cause [end] of the world [nature] will discern a multitude of uses that enter as parts into the result. They all admit of being thrown into the following classes: Commodity; Beauty; Language; and Discipline" (15). In each of these chapters he ponders the question of nature's purposes and seems to conjure an answer; however, he then questions the answer in the following section. In "Commodity," for instance, he claims that "All the parts [of nature] incessantly work into each other's hands for the profit of man" (16). Then, at the beginning of "Beauty," the next chapter, he undercuts this statement by proclaiming that "A nobler want of man is served by nature, namely, the love of beauty" (19). However, he soon suggests that the purpose of nature is to provide man with language (32-45). Yet, right after he concludes the "Discipline" section, he states that "To this one end of Discipline, all parts of nature conspire" (59), as if he has answered the question once and for all. Indeed, "Discipline" was the final category in the list of ends he said he would consider. However, he disrupts his early plan of considering the question in four chapters by invoking it in three more, "Idealism," "Spirit," and "Prospects." A few paragraphs after his assertion that nature's end is discipline, he again revises, announcing that "Nature is made to conspire with spirit to emancipate us" (63), a statement that works against discipline and toward liberation.

When Emerson again comes to the inquiry in the penultimate chapter "Spirit," he hints that the end of nature, both the essay and the natural world, is, paradoxically, endless: "Uses that are exhausted or that may be, and facts that end in the statement, cannot be all that is true of this brave lodging wherein man is harbored, and wherein all his faculties find appropriate and endless exercise" (76). To question nature is to enter into an "endless exercise" that yields an "infinite scope." In fact, in the final paragraph of the essay, Emerson observes that questions about ends are endless: "So shall we come to look at the world with new eyes. It shall answer the *endless* inquiry of the intellect" (93) (italics mine).

Emerson's cabinets are dangerous, full of trap doors, hidden entrances, and distorting windows. Perhaps the specimens in his cabinets are safer; perhaps his simple statements of definition, another essential element of classification, are stable. Certainly, we would expect Emerson to define the primary specimen of his essay, the word "nature," clearly and consistently. In the "Introduction," Emerson refers to "nature" several times before offering definitions of the term. The word first appears in the fourth sentence of the essay, already quoted: "The foregoing generations beheld God and nature face to face, we, through their eyes" (5). Here nature is a person, a face. The word appears again a few sentences later in the clause "Embosomed for a season in nature, whose floods of life stream around and through us . . . why should we grope among the dry bones of the past . . ." (5). Again, nature is personified, compared to a person with a bosom, but then is suddenly turned into a liquid flood. "Nature" soon after appears in the sentence that claims that nature, like a human being, is a form of sacred writing that "describes its own design" (6). Nature as liquid is suddenly turned into a hieroglyph. In the opening paragraphs, "nature" already is hopelessly protean: visage, breast, flood, carved stone.

The next prominent uses of the word occur in the final paragraph of the introduction, ostensibly meant to pin down the word's meaning, to save it from the semantic floods overwhelming it. In this paragraph, the word "nature" is inscribed in several forms: "Nature," "nature," "NATURE," and "*Nature*." What are the differences among these inscriptions of the term? The universe is comprised of "Nature" and "Soul." All that is distinguished from the human as the "NOT ME," is "nature," among which is "NATURE." The word denotes both a common and philosophical import. "NATURE" is the philosophical form of the word, while "*Nature*," "essences unchanged by man," constitutes common one. What are the differences between the common and philosophical senses of the word? What does "nature" with a small "n" signify?

"Nature" dissolves apace as the essay moves forward. In the first chapter, Emerson asserts that "Nature never wears a mean appearance. . . . Nature never became a toy to the wise spirit" (10). So, nature displays noble, beautiful qualities. However, later, Emerson challenges this thesis. He favorably quotes a sentence from Guillaume Oegger: nature is but the "*scoriae*"— dross, refuse—of the thoughts of God (44). Likewise, still later, he praises religion and ethics for "put[ting] nature under foot" (72). Is nature refuse or a servant to man? Or is it beautiful, integral for his happiness and wisdom?

Work of Ecstasy

Emerson once wrote that "Every thought is . . . a prison; every heaven is also a prison" (*CW* 2:201). *Nature* emancipates us from static thoughts and heavenly principles alike. Inviting us to attend to its cabinets and specimens—

much as Emerson observed the arrangements in the Jardin—the essay holds us in tension, resisting our interpretations. "Attention" and "tension" both derive from the Latin *tendere*, "to stretch." *Nature* indeed stretches us, makes us elastic, loosens us from our discrete island into global floods. Overtaxing our faculties, overwhelming our hermeneutical strategies, it pushes us not to stable meanings but to nebulous drifts. While this version of the sublime may lead to pessimism—despair over inability to fix meaning—for Emerson it is ecstatic and emancipating. As Emerson intones in "The Method of Nature," nature is a "work of ecstasy" (*CW* 1:125). To participate in Emerson's *Nature*—through tense attention—is to be placed out (*ek*) of stillness (*stasis*), to be displaced, to circulate again with the chaos out of which our temporary microcosms emerge. Commenting on the paralogical sublime, Lyotard remarks that one can face the flight of stable principles in one of two ways: by lamenting over a failure to represent the cosmos, or by celebrating an "increase of being and jubilation which result form the invention of new rules of the game."[30] Emerson exemplifies the latter, ecstatic to have his walking papers from idealist prisons, glad to play in fields of force. Evolving in his tropes and figures, we risk losing ourselves—our mean egotism—in a similar way, only to find our etymology in the vitalizing winds of the abyss.

Invoking the "sublime" as a liberating force, Emerson fittingly recalls the word's scientific, alchemical associations: sublimation is the process by which a solid turns directly into a gaseous state without liquefying. For Emerson, the sublime vision results in sublimation: in being freed from a discrete solid into a nebulous gas, in becoming an eddy (a transparent eyeball) in the currents of being. Likewise, words detailing the sublime world are sites of sublimation, alembics transmuting discrete meanings into intensities, energies, and actions. We as attentive readers are sublimed as well. As we stand tense before Emerson's currents, our interpretive categories, our ideas of unity, are dissolved, sent back to the gaseous flux from which they arose.

Sublime and sublimating, endlessly moving back and forth between solid and gas, pattern and flux, Emerson's *Nature*, like James Joyce's *Finnegans Wake* (1939), is a *chaosmos* in which figures are, in Philip Kuberski's words, "unitary and yet untotalized," fields of "mutual and simultaneous interference and convergence, an interanimation of subjective and objective, an endless realm of chance which nevertheless displays a persistent tendency toward pattern and order." In this chaosmic world, we learn that nature, texts, and reading are endless activities, that order is never simply order; chaos, never merely chaos. To quote Kuberski further:

Everything in the world can be seen as chaosmic: the subatomic microworld may not be susceptible to particular determinism but in the macroworld of large-scale objects Newton's laws remain in force; the conception of a human being involves the combination of two strands of DNA in which chance and law interact to initiate epigenseis along certain fixed lines while remaining conditioned by the environment; and poems are composed (and sometimes seem to compose themselves) according to the play of chance and the emergent necessities of pattern, just as a reader never quite reads the "same" poem each time he returns to it.[31]

Put another way, from Emerson: "Under every deep a lower deep opens" (*CW* 2:179). Orders perpetually dissolve and resolve, unpredictably and spontaneously. In the same way, *Nature* is different on every reading: sometimes a transcendentalist treatise, sometimes a quantum experience—both Genesis and *Finnegans Wake*.

My interpretation of *Nature*, like any, is an approximation, a hypothesis, a temporary order. But I hope I have at least suggested that Emerson is far from a transcendentalist museum piece (a specimen in a dusty cabinet). Rather, he is alive to primary events in our century in aesthetics, poetics, and science. Without taking him out of historical context or casting him as a prophet, I want to suggest that his work deserves a different sort of attention than it has generally received. Not only *Nature* but also other pieces are far more complex, turbulent, and rich than the traditional transcendentalist readings of him have shown. Reading him in light of his poetic engagements with nineteenth-century science—as Lee Rust Brown and Laura Dassow Walls have recently and richly done[32]—we might continue the fruitful reassessments of Emerson undertaken during the last two decades. The reward of this endless inquiry, of this ecstatic work is an ecological gnosis— a precipitous dive into the abyss of life.

2 >>>
Fuller's Metamorphoses

Caesar in the Garden

One of Fuller's first works, her "Autobiographical Sketch" (1840; 1852), establishes a distinction between Roman imperialism, embodied by her father, and classical mythology, incarnated by Ovid's *Metamorphoses* (ca. 1-8 CE). Her Roman father, she complains, stifled her when she was young by imposing a pedagogical regime that checked "the natural unfolding of her character" and the "subtle and indirect motions of imagination and feeling." Like a nineteenth-century Caesar, he did not let "nature play freely through him" or her but rather controlled himself and his environment by "a single thought, an earnest purpose, an indomitable will." He hated uncertainty and transience, nature's "soft mediums" and "lines of flight"; he loved death and stasis, avoiding the "green garden" to live among the ruins of the past. He was a despot, reducing blooms to "stones."[1]

The alternative to imperialism is the shifting world detailed by Ovid. As a youth, Fuller escaped the rules of her father by "creep[ing] from amid the Roman pikes to lie beneath this great vine [of Ovid], and see the smiling and serene shapes go by, woven from the finest fabric of the elements." From the "mailed clang of Roman speech," she would flee to energies "born of the sunbeam, the wave, the shadows on the hill." In Ovid, she found a universe where "lines of flight" and blurred mediums hold sway, in which things simmer and slide like waves.[2] Merging with Ovid's pages, she understood that stability and order are temporary, tenuous shapes—evanescent convolutions in a jostling cosmos.

The "Autobiographical Sketch" foreshadows a primary conflict of Fuller's intellectual career. During her writing life, she labors to resist the powerful influence of her father while she strives to embrace the liberating nebulae of Ovid. This is not easy. Her father holds her with the ponderous anchors of traditional Western thought while Ovid, in spite all his emancipating energy, unleashes unsettling floods. Yet, Fuller persists against Roman law, labors to metamorphose. She must do this, for in Ovid's conversions lies her redemption: from Platonic being to Nietzschean becoming, from systematic philosophy to edifying conversation, from tyranny to freedom.

Certainly, as Christina Zwarg and others have shown, Fuller in her two books, *Summer on the Lakes, in 1843* (1844) and *Woman in the Nineteenth Century* (1845), contends with patriarchy.[3] But in undercutting the rules of men, she also upsets the categories that have tended to dominate Western philosophy from Plato to Kant: transcendent order, stable hierarchy, and rational certainty. Practicing this iconoclasm, she hopes to affirm alternative values drawn from Ovidian terrain: heterogeneity, polarity, and transformation. Grasping—in intuitive perceptions, gnostic moments—these disturbing forces, she recovers the palpitations of life.

In both essays Fuller channels these currents, in meaning and method. In *Woman in the Nineteenth Century*, penned in the civilized confines of New England, she feels the shock of agitating electricity but persistently tries to harmonize it with Platonic form. The result is a contradictory book, one trying to break free from fixed order but still constrained by its rules. In *Summer on the Lakes*, however, conceived on the prairies of the American Midwest, animated with Goethe's abysmal energies and luminous eddies, she no longer holds to ideal forms. Even though this book was written in 1844, one year before *Woman in the Nineteenth Century* was published, it is less restrained than her later work, perhaps because Fuller based her 1845 feminist tract on an 1843 essay ("The Great Lawsuit") written before she went to the frontier. Whatever the reason for this discrepancy, Fuller in *Summer on the Lakes* draws on Goethe's gnostic ecology to relinquish the ethereal harmonies of Plato, to overwhelm the columns of Rome. In this largely ignored book, we find a Fuller who leaves the trappings of Concord transcendentalism for the open plain.

Ovid's Chaosmos

Ovid's *Metamorphoses* is a coincidence of chaos and order. It depicts a universe in which order unpredictably arises from chaos only to return to disorder again. Though the poem begins with the metamorphosis of chaos into order, this order is not final: it lasts only until the next transformation threatens to return the world to strife.

> Before the sea and lands began to be,
> before the sky had mantled every thing,
> then all of nature's face was featureless—
> what men call chaos: undigested mass
> of crude, confused, and scumbled elements,
> a heap of seeds that clashed, of things mismatched.
> There was no Titan Sun to light the world,

no crescent Moon—no Phoebe—to renew
her slender horns; in the surrounding air,
earth's weight had yet to find its balanced state;

[N]o thing maintained its shape; all were at war;
in one same body cold and hot would battle;
the damp contended with the dry, things hard
with soft, and weighty with weightless parts.[4]

In this noisy mass of uncultivated seeds, nothing can maintain a definite shape. No rhythms organize the soup into discernible patterns.

Suddenly, however, out of nowhere and from an unknown source: division and organization appear.

A god—and nature, now become benign—
ended this strife. He separated sky
and earth, and earth and waves, and he defined
pure air and thicker air. Unraveling
these things from their blind heap, assigning each
its place—distinct—he linked them all in peace.

When he—whichever god it was—arrayed
that swarm, aligned, designed, alloted, made
each part into a portion of a whole,
then he, that earth might be symmetrical,
first shaped its sides into a giant ball.[5]

This god—unknown, who may be the same as nature itself—defines "limits" and sets boundaries.[6] He places like seeds with like and cultivates them: he is a cosmic gardener. This god does not create *ex nihilo* but gives form, clarity, and division to preexisting energy. Indeed, Ovid suggests that nature itself—not necessarily a transcendent god—is responsible for arranging this primal formlessness: patterns organize themselves unpredictably, islands of negentropy rising in an entropic sea.

These opening lines inaugurate a creative tension between order and chaos that structures Ovid's poem. Soon after chaos forms itself (or is formed) into order, a "Golden Age" ensues. Strife is vanquished but along with it, change. All is harmonious. No laws are required to control unruly men. There is no death, no decay. Storms, blight, and plague do not exist. Spring is never ending. Yet, this world is static: no transformations, no creativity, no difference. Men have no need for shelter or planting. They lie in the sun and consume nature's bounty.[7] Is this *living*, this languishing status quo? Isn't the universe threatened with stasis, which would reduce difference to the same, produce a heat death?

Only the return of strife sets things in motion. Jove wars with and defeats Saturn, beginning the "Silver Age." The four seasons arise. Men must build houses and plant seeds, become artists and technicians. Strife continues to reorganize: after the Silver Age comes the Bronze and then the Iron, a return to chaos. Men become warring elements, endlessly fighting; guests are unable to tell if their host is friend or foe, sons attempt to become the fathers through patricide. Again, as in the beginning, the seeds are scattered, unable to grow: disorder reigns once more.[8]

Order unmoved by chaos is static; chaos unorganized by order is an "undigested mass." Both conditions constitute universes of death. Life consists of their antagonism, a contest in which neither vanquishes the other. Jove becomes the referee for this competition. He curbs the pervasive strife of the Iron Age but does not recommence the Golden. After plunging the earth again into disorder by flooding it, Jove starts fresh, with Deucalion and Pyrrha, the only ones whom he allows to escape the water. Standing alone in the swamp, they, like the mysterious god of order, like Jove himself, must organize and cultivate. This they do by throwing stones into the mud (at the behest of the oracle of Themis). These stones metamorphose into humans, growing from the soup. Soon after, animals likewise are born "spontaneously" from the muddy womb of earth. In time, several seeds in the muck emerge into form. Again, coherent shapes arise from formlessness. This time, though, order does not vanquish its chaotic source. Rather, the universe will be a "discordant concord."[9]

Now, the world is a struggle between concord and discord—discord is the muse, the energy; concord is the poet, the form. Repeatedly, Ovid describes how new shapes arise from strife. From the struggle between Daphne and Apollo emerges the laurel, a mixing of human and plant; from the war among Jove, Juno, and Io arises Isis, part woman, part cow; from her perturbed mourning for her fallen brother Phaeton, Lampetia turns into a tree, half person, half wood; and so on.[10] Each metamorphosis grows out of chaos and becomes a pattern of it: a dynamic form that mixes opposites into a cogent structure. Some of these changes are liberating, forms of escape (Daphne); others are tragic, imposed on innocent victims (Io); still others are forms of punishment for hubris (Phaeton); and some are random (Lampetia). Change is unpredictable: destructive as well as creative, emancipating as well as confining. Terrible beauties are born from the muse of discord.

Plato and the Hermaphrodite

The young Fuller knew that Ovid's cosmology resists the status quo. Confined in a rigid system—the Roman one of her father—she concluded correctly that Ovidian turbulence was her salvation.

Her 1843 essay "The Great Lawsuit: Man versus Men; Woman versus Women" and its 1845 extension, *Woman in the Nineteenth Century*, are her first efforts to undam Ovid's swells. Yet, these texts, for all their turbulence, are still constrained within a Platonic paradigm—a place for everything and everything in its place. In her preface to *Woman in the Nineteenth Century*, Fuller announces her intention to sue for growth: "man" has been confined by the stereotypical definition of "men," "woman," by traditional accounts of "women." She believes that the categories of "men" and "women" should be metamorphosed, blurred into one another. If we could take the virtues from each gender, an appropriately flexible and ennobling definition of the "human" would emerge, an androgynous being featuring the strengths of "man" and "woman." Shattering traditional gender differences into creative nebulosity is of course iconoclastic, especially in the nineteenth century. Yet, the source by which Fuller sanctions androgyny is not disruptive at all. She draws her inspiration from Plato's myth of the primal human in the *Symposium* (ca. 387-67 B.C.E.).

> By Man I mean both man and woman; these are the two halves of one thought. I lay no especial stress on the welfare of either. I believe that the development of one cannot be effected without that of the other. My highest wish is that this truth should be distinctly and rationally apprehended, and the conditions of life and freedom recognized as the same for the daughters and sons of time; twin exponents of a divine thought. (*WN* 5)

Proclaiming that the ideal "man" is both "man and woman," Fuller recalls Plato's myth of the hermaphrodite, spoken by Aristophanes to account for the origin of love. In the beginning, hermaphrodites roamed the earth. They were "globular in shape, with rounded back and sides, four arms and four legs, and two faces, both the same, on a cylindrical neck, and one head, with one face one side and one the other, and four ears, and two lots of privates, and all the other parts to match." Yet, soon these beings became arrogant and tried to usurp the places of the gods. To punish this insolence, Zeus and the other gods sliced the hermaphrodites in half to weaken them, separating them into males and females. So arose the origin of love: ever since the severing, males and females have longed for this primal unity.[11]

Of course, this myth does not necessarily reflect Plato's views. Indeed, later in the dialogue Socrates (Plato's usual mouthpiece) recounts his conversation with the sage Diotima, during which he provides his own account of earthly desire as a prologue to heavenly love. Physical desire is a preparation for spiritual desire, as one's yearning for particular beauties is progressively translated into a wish to merge with universal Beauty.[12] In the end, though, the myths of Aristophanes and Socrates are similar. Both suggest that proper love is a quest for a primal unity that transcends difference, where opposites, like male and female, are indeed inseparable and nonpolarized, "twin exponents of a divine thought."

Fuller's use of Plato to sanction her androgynous ideal sets her book against itself. On the one hand, she endorses Ovid's metamorphosing chaos, which blends man into woman, same into other, identity into difference. On the other hand, however, she assumes that this disturbing vagueness will be resolved in the eternal harmony of Plato's ideal realm. While the former proposal suggests strife, change, and future revolution, the latter assumption intimates unity, stasis, and a return to a pristine, Edenic past. This tension revolves around a primary question of *Woman in the Nineteenth Century*. What is nature? Is it an interplay between chaos and order? Or is nature a pattern of a preexistent harmony? If the answer to the first question is yes, then most anything can happen: possibilities for transformation are legion. If the answer to the second is affirmative, then change is illusory: the best men and women can hope for is that they return to their primal harmony, in which "man" manifests divine thought in his proper way, "woman" in hers. Though this latter condition would certainly be more ennobling and equitable for men and women alike, it would nonetheless limit the sphere of the man and the woman, reducing them to ciphers of a fixed structure.

This contest between Plato and Ovid persistently agitates Fuller's *Woman*, stifling the energies of Ovidian metamorphosis, yet also threatening Plato's forms. Ultimately, the book is *Hamlet redivivus*, a study in philosophical paralysis. For example, here's Fuller, early in her book, validating the liberation of women with a theory of universal harmony.

> We would have every arbitrary barrier thrown down. We would have every path laid open to Woman as freely as to Man. Were this done, and a slight temporary fermentation allowed to subside, we should be crystallizations more pure and of more various beauty. We believe the divine energy would pervade nature to a degree unknown by the history of former ages, and that no discordant collision, but a ravishing harmony of spheres, would ensue. (*WN* 20)

Fuller is clearly radical for nineteenth-century readers in claming that the oppression of women is arbitrary and that liberation is natural. If women were as free as men, then we would return to the harmony from which we arose—men and women would be "twin exponents" of the divine. Yet, this "ravishing harmony of spheres" would also necessarily delimit the roles of men and women. For symmetry to exist between any two elements, both elements must retain clearly defined shapes—women would have their predetermined circuit, men, theirs.

Later, Fuller suggests what the eternal round of women might be: their sphere requires that they be electrical, lyrical, emotional. Again, Fuller is revolutionary: the qualities of women that have traditionally vexed men should be valued as divine. At the same time, however, her Platonism reduces the potential of the feminine. According to the dictates of the preexisting harmony, women possess the "electrical" element more than men; "her intuitions are more rapid and more correct" than those of men, who are ruled by "intellect" and thus "absolutely stupid in regard to . . . the fine invisible links which connect the forms of life around them" (61). While the "soul," or Platonic spirit, is androgynous when unbodied, when it rushes into a woman, it "flows, it breathes, it sings, rather than desposits soil, or finishes work" (68). This "electrical" genius of women does not excel in "classification" or "the selecting and energizing of art" (68). Naturally, spiritually, ideally, woman intuits and lives; man thinks and creates.

Fuller is careful to emphasize, however, that the eternal feminine is not always and exclusively embodied by particular women: "[I]t is no more the order of nature that it [the "feminine element"] should be incarnated pure in any form, than that the masculine energy should exist unmingled in any form" (*WN* 69). In other words, woman can embody masculine elements: she may discipline her Muse-like flows with the intellect of "Minerva," the shape woman takes when she becomes masculine. Likewise, men can partake of the feminine element, blurring their stable intellectual categories with the music of "Apollo." While "[m]ale and female represent the two sides of the great radical dualism," "they are perpetually passing into one another," as "[f]luid hardens into solid, solid rushes into fluid." "There is no wholly masculine man, no purely feminine woman" (68-9).

This is Fuller's tension: between eternal symmetry, in which a woman must do one thing, a man another; and shifting shapes, in which men and women are male and female, androgynous vortices. Indeed, only a paragraph after her description of the grand Platonic dualism, Fuller floods the *Symposium* with the *Metamorphoses*.

History jeers at the attempts of physiologists to bind great original laws by the forms which flow from them. They make a rule; they say from observation what can and cannot be. In vain! Nature provides exceptions to every rule. She sends women to battle, and sets Hercules spinning.... Of late, she plays still gayer pranks. Not only she deprives organizations, but organs, of a necessary end. She enables people to read with the top of the head, and see with the pit of the stomach. Presently, she will make a female Newton, and a male Syren. (*WN* 69)

Nature here is a prankster, fortuitously jumbling Plato's forms. Radically new forms arise from its mixtures, surreal ones worthy of Ovid: a reading head, a stomach with eyes. With possibilities like these, it is not unreasonable to suppose that a female Newton might arise. With chaos in the system, brave new orders can emerge that significantly alter the terrain.

The "Muse" is not now feminine energy sent from Plato's stars. She is the turbulence generating a wavering cosmos, the oceanic matrix from which Minerva arises as waves—fleeting patterns.

Goethe's Unsystematic System

The interplay between Muse and Minerva can be read, then, in two ways. These two vectors can be construed as ciphers of what Nietzsche calls *being*—mere signs of a transcendent order that constrains "change" and "transitoriness." Or they could be understood as complementary polarities whose dynamic interactions generate Nietzschean *becoming*—a dance of accident and law.[13] The time of being—the temporality of Plato—is static: change is illusory, only a moving image of eternal forms. However, if nature *becomes*, then time—as Ovid would say (predicting Nietzsche)—is a realm of real change, in which chance metamorphoses form new laws, and laws solidify random swerves into novel shapes.

Fuller's descriptions of becoming, of creative time, are not only harbingers of Nietzsche; they also, of course, reach back to Goethe, who, as we know, made the metamorphoses of nature his prime subject. As Frederick Augustus Brown showed at the beginning of this century, Fuller's study of Goethe was a profound event in her development, awakening her "feelings and inner life." In fact, according to Perry Miller, Fuller was probably the first American thinker to realize the power of the great German poet.[14] In an 1841 essay in the *Dial* entitled "Goethe," the earliest American piece to appreciate Goethe extensively, Fuller claims that *Faust* contains the "great idea" of Goethe: "the progress of a soul through the various forms of existence."[15] She might have said more tersely that this great idea was "metamorphosis," the passage of life through change—this is certainly the word Goethe himself probably would have used. Indeed, as Mary-Jo Haronian has recently demonstrated in a study of Fuller and optics, Fuller was profoundly aware of the scientific issues that Goethe explored.[16] Interested in Goethe's studies of seeing and color, Fuller would also have been cognizant of his other great scientific undertaking: to understand the metamorphoses of flora and fauna, to find the primal forms through which life spirals.

Fuller refers to Goethe constantly through *Woman in the Nineteenth Century*. She primarily extols him for acknowledging the "electrical" virtues of women (like Margaret in *Faust*, Iphigenia in *Iphigenia in Tauris*, and Mignon in *Wilhelm Meister's Apprenticeship*) but perhaps also holds him close as a supporter of her efforts to marry Plato's harmonies to earthly men and women. I say this because Goethe's science and the "transcendental anatomy" it influenced are often read as examples of naturalistic Platonism: efforts to combine Plato's stable ideas with the flux of nature. In the words of Ernst Mayr, the recent historian of biology, Goethe's science was "a fusion of Plato's essentialism with aesthetic principles," a "search for an underlying *eidos*."[17] Certainly Mayr (and others)[18] have good reason for supposing Goethe a Platonist disguised as a biologist. After all, he spent his youth immersed in Plotinus and quite clearly posits the *Urpflanze* and *Urtier* as invisible (though physical) forms unifying diversity.

Yet, as I have suggested in the introduction, there is another way of reading Goethe's science: as a gnostic ecology influenced by Boehme's abysmal natural philosophy. It is conceivable—though I cannot verify it—that Fuller understood Goethe in this way, that the Ovidian passages in *Woman in the Nineteenth Century* and the vigor of *Summer on the Lakes* are conversions of the gnostic Goethe. Taking this possibility seriously, let us again look at Goethe's science of the abyss, for it will be a helpful guide through the falls, rapids, and cataracts of *Summer*. As we know, Goethe set out to Italy in 1786 in search of the *Urpflanze*, the invisible pattern organizing and sustaining metamorphoses of plants. As he records in his *Italian Journey*, during a walk through the Public Gardens at Palermo, it came to him in a flash: each plant is an unfolding of the primal leaf.[19] But what is this Ur-leaf? Is it a Platonic idea immanent in nature? Or is it one side of a fundamental polarity organizing the unruly and disruptive abyss of life, the unifying, negentropic pole complementing a diversifying and entropic opposite? As we have seen, the latter possibility is quite viable when we look at the essay "Problems," part of *On Morphology*.

In that essay, Goethe records a passage that sounds remarkably like Fuller's descriptions of playful nature and electric soul: "Natural system: a contradictory expression. Nature has no system; she has—she is—life and development from an unknown center toward an unknowable periphery" (*SS* 43). Here Goethe suggests that nature is too unruly to be organized by a stable form. However, this does not mean that nature is utter anarchy or blind force. Rather, this abyss organizes itself into polarities—the dance of Minerva and the Muse. As he continues in "Problems": "The idea of metamorphosis . . . leads to formlessness; it destroys knowledge, dissolves it. It is like the *vis centrifuga*, and would be lost in the infinite if it had no counterweight; here I mean the drive for specific character, the stubborn persistence of things which have finally attained reality. This is the *vis centripeta*" (*SS* 43). Nature, bubbling up from an unknowable source, has no stable system, no firm form, but it is, however, organized by centrifugal and centripetal forces in perpetually creative strife. It is a formless ocean periodically coalescing into individual waves and then spreading again into the boundless. The principle of coherence, the *vis centripeta*, is the *Urbild*, the primal plan that is dependent on and complements the essential turbulence, the *via centrifuga*. Both are contingent themselves upon the ungraspable gulf of life.

Fuller, out in the forests west of New England, with her head uncovered and her Plato gathering dust in her library, experiences Goethe's problems with systematic nature. There, perhaps with Goethe's gnosis flowing in her psychic undertow, she realizes that there is no stable being, no *eidos* over which time slides. Rather, as she recognizes in the glaring grain, time that lives is time that becomes. The true temporality is Ovid's, growing, as Allen Mandelbaum has written, from a "reverence for the flow of rivers and surge of seas, for abundant forests, and for entrancing groves." Beyond the confines of civilization, Fuller fosters such a reverence and comes to embrace time as becoming. She metamorphoses into an avatar of the abysmal science, succeeding Goethe and preceding Nietzsche, and moving with the ghost of Ovid, "the totemist-metamorphosist and . . . the delirious Buffon-cum-Linnaeus-cum-Vesalius of animal and plant and man—and, above all, of nomad forms, forms in movement from human to plant to animal."[20] If *Woman in the Nineteenth Century* strains to leave behind the sunny walks of reason and plunge into the sea—not only in content but also, as Annette Kolodny, Marie Mitchell Olesen Urbanski, and Jeffrey Allen Steele have shown,[21] in form—*Summer on the Lakes* takes the dive.

Perpetual Trampling of Waters
Confronting an eagle, waterfalls, a whirlpool, and rapids in the first chapter of *Summer on the Lakes*, Fuller quickly moves from simple harmony to concordant discord. She's in Niagara—the eastern-most stop on her 1843 West-

ern tour—a liminal region where civilization and wilderness clash. This struggle is manifest in a captive eagle. Like the Roman imperialists, who harnessed the bird for their symbol of martial domination, some inhabitants of Niagara have captured an eagle. Fuller is surprised to see this tyranny so far from the settlements of New England. It reminds her of a horrible scene from her childhood: an eagle chained to a balcony of a museum near her home. The unfortunate bird consistently underwent abuse that rendered its eyes "dull" and its "plumage soiled and shabby." The eagle of her childhood resembles the one in Niagara, also a victim of human cruelty. Yet, Fuller notices that the strictures of civilization cannot entirely oppress the powers of the bird. Though subdued, the eagle retains its regal carriage, ignoring the humans, listening, Fuller imagines, "to the voice of the cataract," "feeling that congenial powers [flow] free," "consoled, though his own wing [is] broken" (*SL* 6-7).

This liberating water pervades Fuller's opening chapter, which figures Muse and Minerva twisting. A product of civilization, reared on Plato, Fuller initially labors to embrace the energies of the waters saturating Niagara. She embodies this *agon* on the first page. Upon first reaching the falls, her nerves are taxed,

[f]or here there is no escape from the weight of a perpetual creation; all other forms and motions come and go, the tide rises and recedes, the wind, at its mightiest, moves in gales and gusts, but here is really an incessant, and indefatigable motion. Awake or asleep, there is no escape, still this rushing round you and through you. It is in this way I have most felt the grandeur—somewhat eternal, if not infinite. (*SL* 3)

This indefatigable water figures the unsystematic throbs of nature—the electric soul. Though Fuller first finds it disturbing, she quickly discovers in its cadence hidden orders that are "sublime, giving the effect of a spiritual repetition through all the spheres" (4).

This initial conflict and ensuing celebration of wild water occurs three more times in the first chapter. Again thinking of the waterfalls, Fuller is overcome by the "perpetual trampling of the waters" and begins to fear annihilation by untamed nature, here figured by "savages stealing behind [her] with uplifted tomahawks." Yet, at the same time, she quickly realizes that this "undefined dread" is "such as may be felt when death is about to usher us into a new existence" (*SL* 4). Similarly, in viewing the whirlpool below the falls, she feels both fear, knowing that it is destructive, and awe, for the whorls "whisper" engaging mysteries (5). The rapids inspire tension as well. In "enchanting" her, they threaten her autonomy, casting her under their spell. Yet, they also attract her, offering a vision of the fluid process by which nature is produced. In the rapids, nature seems "to have made a study for some larger design. She delights in this, a sketch within a sketch, a dream within a dream." In the midst of the rapids, "all the lineaments become fluent, and we mould the scene in congenial thought with its genius" (5).

Fuller has had her gnosis—similar to that of Goethe in Palermo and Emerson on the common—seeing in the water the process by which nature functions. No harmonizing principle, no *eidos* can contain these waters. The falls are flux: "perpetual creation," simultaneously destructive and creative, somewhat permanent in shape while utterly transient in function. Likewise, the whirlpool is a mix of centrifugal and centripetal forces. So are the rapids: destroying and creating, stable and transient, they harvest the virtues of all water, indeed, as Fuller claims, of all creation. They are a "sketch" of nature's vast "sketch," a "dream" of its huge "dream." Nature is incomplete, a work-in-progress playfully revising itself; likewise, it is a reverie, a vague vision produced while reason and logic sleep.

Conversation

The method by which Fuller achieves her gnosis is dialectical: she is initially drawn to the turbid waters, then recoils in fear, only to overcome her anxiety and embrace the rapids more intensely, with deeper understanding. It's as if she enters into a conversation with herself, positing claims, disagreeing with them, then reaffirming them with more conviction and knowledge. In entering into such a method of thinking, she participates in the process of nature, which, as a work-in-progress (an evolving sketch, essay, poem) must endlessly revise itself—criticize in order to reach more powerful forms, destroy to create.

Aptly, Fuller got her living through conversation. In 1837, she went to work at Bronson Alcott's Temple School, notorious (and scandalous) for its discussions with children on "adult" subjects of a physiological nature. These talks were a centerpiece of Alcott's radical educational theory. Following Plato and Wordsworth, Alcott believed that children were closer than grown-ups to divine knowledge. Their immortal souls had only been in their bodies a short time, so they were more likely to remember the true, beautiful, and good spiritual realms where their eternal parts dwelt before descending into flesh. Also, children were not yet perverted by the prejudices of society, so they were more likely to speak honestly about their spontaneous feelings and instinctive beliefs—sentiments and senses that would reveal the eternal knowledge of the soul. Putting these theories into practice,

Alcott opened his academy in 1834, hoping to play the midwife to his students by entering into "conversations" with them on serious subjects. Just about the time Fuller came to work for Alcott, as his assistant, he had published *Conversations with Children on the Gospels* (1836-7), an edited transcript of one of his discussions with his pupils on the four Gospels. Though this document spawned moral outrage from New Englanders—primarily because of passages on sex and birth—Fuller nonetheless defended the text and its author.[22]

By 1839—and no longer one of Alcott's employees—Fuller decided to conduct her own Socratic conversations, not with children but with the women of Boston and Concord. Drawing from Plato's (and Alcott's) theory of conversation as revelation (Fuller reported reading Plato to get "tuned up" before one of her meetings[23]), Fuller hoped to get her living not by "*teach*[ing] anything" but by "call[ing] out the thought of others."[24] Like Socrates, she did not wish to be a didactic pedagogue but rather a midwife, a cultivator of seeds. She likely had the Socrates of Plato's early period (ca. 399-387 B.C.E.) in mind—the Socrates of the *Euthyphron, Laches, Charmenides,* and *Lysis*—for this Socrates engages in conversation not so much to reach a conclusion as to explore and develop a subject from several angles. In each of these dialogues, Socrates achieves no result but ends in ambiguity, leaving the dialogue in process, in a condition of becoming. While the later Socrates (of Plato) is more likely to drive a dialogue to a finale—the closure of being—this early one (perhaps closer to the actual Socrates) is happy to emphasize process as much as product, the dynamic activity of thinking as much as stable definitions.

For five years, during which time she was writing "The Great Lawsuit" and *Summer on the Lakes,* Fuller, Socrates in New England, led dialogues on a variety of subjects ranging from mythology to religion to philosophy to psychology to morality. According to transcripts of these conversations, Fuller was a brilliant interlocutor, able to shift perspectives quickly, to range over numerous disciplines, to digress and return, to avoid dogmatic theories.[25] These qualities—flexibility, heterogeneity, spontaneity—were necessary for her primary aim (which was perhaps the aim of the early Socrates): to push herself and her interlocutors beyond the conventional ideas of her time into the abysses of their own souls. After five years of engaging in these conversations, she sums up the primary motivation behind her colloquial philosophy, emphasizing self-reliance: "My wish has been more & more to purify my own conscience when near [my interlocutors], give clear views of the aims of this life, show them where the magazines of knowledge lie, & leave the rest to themselves & the Spirit who must teach & help them to self-impulse."[26]

According to Christina Zwarg, the transcripts and reports of Fuller's conversations help to explain her "unusual compositional strategies," characterized by "shifting frames of reference," by what Jullie Ellison has called a "'Both/and' policy."[27] These strategies, carried out in the conversation parlor and on paper, are certainly powerful feminist tools, as Zwarg argues, upsetting as they do the traditional ("masculine") hierarchies of thinking: either logical or fallacious; either lucid or worthlessly vague. But Fuller's theory and practice of conversation also reflects a major element in European Romanticism: dialectic. Dialectic—both a structure of nature and a method of thinking—is pervasive in the canons of German Romanticism. One finds it developed philosophically in Fichte's *Science of Knowledge* (1797), Schelling's *System of Transcendental Idealism* (1800), and in Hegel's *Phenomenology of Spirit* (1807). Each of these philosophers describes the cosmos as a "self-moving and self-sustaining system," to use the phrase of M. H. Abrams. Drawing from Boehme, each maintains that the cosmos is comprised of an endless, agitated dialectic between opposing principles: ego and non-ego, ideal and real, infinite and finite, master and slave. These polarities, like interlocutors in a vigorous conversation, perpetually push each other to higher levels of consciousness, ever striving to achieve absolute awareness. In this view, history itself is *Bildungsgeschichte,* an educational process by which the spirit instructs itself in time. In the beginning, spirit is pure but not fully aware of its powers (omnipotent without being omniscient, potential without being actual). To become conscious of itself, to grow into its fullest actuality, it must perpetually posit oppositions through which it perceives itself with increasing clarity. This process of intensification—found in Boehme and Goethe—is described by Hegel as an instance of *das Aufheben:* negation, preservation, and ascension. Each form of spirit (be it organic, historical, or philosophical) is temporary, limited. As it develops over time, the form eventually opens to its own opposite, or antithesis. But this antithetical form does not merely obliterate the prior form. On the contrary, the new form retains what was most valuable in the earlier form—indeed, the new form is dependent on the earlier one form its own evolution. This interaction of antithetical forms increases the self-consciousness of both. Both realize their own limitations; both understand their dependence on a larger whole. The master initially controls the servant. Yet, over time, the servant evolves into a self-reliant worker and realizes that the master is dependent upon his labor. Likewise, the master eventually faces his own dependence on the servant and understands that the servant is actually independent. Both forms have opened into their opposites and become more self-conscious in the process. This dialectical interaction between master and servant is analogous to similar conversations between opposing philosophical world views (realism and idealism), historical movements (Marxism and capitalism), and organic processes (acorn and oak). Each of these forms is a way station for the spirit, a temporary junction in its cosmic evolution.[28]

As the cosmos, so the thinker: the individual mind itself develops by engaging in a dialectical process, entering into a dynamic conversation with itself and others. This "logic" is developed by Fichte, Schelling, and Hegel, but it is also declaimed by more literary minds, like Goethe, Schiller, and F. Schlegel. As we have seen, Goethe, like Fichte, Schelling, and Hegel, believed that nature is a polarized conversation between centrifugal and centripetal forces, intensifying with each further turn of phrase. His method of observation—intuitive perception—was an extension of nature's dialectic: to apprehend nature—both its eddies and its oceans—one must place parts and wholes in dialogue, attending to how the parts are informed by the whole, how the whole is affected by the parts.

Goethe's friend Schiller explores similar dialectical processes in "Letters on the Aesthetic Education of Man" (1795). In this piece, Schiller argues that man achieves his fullest potential as thinker and artist by placing his sense drive (*Stofftrieb*) (his impulse toward nature, the finite, change) and his formal drive (*Formtrieb*) (his desire for spirit, the infinite, stasis) into conversation. The result is the play drive (*Spieltrieb*), the artistic impulse. Playing (creating art), one draws from the energies of nature (palpable flux, unconscious force) without being overwhelmed by them, and embraces the forms of the mind (abstract pattern, conscious composition) without becoming static. Perpetually moving back and forth between these two modes, one both engages in and produces artistic forms of Kant's aesthetic "purposiveness without a purpose"—controlled accident, spontaneous discipline.[29]

Throughout his *Athenaeum Fragments* (1798-1802), Schlegel invokes similar dialectical activities to detail ideal thought and art. For example, the "naïve," which is "beautiful, poetic, and idealistic," is a polarized blending of "intention with instinct." If the artist is compelled only by instinct, similar to the sense drive, then he is "childlike, childish, or silly." If he is motivated solely by "intention," analogous to the form drive," he is beset by "affectation," overly artificial gestures. To achieve powerful art—naïve, natural art—one must convert instinct into intention, intention into instinct. One does this through irony, a "continuous alternation of self-creation and self-destruction"—a perpetual expression of instinct endlessly criticized by intention.[30]

These ideas—centering on nature, philosophy, and art as conversation and dialectic—did not fade away when Romanticism was incorporated into

Modernism. On the contrary, Romantic dialectic thrives, in less idealistic forms, in the work of Nietzsche and Heidegger. Even though Nietzsche criticizes Romanticism for its hunger for spiritual comfort in a painful world, and even though he attacks Socrates's dialectic as a violent, vengeful argumentative tool, he nonetheless draws from Romantic dialectic and the playful conversational forms of Socrates throughout his philosophical life.[31] For instance, the notion that the sense drive and the form drive merge into the play drive appear in Nietzsche's *Birth of Tragedy* (1872) as the Dionysian and the Apollinian converging into tragedy. Later, Nietzsche would elevate this aesthetic opposition into a cosmological one: nature is a perpetual conversation between Dionysian turbulence and Apollinian patterns.[32] Heidegger, a deep student of Nietzsche, likewise purveys dialectical forms. In *Being and Time* (1927), Being is a playful oscillation between unknowable abyss and palpable presence, ungraspable whole (*lethe*) and revelatory parts (*aletheia*). Rich thinking—which Heidegger will later connect to poetry—must itself place part and whole in dialogue. It is circular, a hermeneutical conversation, moving back and forth between Being and beings, whole and parts: one can only understand the parts from the perspective of the whole; one can only glimpse the whole by studying the parts.[33]

Now we come full circle: Richard Rorty, the American neo-pragmatist, thinking out of Heidegger (and Dewey and Wittgenstein), establishes conversation as the primary power of living philosophy. In *Philosophy and the Mirror of Nature* (1979), Rorty admonishes philosophers not to establish an absolute in static systems but instead to wonder about transience in edifying conversations. For Rorty, philosophy from Descartes through Locke to Kant has been "systematic": it has bifurcated mind and nature, defined knowledge as the mind's correct representations of the nature external to it, and established these representations as the foundations of objective truth. Once this system is in place, all questions are answered, all conversation unnecessary; language need only be commensurate with the representations of the mind. The world becomes fixed and dead. The "edifying" philosopher (like Heidegger and Dewey), however, reacts against these systems. He finds that objective truth is not only myth but also alienates thinkers from history and creativity. For him, philosophy is not a science but a conversation, an open-ended, dynamic process that creates fresh descriptions of the world instead of merely mimicking conventional ones, that keeps a space open for wonder and innovation instead of simply resting in static conclusions. Without conversation, the mind stagnates and the universe monotonously ticks.[34]

Conversing assiduously with Emerson—a key source for American pragmatism (as Richard Poirier has shown) and for Nietzsche's philosophy (as

George Stack has demonstrated)[35]—Fuller is a major, though neglected figure in this canon of conversational thinkers. Like the German Romantics she studied and loved,[36] like Nietzsche and Heidegger, she sees nature itself proceeding in the form of an agitated conversation, perpetually metamorphosing its deep force into different forms, endlessly revising these forms into more complex, richer patterns, ever moving back and forth between ungraspable energy and discrete figure. Wishing to participate in nature's rhythms, her thinking and speaking are likewise dialectical. Throughout *Summer on the Lakes*, Fuller enters into a philosophical colloquy with herself, challenging her upbringing, trying to undulate with Ovid and Goethe. She proves a conversational stylist as well, her book taking the form of a long dialogue among several heterogeneous interlocutors.

But Fuller's conversational gnosis and her related style are dangerous: edification always threatens the system. While Fuller by the falls realizes that life is in the wild, people tend to love death, afraid of drowning in the voice of many waters.

Universe of Death

After her embrace of Ovid's nature by the rapids, Fuller spends the remainder of *Summer on the Lakes* considering both the virtues of the wild and the dangers of controlling it.

For example, farther west, on the Manitou Islands (located in northern Michigan), Fuller refines her watery vision by realizing more deeply the "mighty meaning" of the wild, Western "scene." Here one might foresee the laws by which a "new order, a new poetry, is to be evoked from this chaos" (*SL* 18). Later, even deeper in the wild in a rough settlement on the outskirts of Chicago, Fuller allows her mental geography to correspond to her physical one. She perceives in this frontier scene a "mixture of culture and rudness" that "gives a feeling of freedom, not of confusion" (24). Later, after spending a day on the prairies of Illinois, Fuller is now prepared to apotheosize the chaos of the plains, to canonize her revelation in Niagara. Countering a scholar who once said that "limits are sacred," Fuller intones, "what is limitless alone is divine" (40).

There are many such overt paeans to turbulent nature throughout *Summer*. However, Fuller perhaps shows her deepest understanding of the wild in three stories about the dangers of constraining edifying conversation with systematic grids.

In Chicago, Fuller has a conversation with a Mrs. Z., in which she learns the plight of Mariana, a former schoolmate of hers (but likely based on Fuller herself). Mariana is the embodiment of the play of the wild, the electricity of the soul, the trampling of the waterfalls. She is "always new, always surprising" (51). She engages in dervish-like dancing, whirling until giddy (51). Hers is a "wild and exuberant life," pervaded by "electric sparks" (60). Yet, like her prototype Cassandra, she suffers resistance from society, for her nature threatens the security of the world in which she lives. She never finds a medium through which to express her genius. Rather, she agonizes while her energies are stifled by her overly rational friends, husband, and society. She wilts and dies (58-64).

Later, still farther in the wild, in the territory of Wisconsin, Fuller finds another oppressed Cassandra in a book by Justinus Kerner called *The Seeress of Prevorst* (1829). Like Mariana (and Cassandra), the Seeress, named Frederica Hauffe, born in 1801 in Prevorst, is imbued with electricity. In her galvanized mind exist the seeds of "poetic creation and science" (94). She is a visionary, a conduit for universal forces, a perpetual transparent eyeball. Yet like Mariana she suffers societal misunderstanding that suffocate her powers. Those close to her, misapprehending her gift as madness, deprive her of the nourishment she most needs: the mountain air and sympathy from her loved ones. She dies at twenty-nine (82-102).

Fuller meditates on a third instance of oppressed wildness during her time on Mackinaw Island in Lake Huron. There, witnessing the cruel treatment of the Chippewa and Ottowa tribes at the hands of white civilization, she spends the entire "Mackinaw" chapter philosophizing on the plight of the Native Americans. Unlike her fellow Americans, she appreciates the Indians' beauty. While the forces of white society would subject them to "ignominious servitude and slow decay," Fuller would depict their "world of courage and joy" (107-8). Indeed, she notices that the Indians, like Mariana and Frederica, possess considerable creative powers. While they may be stoic among the whites, amidst their own people, they often "declaim" or "narrate at length," clearly possessing "great power that way" (108). Fuller also recognizes the beauty and grace of the tribes' customs, finding them fascinating symbols of a rich culture (108-13). Yet, sadly, she understands the effect of tyranny: after years of subjugation and degradation, the Indians are "no longer strong, tall, or finely proportioned" (113).

Each of these cases illustrates the danger of a world without polarity. In all three cases, Minerva and Muse, centripetal and centrifugal, are not allowed to enter into conversational interaction. Instead, form rebels against and dominates energy, center counters and controls circumference. In this hierarchical relationship, half the world is stifled, invigorating electricity is smothered. This is the world of Fuller's father returned: bodies must be disciplined by spirit, women by men, people of color by whites. But, as Fuller suggests, this world is a universe of death, a flat-lander's hell.

Vagrancy

To keep the lands warm and living, we must turn vagrants, keeping our legs and minds nimble: readiness is all. After her account of Mariana and before the description of the Seer, Fuller details this ethic of vagrancy in the midst (appropriately) of a conversation among "Old Church," "Good Sense," "Self Poise," and "Free Hope." After a long speech by "Self Poise" (probably meant to be Emerson, whom Fuller often found to be emotionally distant) on the illusory nature of emotion and the true one of intellect, "Free Hope" (a likely mouthpiece for Fuller) replies:

> I find not in your theory or your scope, room enough for the lyric inspirations, or the mysterious whispers of life.... [I]t is madder never to abandon oneself, than often to be infatuated; better to be wounded, a captive, and a slave, than always to walk in armor. As to magnetism, that is only a matter of fancy. You sometimes need just such a field in which to wander vagrant, and if it bear a higher name, yet it may be that, in the last result, the trance of Pythagoras might be classed with the more infantine transports of the Seer of Prevorst. (*SL* 149)

In response to Self Poise, who platonically (and perhaps perniciously) values serenity of mind over tumult of body, Free Hope stresses the importance of balance between mind and body, reason and emotion. To organize the body hierarchically is death. It is the way of the pilgrim, who journeys only to find eternal rest, who circulates to settle. To cultivate reason and emotion, stasis and motion, habit and risk—this is life. It is the way of the vagrant. She moves because incessant motion is the principle of the cosmos; she takes pleasure in merely circulating because the spiraling vortex is the shape of all beings. This ethic of vagrancy is not easy but risky. One is vulnerable to wounds, captivity, insanity; it requires great discipline, the rigor of remaining open to change. Her reward is not quiet retirement in the holy city—the goal of the pilgrim—but an apprehension of the waters of life.

Fuller's primary mode of practicing vagrancy—an *askesis*—is her writing style in *Summer*—an aesthetic. This style—which, like her actual motion westward, is a conversational tension of *vis centripeta* and *vis centrifuga*—illuminates for readers the energies of polarity and the dangers of hierarchy. Her commitment to wild writing primarily takes the form of a polyvocal style (a cacophonous conversation), as Joan von Mehren and Marie Mitchell Olesen Urbanski have shown in other contexts.[37] Not wishing to impose her voice on the fecundity of her own textual landscape, Fuller selflessly becomes a vortex through which multiple voices flow. The book is less a travel narrative than an organized cacophony of styles, speakers, stories, and digressions. It overwhelms readers as the apocalyptic waterfall—voice of many waters—unsettles the author.

For example, after spending most of the opening chapter exploring the virtues of water, near the chapter's end Fuller invokes another voice to elucidate her feelings upon leaving the falls: "I will add a brief narrative of the experience of another here, as being much better than anything I could write." She then quotes a brief paragraph of a writer she does not name. This anonymous writer's anti-humanistic passage expresses a sense of being dwarfed by vast natural powers and warns readers against being overly egocentric in viewing immense vistas (*SL* 7). Fuller's staging of this other voice undercuts, of course, her own ego, displaces her own authority.

This is the first of several invocations of alternative voices, often quoted at length, sometimes rendered in verse. Indeed, she opens her second chapter with a three-way conversation among herself, Sarah, and James (*SL* 10-2). Later, she fashions the lengthy conversation among "Old Church," "Good Sense," "Self-Poise," and "Free Hope" (78-82). In neither dialogue does Fuller favor one voice. Rather, she lets each interlocutor have his or her say, leaving readers to decide for themselves which one they value most.

These local dialogues are microcosms of the global *heteroglossia* throughout the book. Repeatedly, Fuller summons voices not her own to offer fresh perspectives on the landscape. For example, while describing the prairie, she quotes at length extracts from other travelers (*SL* 46-50). Other times, as in the stories of Mariana and Frederica, told to her by others, Fuller digresses at length into tales that relate conceptually to the wild. Yet, other times, Fuller relays scenes or stories that seem rather arbitrary. For instance, she digresses into a long and tragic story of a Captain P., a noble man married to a "vulgar," alcoholic woman, simply because a random passenger told the story to her (13-7). Likewise, upon seeing some wild roses in Milwaukee that remind her of Venus, she quotes, "with no excuse," a long excerpt from a book describing Titian's *Venus and Adonis* (69).

These competing voices are accompanied by competing styles. Fuller in several places breaks into poetry to offer alternative vistas; for instance, she versifies on wild pigeons (*SL* 30) and on Ganymede speaking to his eagle (34-5). Often, she cites poems by other authors, some of whom, as with the prose writers, remain anonymous.

By the end of her book, when Fuller reaches her wildest destination, Mackinaw Island, a waterfall of voices and styles floods the text. In this penultimate chapter (*SL* 105-44) in which Fuller celebrates Native Americans, we are beset by at least sixteen different authorities on the Indians, not counting Fuller's own, in the space of about fifty pages, rendered in myriad modes—ranging from anthropological analysis to travelogue to mythology to oration to poem. We hear from white men (Carver, McKenney, a Mr. B., Henry, Adair, Drake); white women (Schoolcroft, Grant); anonymous Native Americans (commenting on dogs, delivering the myth of Muckwa); an anonymous writer (of *Life on the Lakes, or, a Trip to the Pictured Rocks*); an unidentified observer, a British Lord (Fitzgerald), an American governor (Everett). Reading through this array of voices, we experience a full gamut of opinions on Native Americans, ranging from positive (Schoolcroft) to neutral (Grant) to negative (Adair).

In the midst of this varied assemblage, we find it impossible to gain a stable form, a homogenous reading of the subject. Exhibiting a radical pluralism, Fuller pushes us into the textual abyss. Should Native Americans be extolled for their virtues? Should Native Americans realize that their customs and ways are likely to perish at the hands of whites and therefore try to assimilate themselves into mainstream American culture? Should Indians be treated as heathens or displaced Jews and converted to the Christian religion? Fuller leaves these questions unanswered.

Just as the final pages defy closure, the overall book resists classification. It is a travelogue, an anthology of prose and poetry inspired by the West, a collection of philosophical dialogues, a bibliographic essay on books on the West, a treatise on philosophy, a work of natural history, a social science of the Native Americans, a manual of vagrant ethics, a wild cosmology. And this list is not exhaustive. Like Ovid's regions and Goethe's unsystematic systems (Emerson's *de*-scriptions of nature's *de*-signs), *Summer on the Lakes* is Protean—a cloud on the prairie, a green gush of water. These turbulent scenes, Fuller suggests, could edify the true genius of America. But, as she is well aware, America does not realize its wild potential, its promise of vagrancy. While the country contains ample wilderness for reflective wandering, its inhabitants speedily impose static grids, wishing to destroy or tame elements beyond their control. The Marianas, the Fredericas, the Native Americans are more likely to perish than thrive. However, this oppression of the wild, Fuller reminds us, is not a triumph of civilization but a tragic failure of philosophical courage.

3 >>>
Melville and the Ungraspable Phantom

Pilgrim and Nomad

In 1856, Melville, alone, made his way to the deserts of Egypt and Palestine. By this time he was an outcast, a failed literary man. His masterpiece, *Moby-Dick*, only five years old, was already gathering dust. Subsequent books were critical and commercial disasters. His appetite for worldly embrace unrequited, he set out for the ancient sands. Like his fellow exile Ishmael, he hoped to find sustenance amidst the dunes.

In the course of his journey, he stopped to visit his friend Hawthorne, serving as American consul in Liverpool. Hawthorne later described the visit in his notebook. During a walk together along the Irish Sea, Melville had told him that he had "pretty much made up his mind to be annihilated." Hawthorne comments:

> [B]ut still he does not seem to rest in that anticipation; and, I think, will never rest until he gets hold of a definite belief. It is strange how he persists—and has persisted ever since I knew him, and probably long before—in wandering to and fro over these deserts, as dismal and monotonous as the sand hills amid which we were sitting. He can neither believe, nor be comfortable in his unbelief; and he is too honest and courageous not to try to do one or the other. If he were a religious man, he would be one of the most truly religious and reverential; he has a very high and noble nature, and better worth immortality than most of us.[1]

Hawthorne details a primary tension in Melville (one we've just seen in Fuller): between the desire to be settled in belief and the acceptance of uncertainty. While Melville wants to rest in faith, he realizes that unshakable convictions come hard, are perhaps impossible, in the strife-torn world. In his wanderings "to and fro" over literal and figurative deserts, Melville struggles between the urge to be a pilgrim and the impulse to be a nomad. While the pilgrim journeys with a definite end in sight, a holy place—either on heaven or earth—where he finds repose, the nomad wanders with no ultimate *telos*. He takes pleasure in circulating. While the pilgrim undergoes risks to be rewarded by security, the nomad accepts insecurity as a primary condition of existence. The pilgrim is really a settler en route; the nomad is a wanderer for life. For the pilgrim, the desert is where *being*—the one—is achieved; for the nomad, dunes betoken perpetual becoming, the abyss rippling forward.

While Melville himself was beleaguered by an unresolved conflict between these two impulses, in *Moby-Dick* he temporarily favors the nomad. He turns intellectual agitation into a virtue in Ishmael, who perpetually spirals in the convoluted ocean, who is open to the unexpected, the foreign, the mystery of the white whale. Ishmael is countered by Ahab, who is on a quest for certainty, traveling over uncharted seas in hopes of resting in the absolute upon slaying Moby-Dick. Loathing insecurity, throughout his hunt Ahab imposes the charts in his mind onto the labile waters, reducing currents to lines, wishing to enweb whale and nomad alike: unmanageable elements. While Ishmael oscillates with the tides, Ahab longs for repose, a noumenal principle behind the pasteboard masks of phenomena. Perhaps reflecting Melville's deepest hope, the nomad thrives and the pilgrim dies: Ishmael in the end is buoyed by the profound matrix; Ahab sinks, his mind weighted with madness.

The various, rich contrasts between the captain and his reflective crewman have been the subject of important readings of the *Moby-Dick.* Most versions of this contrast—like those exemplary ones of Charles Feidelson Jr., Alfred Kazin, and Robert Zoellner—have appropriately emphasized Ahab's rage for order and Ishmael's affirmation of wavering.[2] In this chapter, I shall extend these past interpretations by treating the fundamental antagonism between Ishmael and Ahab in several fresh contexts, primarily focusing on their opposition as one between nomad and pilgrim, terms inspired here by Gilles Deleuze and Felix Guattari.[3] These two categories are more than illustrative tropes. They are what Zoellner, following M. H. Abrams, calls "constitutive metaphors"; that is, they are essential structuring devices, matrices generating and patterning key elements of *Moby-Dick.*[4] "Ishmael: nomad" and "Ahab: pilgrim" organize several oppositions that produce significant meanings on cosmological, scientific, philosophical, mythological, imagistic, and narrative levels. These primary antimonies pattern tensions between the following: Gnostic and ecologist, organ and machine, Darwinian evolution and the essentialism of Agassiz, Heraclitus and Plato, spiral and line, recursivity and discursivity. Throughout his novel, Melville referees this vast antagonism, in the apocalyptic finale celebrating the victory of Ishmael—of spiraling, decentered, ecological thinking.

The Ungraspable

"Call me Ishmael." We immediately learn in the first sentence that the narrator is a principle of nomadism, an avatar of his biblical namesake who was ousted from family and settlement, condemned to wander chartless deserts, yet chosen by God to originate a great nation. From the outset, the biblical Ishmael is an exile from tradition, denied by Abraham himself—the great father of Judaism, Christianity, and Islam; the progenitor of the formidable monotheistic quests of Western metaphysicians from St. Paul to Kant; the pilgrim of God who journeys to establish a heaven on earth.

Unlike his father, who journeys to the promised land under God's guidance, Ishmael roves in the desert with no clear *telos*. So does his literary incarnation. Melville's Ishmael takes to the sea not as a pilgrim bent on resting in God's bosom but as a nomad in search of motion itself, desirous to release his pent up "spleen," to enjoy "circulation" (*MD* 3). For him, land, maps, and stable edifices stagnate the bile and blood, inflict the "*hypos*," keep him under the weather. The sea, however, swirls his fluids, giving vent to bile and currency to blood. Churning in the ocean, his body and mind regain vigor—the lines of *melancholia* reeled into ecstatic spirals.

Like his biblical double, Ishmael finds the primal, the sacred, in the midst of the maelstrom. Ishmael circumambulates to the sea to sound the spring of everything, to experience a gnosis of the abyss of life. As he proclaims, he sails before the mast to know the "image of the ungraspable phantom of life" that "is the key to it all" (*MD* 3-5). He embraces the disturbing fact that one finds in water not a static truth or maxim on which one can base a systematic philosophy, but rather an ineffable origin of being, fathomed only by embracing the gyrations it generates. This abysmal power of life is indeed glimpsed only in its paradoxical manifestations: it appears in the ocean, both mild and tormenting, beautiful and annihilating, attractive and repellent, seductive and horrifying, ubiquitously familiar and exotically unfamiliar. Moreover, the abyss is figured by the whale, itself a synecdoche for the sea, a "grand hooded phantom . . . a snow hill in the air," duplicitously white, both pure and terrifying (5,7). To this watery gulf Ishmael is drawn, feeling the "magnetic virtue" of it, eager not to reduce the riddle to an answer but instead to "sail forbidden seas, and land on barbarous coasts," to be social with "horror" (4,7). Richard H. Brodhead has well expressed Ishmael's desire: to know "the mystery of primordial nature" in an oceanic world of "continuous sublimity, inhabited, in Wordsworth's words, by 'huge and mighty forms, that do not live/ Like living men.'"[5]

Choosing for his meditations the paralogical ocean, the refractory Leviathan, Ishmael honors his nomadic heritage: his thought must remain inconclusive. Throughout the novel, he celebrates living mysteries, for they keep his inquiries circulating. He spurns the land for the "magnanimity of the sea which will permit no records" (*MD* 60); he believes that "in landless-ness alone resides the highest truth, shoreless, indefinite as God" (107). As we have seen, the whale, especially the sperm whale, becomes for Ishmael an essential trope for the evasive ocean. The sea beast is beyond the categories of natural history, frustrating the Linnaeuses, the Cuviers, the Agassizes of the world, inspiring only incomplete classificatory systems (134-45); it remains "wholly inexplicable," "unaccountable," beyond the disciplines of art, science, and religion (264). These puzzles are not limited to waves and whales but, as manifestations of the original "key to it all," they haunt the human, whose innermost truth, whose "awful essence," is figured by an antique, bearded king, grand and broken in his tantalizing silence (185-6). All true places, Ishmael asserts, are not "down in any map" (55).

This brief resume of Ishmael's ruminations demonstrates his philosophical bent. He is an ecological gnostic, with pre-Socratic leanings (*not* an anti-mate-rialist Gnostic, a view amenable to Ahab, as we shall soon see). Ishmael locates the origin of life not in Platonic idea (or Christian heaven or Newtonian law) but in the flux of phenomena rising from an ungraspable reservoir. One might well say that the famous "mast-head" passage suggests otherwise, for there Ish-mael admits he keeps sorry watch for whales because of his propensity for Pla-tonic speculation. However, while Ishmael may have begun his voyage on the *Pequod* as a "romantic, melancholy, and absent-minded young m[a]n," he quickly learns from the sea to attend to the world differently, to change from Plato's degradation of phenomena as shadow of the real to an embrace of the visible as habitat of life. In what is likely a description (in third person) of one of his masthead reveries, the dreaming young transcendentalist eventually "loses his identity," and takes the ocean underneath for a visible image of the "bottomless soul" pervading the cosmos. In this mood, he dissolves into this ubiquitous spirit. Yet, such a state is dangerous, a prelude to death:

> But while this sleep, this dream, is on ye, move your foot or hand an inch, slip your hold at all; and your identity comes back in horror. Over Descartian vortices you hover. And perhaps, at mid-day, in the fairest weather, with one half-throttled shriek you drop though that transparent air into the summer sea, no more to rise for ever. Heed it well, ye Pantheists! (*MD* 172-3)

Often read as Melville's parody of Emerson's "transparent eye-ball" sequence (a valid enough interpretation, though one that oversimplifies both Emerson and Melville), this passage is subtle rejection of the two masters of Western metaphysics, Plato and Descartes.[6] These thinkers, for all their differences in time and temperament, are dualists, bifurcating the world into a hierarchy of superior *res cogitans* (thinking things, mind, spirit, soul, realm of forms and ideas, *noumena*) and inferior *res extensa* (extended things, body, matter, materials, illusory region of palpable elements, phenomena).[7] The young Pantheist (Melville's idiosyncratic synonym for metaphysics here; strictly speaking, a pantheist is monist, believing spirit and matter to be one, continuous) has attempted to annihilate the body and merge with spirit, reducing the visible world to a mere image of his thoughts. Yet this condition does not disclose the real but is illusion itself, a siren song, a dose of lotus, seducing the thinker to deny fundamental facts like the burden of gravity and the horror of the sea and death. The dualist, the metaphysician, is suicidal, wishing to escape the complexities of the world, denying the rich—though paradoxical—vitality of the ocean's "ungraspable phantom of life."

(Yet, though Ishmael leans toward the swells, early in the novel, before shipping, he proposes the following Platonist possibility:

> Methinks we have hugely mistaken this matter of Life and Death. Methinks that what they call my shadow here on earth is my true substance. Methinks that in looking at things spiritual, we are too much like oysters observing the sun through the water, and thinking that thick water the thinnest of air. Methinks my body is but the lees of my better being. (*MD* 37)

One can account for this passage by arguing, as John Wenke has,[8] that Ishmael begins the novel as a Platonist but ends it as a pagan [that is, naturalistic] thinker. Or, one can simply say that Melville, like Whitman [and Emerson and Fuller and Thoreau] contains multitudes and contradictions. "Do I contradict myself?/ Very well then . . . . I contradict myself" [SM 51:1314-6].)

Early Greek Thinking

Generally locating reality in the physical (ocean and whale), Ishmael leaves the halls of traditional Western metaphysics and returns to landscapes of pre-Platonic thought, the meditations of such early Greek thinkers as Thales, Anaximander, and Heraclitus. Before Plato transformed philosophical truth into eternal idea, these sixth-century (B.C.E.) thinkers found the mysterious principle of life in space and time, coursing equally through mind *and* matter. Thales, a Milesian, believed the substance of the universe to be water, *hydros*: earth is water in condensed form, air, in rarefied. Anaximander, also from Miletus, maintained that the four qualities of matter— hot and cold, wet and dry—arose out of an undifferentiated, primal mass, called the "unlimited," *apeiron*. Heraclitus the Ephesian, known in antiquity as the "dark one," proclaimed that the warring many is organized by a hidden principle called *logos*.[9] Each of these principles—*hydros, apeiron, logos*—is mysterious, paralogical, and ungraspable. Each hides: water is invisible in earth and air; the unlimited by definition beyond the grasp of perception or conception; the *logos*, as Heraclitus himself says, a "hidden harmony," principle of a nature that "loves to hide." Each is beyond logic, manifesting itself in paradoxical patterns: water is simultaneously earth and air; the unlimited is hot and cold, wet and dry; *logos* is a site of opposition and concord, discord and harmony.

In moving toward such a principle, an unreachable "key to it all," Ishmael harbingers the pre-Socratic meditations of Nietzsche and Heidegger, each of whom wished to move philosophy beyond Platonism by returning to pre-Platonic springs. In his posthumously published *Philosophy in the Tragic Age of the Greeks* (1873), Nietzsche reads Heraclitus, for example, as a precursor of his own thought. According to Nietzsche, Heraclitus did not, like Plato, divide the world into metaphysical and physical realms; rather, the Ephesian denied metaphysical being entirely and set up the physical world as the actual, claiming that playful strife activates the cosmos.[10] Drawing from Heraclitus, the mature Nietzsche of course develops a philosophy of becoming in hopes of freeing thought from its pervasive Platonism. As he asserts in *Will to Power* (1901) metaphysicians from Plato through Kant have attempted to subdue the agitated *physis* of Heraclitus, fearing and loathing that which they cannot know or control. Devaluing the palpable universe in favor of an impalpable one, these metaphysicians perform acts of revenge on time, denying life, nihilistically murdering creative strife.[11] According to Nietzsche's Zarathustra, the path to redemption, the way to escape this philosophy of dearth, is to relinquish the spirit of revenge and to affirm becoming.[12] This Dionysian embrace of unreason, change, and strife is really a celebration of life—full life, not just the sides of it amenable to security, but all sides, all polarities.[13] Like Ishmael, the Dionysian thinker hallows difficult beauties and animating horrors.

In "Who Is Nietzsche's Zarathustra?" (1967) Heidegger develops Nietzsche's meditations on Platonism and revenge. Like Nietzsche, he believes that Plato and philosophers after him (including Nietzsche) have diminished the full enigma of the earth to logic or representation.[14] In *On Time*

and Being (1972), Heidegger claims that Plato and the philosophical tradition he inaugurated have cherished only the light, forgetting the hidden
source—which Heidegger calls "Being"—from which beings primordially
emerge: metaphysics has chosen the brightness of the sun and neglected the
wine-dark sea.[15] The task of philosophy, Heidegger maintains elsewhere in
Discourse on Thinking (1966), is to "step back" from metaphysics, to leave it
"to itself," "to think Being without regard to metaphysics." The philosopher
should "step" from presence itself to the abyss that grants presence. Meditating in the region of the unthought, the thinker cannot exert a will to power
over the world and must not attempt to fit it into his procrustean notions.
Rather, he must practice "releasement" (*Gelassenheit*), letting the world *be*
on its own terms, without imposing anthropocentric notions, refusing to
manipulate it as commodity.[16]

Stepping back, releasing, the thinker experiences Heraclitus's *logos*.
According to Heidegger in *Early Greek Thinking* (1975), Heraclitus's *logos* is
his name for Being: the power "by which [beings] become and remain
observable," the "original unifying unity of what tends apart." This *logos*,
Heidegger urges, is prior to metaphysics; it is a source of existence irreducible to Platonic concepts. In bestowing presence to individual beings, it
conceals itself, hides from thought and sight. It is the same as *aletheia*, Greek
for the principle of unconcealment that conceals itself (bearing within it
lethe, oblivion, a forgetting, a hiding) in disclosing phenomena. Heraclitus's
logos, inflected through Heidegger, *corresponds* to (is not equal to) Thales's
metamorphosing water, Anaximander's unlimited, Nietzsche's becoming: it
is the intractable key to existence.[17] It is Ishmael's "ungraspable phantom of
life."

Discursive and Recursive

Ishmael struggles to become a Dionysian thinker, to step back from traditional notions of man's supremacy over the physical, to sound the *lethe*.
Unlike Plato, he cannot employ logic to move from hypothesis to conclusion
in a linear fashion; distinct from Descartes, he does not attempt to deduce
absolute truth through the strict geometrical axioms in his mind. For him,
inquiries without rational answers take priority. Releasing the ocean, the
whale, to remain concealed, he must be content with approximation and
partial interpretation. He must enter, like Fuller, into Heidegger's
hermeneutical circle.

In *Being and Time* (1927)—as we have seen—Heidegger asserts that all
profound inquiry is circular. In asking about Being, for example, one must
already possess an everyday, tentative sense of what Being is: the question

already partially presupposes and delimits an answer. Yet, if one is an active thinker, this answer never fully corresponds to the assumptions behind the question. New information and fresh thoughts arise, urging one to revise his sense of Being and thus the way he asks the question.[18] Put another way, by Hans-Georg Gadamer in *Truth and Method* (1960), all knowledge is provisional interpretation: one can only understand parts from the context of a whole, but a whole is revealed only through parts.[19] According to James S. Hans, this circularity between part and whole is recursive, a "regular return with a difference." Starting with a whole, proceeding to parts, the thinker constantly returns to the whole to relate it to new parts. When he notices a difference between whole and parts during this return, he gains new understanding and revises the whole, which in turn leads to an alteration of the parts.[20]

Ishmael's inquiry into the ungraspable phantom of life is recursive, a circulation, and figured by the spiral, a return with a difference. His primary question in the novel is the same as Ahab's, the same as Heidegger's and Heraclitus's: "What is the key to it all?" While Ahab answers this question once and for all in the "Quarter-Deck," Ishmael asks it endlessly, from several different perspectives, never receiving a final answer. Turning the whale into a synecdoche for life's deepest mystery and source, he examines the Leviathan from various contexts, enters into conversation with it, placing the whole (his overall sense of the whale) and the parts (his particular answers) into a circular dance. In "Cetology," he asks his question from the perspective of scientific classification, realizing that his "cetological System" must remain unfinished, a tentative and partial map of the vast terrain of the whale (*MD* 145). He asks again in "The Whiteness of the Whale," concluding that there may be an "indefiniteness" at the heart of the universe (195). Inquiring into the nature of the whale another time in "Monstrous Pictures of Whales," he claims that it "must remain unpainted to the last." However, while one can never represent or read the whale fully—never totally understand the abyss of life—some "portrait[s]," or interpretations, may "hit the mark much nearer than another" (264).

He continues to ask this inexhaustible question, the parts never meshing with the whole, the whole becoming more mysterious as new parts emerge. Indeed, as Robert M. Greenberg has claimed, following Howard P. Vincent, Ishmael thinks about the whale "from nearly every conceivable angle of formalized knowledge."[21] For example, he considers the whale in paint, teeth, wood, iron, stone, mountains, and stars; he ponders it in anatomy, physiology, physiognomy, and phrenology; he studies it from the angle of history, religion, and myth. While these inquires never yield a final answer, Ishmael's understanding of the whale does deepen with each return to the question. Some answers, again, "hit the mark much nearer than another," are more luminous with gnosis. He apprehends that the whale remains ungraspable; that it is primal and eternal; that it is a source of life and light; that it is polarized, fierce and calm, creative and destructive; that it is sacred.

Ishmael's entrance into the hermeneutic circle is responsible for his reflective digressions that hinder the novel's plot from moving forward in a linear manner. While Ishmael is on land, his plot is linear: in search of a whaling vessel, he travels from Manhattan to New Bedford to Nantucket, developing a friendship with Queequeg along the way. This linear motion ceases, however, once he ships. From the "Cetology" section onward, he perpetually turns to the same question, digressing as his inquiry dictates. If it weren't for Ahab's overtly linear quest—his desire to move directly from point A (not having killed Moby-Dick) to point B (killing the white whale)—the novel's traditional, discursive plot would disappear. The novel's narrative is a contest between Ishmael's recursive circulations, his nomadic intellectual wanderings, and the discursive logic of Ahab, his pilgrimage from movement to repose.

Indeed, throughout the novel, Ahab tries to turn everything he touches into a "Fast Fish," to put a line to it and bind it to his will. A fish of this type, as Ishmael claims in his discussion of whales and property, is one "connected with an occupied ship or boat, by any medium at all controllable by the occupant or occupants" (*MD* 396). On a mission to chart the waters as he makes his way to his destination, Ahab attempts to attach his will to whales, waves and men. This mapping is a result of his metaphysical vocation (to be explored momentarily): he must transform whorls into lines, the cyclical poem of nature into a traditional novel.

Ishmael wants to leave nature loose, a "Loose Fish," unattached to controlling lines—a living *Finnegans Wake*. This is not an easy undertaking. Entering into the hermeneutic circle, thinking recursively instead of discursively, is risky, requiring the thinker to proceed on uncertain terrain, to realize that his map is always faulty and in need of editing. It demands Keats's "negative capability," the ability to remain in "uncertainties, Mysteries, doubts, without any irritable reaching after fact & reason."[22] Certainly Ishmael must labor to remain loose. He must battle his own Ahabian tendencies, his "*hypos*" (*MD* 3). He must war with his own cultural prejudices before he can embrace the "savage" Queequeg (21-4). Most importantly, Ishmael must contend with Ahab's discursive will, which threatens to straighten his digressive spirals into monotonous lines, to turn him into a Fast Fish, a character in Ahab's narrative. This final contest comes to a head late in the novel, which I shall consider later, after we come to understand what Ahabian tendencies from which Ishmael must swerve.

For now, we can recognize that Melville's novel embodies in style the content of Ishmael's vision. Like the ungraspable phantom of life, it is polarized, a tension between Ishmael's centrifugal, massively digressive meditations and Ahab's centripetal, aggressively linear quest. Placing these two modes in conversation, Melville ensures that Ishmael will not circulate endlessly around the mystery of the whale, that Ahab will not bring his narrative to a precipitous close. Rather, driven by the back-and-forth play between these two dialectical forces, the novel spirals forward, a living rhythm. Yet, like an organism, the book is threatened constantly by death and stasis, for Ahab would be the only voice, filling the silence with a chronic monologue.

Revenge against Time

While Ishmael's biblical brother, ousted from tradition, wanders the desert, Ahab's is a king of northern Israel, in the line of the Judeo-Christian tradition inaugurated by Abraham's pilgrimage and supported later by Platonic thought. Yet King Ahab, like any ambitious metaphysical thinker (metaphysical in Nietzsche's vengeful sense), is not content merely to mimic the traditions and ideas he inherits but asserts his own will to revise them: he blasphemously builds groves to Babylonian gods, doing more to provoke God than any other king prior to him.[23]

Captain Ahab takes his namesake's mantle, equating speculation with opposition, violence, and control—his instrument of thought is the lance. As Captain Peleg describes the monomaniac to Ishmael: "Ahab's above the common; Ahab's been in colleges, as well as 'mong cannibals; been used to deeper wonders than waves, stranger foes than whales. His lance! aye, the keenest and surest that, out of all our isle!" (*MD* 79). We learn much from this brief description. Ahab is ascendant, above the "common": he rules the commonwealth of his ship; he transcends democracy, is a monarch; he is superior to the commons (Emerson's "bare common")—natural landscapes and their inhabitants. He has been schooled in landed universities, a master of civilized learning, trained no doubt in philosophy; yet, he has also dwelt with cannibals, the uncivilized, perhaps even partaking in their rituals, consuming human flesh. This curious blend of refinement and rapacity characterizes the metaphysician as Nietzsche and Heidegger define him, a vengeful thinker who uses his sophisticated mind to subdue, objectify, and consume the world. Like Ishmael, Ahab has experienced the wondrous, the strange; however, the captain does not wish to be social with the other but rather stabs it, his lance his weapon against obscurity. He aspires to destroy the "ungraspable phantom of life," which he locates in Moby-Dick, reducing the mighty Leviathan to oil for his study. While this pilgrimage is irrational, a cause or symptom of Ahab's madness, it is carried out in the name of rationality and not entirely different in kind than the grandiose, anthropocentric agendas of metaphysicians from Plato to Aquinas to Descartes, all of whom, according to Nietzsche and Heidegger, have sought revenge against time. For all their differences, these thinkers, like Ahab, use reason to accomplish the irrational goal of explaining and controlling the cosmos. Ahab simply pushes their desires to an extreme and pursues them physically as well as mentally.

Ahab's first extended speech, the "Quarter-Deck" oration, unfolds his cosmology, revealing a violent version of the Platonic/Cartesian dualism Ishmael rejects on the masthead. After Starbuck assails Ahab for blasphemously exacting vengeance on a dumb brute, the captain responds: "All visible objects, man, are but as pasteboard masks. But in each event—in the living act, the undoubted deed—there, some unknown but still reasoning thing puts forth the mouldings of its features from behind the unreasoning mask. If man will strike, strike through the mask!" (*MD* 178). Phenomena are merely masks covering an inscrutable, reasoning force: *res extensa* nothing but outer garments for *res cogitans*. Moby-Dick is meaningless as a whale, as material, and gains significance only as a sign of something invisible, of which it is either an active bearer ("agent") or prime example ("principle"). Because Ahab the metaphysician is unable to understand the force behind the mask of the white whale, he hates it, will kill it, reducing the world only to what can be illuminated in the lights of reason. Like his forebears Plato and Descartes, Ahab wishes to abolish the *lethe*, the "inscrutable"; he has experienced it and wishes to destroy it, leaving for speculation only that which unconceals itself clearly. Philosophy becomes either suicide or murder; either the subject kills and thus controls the object, or the object overcomes the subject. Ahab's ontology suggests that the cosmos is a battlefield, where rational humans are destined to triumph. His epistemology is to divide subject from object and conquer. The pilgrim is a warrior against time.

Ahab's desire to objectify extends not only over elements (the sea) and animals (the whale) but also over humans, including the unlettered harpooners, the other crew members, the lower mates Flask and Stubb, and also over the speculative, devout Starbuck himself (*MD* 178). Indeed, Ahab installs himself at the top of the chain of being. He has segmented the cosmos into a hierarchy over which he rules, beginning with the inanimate ocean, rising through the unconscious whale and the brutish crew, ending with his rational mind. He masters the sea with his navigational tools, his quadrant, log and line, and charts; the whale with his harpoon; the harpooners with his grog; Flask and Stubb, the third and second mates, with his rhetoric; Starbuck, the first mate, with his will. Ahab the pilgrim is on a quest to police each link in the chain. When all is secure, he can finally rest, the world a double of the map in his mind.

It could be argued, however, that Ahab's hubris, his desire to transcend limits and become a god, make him hate the status quo of the hierarchy he posits, in which there is a place for everything and everything in its place. Yet Ahab realizes that in the universe he envisions, he, too, must be determined by an invisible power. Indeed, as William B. Dillingham has observed, Ahab struggles between atheism, which would allow him to ascend to universal command, and God-hunger, the desire to be guided by an invisible principle.[24] Hence, ironically, but consistently given the philosophical framework, the arrogant Ahab humbles himself before a controlling power, Fate. Victim of his own deterministic philosophy, Ahab does not develop in the novel at all, but remains rigid. He does not circulate, is not a spiral: he is a line. When Ahab first appears on deck of the *Pequod*, Ishmael immediately notices a "slender rod-like mark, lividly whitish," a "perpendicular seam" that runs the length of Ahab's body (*MD* 123). Ahab is inseparable from this line. He is an effect of a relentless cause, as inelastic as the whale bone comprising his leg and bolted into place on the deck of the *Pequod* (124). As he soliloquizes after his quarter-deck oration, not even the gods can "swerve" him (164). Every action is controlled by a first cause, God, as Ahab sadly admits to Starbuck on the eve of first lowering for Moby-Dick. A "cozening, hidden lord and master, and cruel, remorseless emperor commands" him; he is not even in control of his own arm. Like his universe, he is dictated by "some invisible power" (545). A machine himself—a cog in the universal mechanism—he loves best mechanical men. As he tells the carpenter who is fashioning him a new leg of bone, he wants a wooden or metal man, animated by the blacksmith's fire (470-1). Organisms are reduced to mechanistic grinding under Ahab's will: dreading the hunt of Moby-Dick, the crew, as Ishmael observes, were "ground to finest dust, and powdered, for the time, in the clamped mortar of Ahab's iron soul. Like machines, they dumbly moved about the deck" (536).

Chain of Being

Ahab's mechanistic cosmos reflects a pre-Darwinian "evolutionary" paradigm that was very popular though beginning to pass away in Melville's time. This paradigm—of which Melville was likely aware (he mentions two of its important proponents in *Moby-Dick,* Baron Georges Cuvier and Louis Agassiz)—is characterized by essentialism: the idea that the cosmos is fixed and full—a place for everything and everything in its place. This theory of a static universe is the biological corollary to the "metaphysical" tradition challenged by Nietzsche and Heidegger.

According to A. O. Lovejoy, until the eighteenth-century, most Western thinkers presupposed a static, spatial chain of being, reaching down from God to minerals. The three ideas ruling this paradigm were hierarchy, continuity, and plenitude. Superior beings exist closer to the top of the chain, inferior ones, nearer to earth. While each link in this chain is clearly demarcated, no gaps exist. The chain is full; there is no need for new creatures to be created. As Lovejoy shows, these primarily Liebnizian ideas were revised during the second half of the eighteenth century when scientists challenged continuity and plenitude by discovering fossils of extinct species. Hence, thinkers—like Buffon—desirous of holding the great chain together, were forced to articulate an early version of evolution. They temporalized the chain, asserting that each species is evolving toward a God-granted perfection: seemingly extinct species are less perfect, earlier forms of currently existing, more perfect flora and fauna. While species appear to change, their essences remain the same—design still rules.[25]

While innovative nineteenth-century scientists like Lamarck in France and Agassiz in America proposed that static essences don't exist and that species do indeed evolve, they still believed that species move toward increasing perfection under God's unwavering guidance—that design rules the universe. Indeed, scientists as different as Agassiz, Lamarck, and Buffon could still posit the same basic claim: man heads a continuous, linear, hierarchy of species determined, directly or indirectly, by God's plan. The cosmos, for all its transformations, remains safely scripted and organized.[26]

Ahab, in his rage for order, instances a tension between both versions of the pre-Darwinian chain: the spatial and the temporal. On the one hand, he yearns for a static scale of nature, in which hierarchically grouped animals and men are fated to be what they are, to move with the regularity of machines. On the other, he wishes to progress himself, to evolve to the very top of the chain from which place he will hold the other species below him. From either position, he maintains, violently, the shared assumption of both pre-Darwinian chains of being: anthropocentrism, hierarchy, and design. Turning the *Pequod* into a pre-Darwinian world in miniature, Ahab places himself, as superior man, at the top of a rigid hierarchy, one for which he finds the sanction of fate. (Indeed, one reading of Ahab's monomania is that he fears that a mere animal might usurp his place on the chain and therefore he must overcompensate by constantly asserting his ascendancy.) Yet, while Ahab revels in a spatial stasis that favors his ascendancy, he also, paradoxically, expresses a desire to evolve temporally, to progress. Traditionally, the sun and the planets and of course God hold higher places on the chain than man. As the oration on the quarter deck shows, however, Ahab is prepared to progress to their places, believing nothing—sun or God—is over him. His hubris is a logical extreme of the temporal chain; if man is evolving toward increasing perfection, what is to stop him from becoming a god? While Ahab wishes to apply the spatial chain of being to those under him, he wishes himself to progress in time to increasing perfection. In both cases, this is clear: Ahab aggressively espouses an "inorganic," "mechanistic" natural philosophy in which permanence is superior to change; predictability is better than uncertainty; reasonable man is greater than other flora and fauna.

Darwin's Organs

Ishmael, embodying yet another nomadic impulse, counters, unsurprisingly, Ahab's chains by espousing a more Darwinian paradigm—that is, a more organic, ecological view of the world. Darwin's evolutionary paradigm indeed shares key affinities with the views of Goethe and Nietzsche that I have been detailing. For all their important differences, Goethe, Darwin, and Nietzsche de-center man, demoting him from the throne atop the great chain of being; they believe that unruly physical energies are the animating forces of the cosmos, driving plants, animals, and humans; they posit a dynamic, evolving universe, generated by becoming (metamorphosis), not held together by being (essentialism); they maintain that polarity is the primary vehicle of this transient cosmos—Goethe's centripetal and centrifugal forces, Darwin's unpredictable *law* of natural selection, Nietzsche's Apollinian and Dionysian energies. Indeed, Darwin himself acknowledged Goethe's contributions to his own views, citing the German scientist's comparative anatomy in as an important step toward his own theory of common descent.[27] Likewise, the Darwin-influenced ecologist Ernst Haeckel even claimed that Goethe was a forerunner of Darwin.[28] Moreover, Nietzsche was a student of Darwin and often celebrated the British scientist's sense that growth arises only from struggle.[29] Also, Nietzsche is often cited as an important philosophical supporter of the ecological tradition inaugurated by Goethe and Darwin, primarily for his devastating attacks on anthropocentrism and his emphasis on *physis* over *pneuma*.[30] But these affinities—almost all based on a shared "biologism"—cannot be pushed too far. As several scholars have correctly pointed out, Goethe differs considerably from Darwin in emphasizing affinities in space (homologies in anatomical structure) and not in time (homologies among different species at different periods), and in caring more about *Urbilden* than common descent.[31] Likewise, Nietzsche himself announced his divergence from Darwin. While Darwin believes that the utility of an organ in its environment explains its origin, Nietzsche thinks that new organs arise regardless of their use—often through "deficiency" and "degeneration"—and are later related to useful activities.[32]

I have digressed here for two reasons. First, I want to account for why I can illuminate Ishmael with Goethe, indirectly, by way of my introduction, and directly, in this chapter, with Nietzsche and Darwin. Each, like Ishmael (like the pre-Socratics), espouses a biological philosophy that counters traditional metaphysics (as Nietzsche and Heidegger define it). Second, I want to justify bringing Darwin, instead of Goethe, directly into the discussion of Melville. While Ishmael entertains the biological view of Goethe, he more resembles Darwin in emphasizing common descent, connections among different species, the difficulty of establishing stable categories of biological classification, and the role of chance in the development of life.

Ishmael indeed harbingers the great event of 1859, Darwin's publication of *On the Origin of Species*. As with Melville, Darwin's first publication was a voyage story, an account of his sea travels around the Galapagos Islands between 1832 and 1836. Melville knew Darwin's *Voyage of the Beagle* (1838), citing it in the extracts to *Moby-Dick* and drawing from it freely later, in "The Encantadas" (1856) as H. Bruce Franklin, Benjamin Lease, and Mark Dunphy have shown.[33] Perhaps Melville sensed in the *Voyage* Darwin's drift, which swelled to an unsettling river twenty years later when the scientist used his earlier data to overwhelm the great chain. Overgrowing the edifices of anthropocentrism, hierarchy, and design, Darwin helped to verify scientifically what Nietzsche would develop philosophically some twenty years later.

The web and the tree are key images for Darwin's ideas on the origin and functioning of species. They both illustrate the fact that all species on the planet descend from a common, ungraspable origin, the same seed; man and animal and perhaps plant are different only in degree, not kind, with none possessing innate superiority over the other. Both images further suggest that different species are not essential, but, like strands on a web and branches on a tree, are variations of a common source that develop into species. The web and the tree moreover illustrate, in opposition to Lamarck, that species do not evolve because of their innate ability to adapt to their environment; rather, they become diversified because of environmental factors beyond their control. The strand on the web is dependent upon the other strands around it; the limbs of the living tree reach toward the sun, bend with the wind. For Darwin, species enter into a creative interchange with their environment—shaping and being shaped, adapting and becoming adapted. Finally, and most radically, natural selection, Darwin's primary mechanism of diversity, is comprised of unpredictable, largely random factors, ranging from genetic mutation to available food supply.[34] (While some evolutionary biologists have read Darwin's natural selection as a deterministic mechanism, other, more recent ones like Stephen Jay Gould and Niles Eldrege, emphasize the role of chaos in natural selection and in other vehicles of modification [like Gould's "punctuated equilibrium"].[35])

These ideas of course precipitated a momentous upheaval. Suddenly, man is no longer unique and superior, but merely one more strand in the web, one more branch in the tree. Moreover, man is no longer a subject in control of a separate, objective world; rather, he lives only as a part of a larger whole, bewilderingly complex and largely unpredictable. Further, this whole is not driven by rational design but rather by random factors— unpredictable pulses are agents of significant changes. In sum, as Darwin famously concludes his *Origin*, the world is a "tangled bank," diverse, sprawling, and confusing; yet it is interconnected, an ecosystem in which each part—plants, animals, worms, men—is dependent on one another as well as the whole.[36]

By no means a positivistic scientist like Darwin, Ishmael nonetheless eschews anthropocentrism, believes in a common, ineffable origin of life, embraces his affinity with other forms of life (human and nonhuman), finds stable classifications untenable, and opens himself to the waverings of chance. As we know, while Ahab believes that life issues from a spiritual principle and that physical specimens are but insubstantial masks, Ishmael believes that living things arise from the sea, the primal soup that is the key to it all.

Likewise, while Ahab perpetually asserts his ascendancy over brutes, Ishmael constantly finds affinities between human and animal. Sharks and man, for example, exhibit similar rapacious behavior, virtually indistinguishable in their eating habits (*MD* 293). Likewise, humans often display a herd-like mentality that betrays their animality (385). While crass humanity seems to sink into certain animal behaviors, other forms of animality provide a standard of nobility for humans. Admiring the whale's ability to remain warm in icy arctic waters, Ishmael exclaims, "Oh, man! admire and model thyself after the whale!" (307). Indeed, the noble brow of the sperm whale suggests that it is a philosopher (335). The brow of the sperm whale is indeed human; like Shakespeare's, it is sublime, betokening a "high and mighty god-like identity" (346). The philosophical virtue of the whale is matched by its capacity for affection: whale babies and mothers appear human in their nursing, in their obvious affection (386-88). Ishmael also finds affinities between civilized and cannibal, sophisticate and savage. Though Queequeg appears as an uncivilized cannibal, the ostensibly civilized, learned Ishmael quickly learns that little difference exists between them. Upon waking from his first night spent sleeping with Queequeg, Ishmael is unable to discover where his body ends and Queequeg's begins because they are so intertwined (25). They are linked by a primordial force; as Ishmael asserts, "[w]ild he was; a very sight of sights to see; yet I began to feel myself mysteriously drawn towards him. And those same things that would have repelled most others, they were the very magnets that drew me" (51). Ishmael finally realizes that there is no difference between himself and the savage: "I myself am a savage, owing no allegiance but to the King of Cannibals, and ready at any moment to rebel against him" (270).

Ishmael not only searches for affinities between and among earth, animal, and human; he also attempts, in scientific fashion, to classify different species of whales, to become a cetologist. Indeed, as Howard P. Vincent, Robert K. Wallace, and Robert M. Greenberg have shown, Melville was well schooled in the whale science of his day.[37] Sifting through scientific sources on the Leviathan and watching the plunging whale itself, he finds, as did Darwin, that classifying species is as difficult as classifying an abyss. In a world constantly evolving, rigid classifications are tentative at best: the line between distinct species and variations within species is blurry and shifting. Of this fact Ishmael is well aware, announcing that his cetological classifications are vain attempts to class "the constituents of chaos" (*MD* 134). He brings forth several noted naturalists to support his conclusion that the whale is beyond classification. All the cetologist can hope for is "to project the draught of a systemization of cetology," to offer a work in progress, possibly never to be finished (136). He then embarks on his classification, attempting to divide whales into books and chapters. After arranging several types of whale, he realizes that "there are a rabble of uncertain, fugitive, half-fabulous whales" irreducible to his system, which must remain incomplete, as the evolving earth is ever unfinished, a rough draft never finding final form. Ishmael concludes his classificatory efforts by deciding that true systems are ever uncompleted, that the world, like his book, is Darwinian—a work in progress (145).

This cosmic text is as chaotic as it is ordered, as much a product of chance as of law. In weaving a mat with Queequeg, he suggests that the universe is comprised of law, freedom, and *chance*: the "unalterable" warp is necessity; the woof he weaves through the warp is free will; and the sword Queequeg "carelessly and unthinkingly" slides between the threads is randomness (*MD* 214-5). We could say that Ishmael here intuits the nature of Darwin's cosmos, which is ruled by a coincidence of law, freedom, and chance. Natural selection is an unalterable law: certain genetic strains will survive in certain environments and other strains will not. Yet, the conditions under which natural selection functions are generated by chance: genetic mutations and environmental changes are unpredictable. Between the necessity of the mechanism and the randomness of its conditions lies freedom, the ability to alter the applications of natural selection through creative (unpredictable) actions. The random swerve of a part (rather conscious or not) can affect the whole, which in turn can change how the whole selects the parts that will thrive.

Serpentine and Spiralize

Ishmael struggles to embody this agitated cosmos by becoming an eddy himself, a human spiral open to abysmal flows, a pattern of turbulence. He must labor, for throughout the novel, Ahab tries to dominate him. The captain almost succeeds, even at one point persuading Ishmael of the philosophical feasibility of the hunt.

Before Ishmael comes under Ahab's command—before he ships on the *Pequod*—he proves himself a figure of coalescence, capable of swerving to gather disparate ideas. After opening himself to the circulations of the ocean in "Loomings," he revolves to the barbaric, the other, embracing Queequeg, paganism, and the whale. Averse to monomania, he gains knowledge throughout the novel by this fusing of the heterogeneous. For instance, in his effort to interpret a "boggy, soggy, squitchy picture" in the Spouter Inn, he is content with a communal hermeneutic, a conjunction of disparate readings, reaching a conclusion (the picture depicts a whaling scene) partly grounded on his own examination, partly based on the opinions of others (*MD* 13). Indeed, Ishmael's mode of living and his method of inquiry are characterized by conviviality, swerving his own body and beliefs to join with those of others. As he declares after merging with Queequeg, "see how elastic prejudices grow when love once comes to bend them" (54).

Yet, after shipping on the *Pequod*, Ishmael risks becoming a cog in Ahab's machine. After the quarterdeck speech, Ishmael "hammer[s] and clinch[es]" his "oath" to Ahab, swearing to participate in the captain's "quenchless feud" against time (*MD* 179). After his oath, Ishmael even attempts to persuade readers of the validity of Ahab's view in the "Whiteness of the Whale" (188-

95). Playing out a philosophical parable, Ishmael for a substantial part of the novel is persuaded by Ahab of the rationality of the hunt for Moby-Dick. Essentialism and the line will again dominate evolution and the spiral. Like an islander in one of Melville's early novels, the ingenuous Ishmael becomes a convert to Ahab's religion, making for a while Ahab's pilgrimage his own.

What saves Ishmael from being completely mechanized by the monomaniacal captain is the hermeneutic circle—philosophy as conversation. Only a few pages after merging with Ahab by taking his oath, he immediately separates from him. After registering Ahab's interpretation of the whale on the quarter deck, he immediately offers his own in the "Whiteness of the Whale," even in the midst of his *apologia* for Ahab. Importantly, Ishmael's interpretation of the whale as a synecdoche for universal indeterminacy is temporary, occasional, held by him only "at times" (*MD* 188). Entering the circle, he continues to sound the whale from a number of disparate perspectives, ranging, as we have seen, from science to religion to history to myth. This willingness to merge with heterogeneous views ultimately frees Ishmael's mind from Ahab's, restoring him to a loose fish in "The Squeeze of the Hand." In this chapter, which comes as the *Pequod* nears its encounter with Moby-Dick, Ishmael and the crew are gathered round a large vat of cooling whale sperm squeezing the coagulated lumps to liquefy them; suddenly intoxicated by the aromatic sperm, Ishmael feels his fingers turn to "eels." They begin to "serpentine and spiralize" with the fingers of his mates. He details his Whitmanesque merging:

> I squeezed that sperm until I almost melted into it; I squeezed that sperm till a strange sort of insanity came over me; and I found myself unwittingly squeezing my co-laborers hands in it, mistaking their hands for gentle globules. Such an abounding, affectionate, friendly, loving feeling did this avocation beget. (*MD* 416)

Ishmael's conjoining of man with man, man with nature redeems him to his world of living vortices, from which he was for a while exiled by Ahab: as he squeezes the sperm, he forgets about his "horrible oath" to the captain (*MD* 416). Ishmael's recursive embraces and cogitations save him from Ahab's "either/or" logic, keeping him open to "both/and" possibilities. Even though he obeys the captain's orders, he rebels in disposition. Countering Ahab's lines, his way of seeing is organic, a balance of centrifugal and centripetal forces, order and disorder: "[t]here are some enterprises in which a careful disorderliness is the true method" (361). This interplay of whim and order is analogous to the growth of Darwin's organisms; his disorderly method—the sequence of his chapters—grows like branches and twigs from a tree (289). This paradoxical method enables him to accept a duplicitous world, in which the whale is both horrible and sublime; the ocean, harmonious and red in tooth and claw; the human, noble and sharkish.

Gnosis at the Tiller

"The Squeeze of the Hand" is Ishmael's baptism in the flows of the abyss. Though he for a time fell away from life and worshipped at the shrines of Ahab, he ultimately returns to the flux. Put another way, he renounces Ahab's traditional, anti-materialist Gnosticism for the true religion of gnostic ecology.

As Thomas Vargish, William B. Dillingham, and Etsuko Taketani have shown, Ahab clearly exhibits Gnostic beliefs. Before writing *Moby-Dick*, Melville likely learned about Gnosticism from Ephraim Chambers' *Cyclopaedia* (1728), Andrews Norton's *Evidences of the Genuineness of the Gospels* (1844), and Pierre Bayle's *Dictionary* (1697) and then proceeded to cast his monomaniac captain as a latter-day *pneumatic* with a serious hatred of *hyle*. Of course, Ahab is not simply a Gnostic, as we have seen. On the one hand, he is a mechanist, espousing the determinism of the spatial chain of being. On the other, he is a progressionist, hoping to evolve above the laws of matter to godhead. This latter component of the complex Ahab is Gnostic. For instance, in the quarter deck oration, Ahab conjectures that Moby-Dick might be the apostate god of matter (Ialtobaoth) attempting to conceal the existence of the true god of the *pleroma*. Likewise, in "The Candles," Ahab addresses the flames as his "fiery father"—the demiurge entrapping him in matter—and asserts that there is "some unsuffusing thing" beyond, the transcendent *pleroma*. Compared to this *pleroma*, this material deity is but time to eternity, a machine to life (*MD* 507-8).[38] These and other Gnostic resonances—primarily in Ahab's invocations to a female principle who resembles the fallen Sophia—shed powerful lights on Ahab's loathing of nature. For him, the flesh, the ocean and the whale are evil artifacts of an evil god.[39] In fact—and this is not surprising—in some Gnostic sects, Leviathan is the world serpent, the *ouroboros* dividing the material cosmos from the *pleroma*, a slimy symbol of the unruly chaos of nature into which the Gnostic has fallen.[40]

(Of course, Leviathan is a pernicious symbol in the Bible as well, always associated with evil enemies of God. The opening of Genesis, for instance, is a rewriting of the Babylonian cosmogonal myth *Enuma Elish*, in which Marduk kills and divides Tiamat, the great sea beast of chaos. Likewise, in The Book of Job, God brags of his ability to capture and tame Leviathan. In

Psalms, moreover, the poet praises God's ability to "split the sea in two" and smash "the heads of monsters on waters." Likewise, the books of Isaiah and Revelation praise God's power to destroy serpents, dragons, and whales—all symbols of evil and ignorance.[41])

Countering Ahab yet again, Ishmael embraces Leviathan as a symbol of life, a numinous type of the key to it all. While Ahab would strike through the material whale to the spiritual abyss, Ishmael would study the whale as a manifestation of the first chaos. As James Baird has shown, Ishmael renounces Western traditions in which the whale is viewed as pernicious chaos and instead turns to Indian and Chinese traditions in which Leviathan is sacred. Versed in F.D. Maurice's *Indian Antiquities* (1800) and William Julius Mickle's "Inquiry into the Religious Tenets and Philosophy of the Brahmins" (found in Alexander Chalmers's *The Works of the English Poets* [1810]), Melville has Ishmael equate the whale with Vishnu, one of the three primary Hindu deities (along with Brahma and Siva). But Ishmael goes further, according to Baird: he sees the whale as "Brahma incarnate, encompassing in his vast being both Vishnu . . . and Siva . . . the keeper of infinite and timeless wisdom . . . the unreasoning force of chaos . . . the primal God." In viewing the whale this way, Ishmael also recalls a Chinese myth of the primal "Dragon of the Great Deep." In Buddhist cosmogony, water is the force of life and death, creation and destruction, the reservoir of all life. Its symbol is the dragon/whale, "the *giver of life*."[42]

Moby-Dick: Leviathan: dragon: ocean: chaos. For Ishmael these are not evil energies to be controlled or destroyed; they are to be worshipped, sacred symbols of the living abyss. Aptly, right after his baptism in sperm, Ishmael proclaims his biological religion in "The Cassock." The whale's huge, jet-black penis is an "idol," a holy object; its pelt, when removed and worn as a bib, is a cassock, a religious robe; the mincer wearing the cassock is an "arch-bishoprick" intent on cutting "bible leaves" from the whale's flesh. Fittingly, the center of this *religio ceti* is the phallus, which is double, beyond logic, an "enigmatical" object: it is both dark (an ebony idol) and light (producer of oil for lamps); both destructive (as life force of the terrible beast) and creative (as semen of the noble whale) (*MD* 419).

Having been baptized in sperm and introduced to its holy rites, Ishmael next, in "The Try-Works," is ready for gnosis: his purification from the forces of Ahabian death result in a vision of the living cosmos. At the helm of the ship while its members are boiling whale blubber in the midnight darkness, Ishmael becomes momentarily mesmerized by the blackened shapes moving in the firelight. He yields to sleep only to awaken to a "bewildered feeling, as of death." In this confused state, he grasps at the tiller, but notices it to be inverted. In his sleep, he had turned around to front the stern, his back to the prow, and would have capsized the ship had he tried to steer from that position. He takes this hallucination as an insight into the nature of things. The flames of the try-works betoken despair and sorrow, the dark, tragic forces of life that have undone Ahab. These powers comprise a major part of Ishmael's paradoxical standard of wisdom: one must feel the world's woe to be wise. However, "there is a woe that is madness" (*MD* 423-5). If one becomes utterly consumed by the woeful fire, he will be Ahab, monomaniacal; true wisdom involves a mix of woe and joy, the tragic and the comic, what Nietzsche calls tragic gaiety. Ishmael can oscillate between tragedy and gaiety, coffin and life buoy; Ahab remains only single, an unyielding bone.

This epiphany at the tiller—akin to Emerson's on the common, Fuller's by the falls—reveals immediately to Ishmael what he had expected throughout the novel. The single science—the reduction of chaos to order, ocean to map—is death; only the double science—blending turbulence and pattern, waves and grids—grants life. Christopher Sten is right. It is indeed Ishmael's openness to the paradoxical mysteries of an organic cosmos that saves him from Ahab's rage. The white whale "vitalizes" Ishmael's imagination with its "force and magnitude," urging him to resist the stasis of Ahab's absolutism, perpetually sending him churning in the hermeneutic circle.[43] The chapter headings following the pivotal sequence of "A Squeeze of the Hand," "The Cassock," and "The Try-Works" bear this out: the living whale has redeemed Ishmael from his captain. After his epiphany at the helm, he meditates on "The Lamp," intimating his illumination; he then reflects on "Stowing Down and Clearing Up," showing that he has purged himself of Ahab's influence. Enlightened and cleansed, Ishmael is ready to be gathered into the ocean's immense cross-currents, safe from Ahab's violence.

The moral of *Moby-Dick*, the victorious philosophical direction: the nomad undoes the pilgrim, the spiral bends the static line. Ishmael is rewarded within the moral economy of the novel, in the end "drawn towards the closing vortex," whirling in the wake of the sunken *Pequod*, drifting to safety, fittingly, on a coffin turned life buoy, death and life. He alone escapes the catastrophe, a new Adam of a race of Loose Fish, welcomed by the whale's flows, unharmed by the sharks in its waters, gaining at last the vortical "vital centre," the key to it all, as John T. Irwin observes, both the "source and the abyss," the beginning and the end.[44] Ahab is consumed in the end by his own violence, destroyed by the enigmatic whale he hated for swimming beyond his dictates, pulled to the ungraspable bottom of the ocean by a rope of hemp: a Fast Fish—live by the line, die by the line (623-5). These are the poles of the apocalypse: the passing of imperialistic metaphysics, the violent dream of anthropocentric thought; the emerging of conjunctive thought, conjugation, a new earth gathering primitive and civilized, a new heaven of natural culture.

Melville himself could not remain nourished for long by his vision of the nomad. Like Ahab, he could not endure lengthy insecurity. Only months after *Moby-Dick*, he published *Pierre*, a novel about a tortured American Hamlet, unable to find certainty or accept incertitude, incapable of resolving into pilgrim or nomad. This was clearly Melville's own tormented condition as he hashed it out with Hawthorne on the bleak rocks of Ireland. The author of *Moby-Dick* was doomed to wander to and fro between nomad and pilgrim in inhospitable deserts. Yet, in this turbulence, Melville showed himself more a bitter nomad than a failed pilgrim, prepared to face, courageously though begrudgingly, the pain of metaphysical abandonment, the maddening mystery of the white whale. Tragically, he experienced mostly the agony of exile, rarely the ecstasy of the wild.

Thoreau Over the Deep

Water in Winter

On New Year's Day, 1851, Thoreau as usual set out on his afternoon walk, exhilarated by another warm day, the third in a row, surrounded, though the sky was sunless, by a luminous mist. He made his way to a deep cut in the bank around Walden Pond, his former habitat. There he beheld thawing clay, the frozen earth melting under the plastic power of midwinter spring: earth returning to first water. Metamorphosing his head to hands and feet, Thoreau dug below the surface of the sliding mud to unearth its subterranean significance:

> These things suggest—that there is motion in the earth as well as on the surface; it lives & grows. It is warmed & influenced by the sun— just as my blood by my thoughts. I seem to see some of the life that is in the spring bud & blossom more intimately nearer its fountain head—the fancy sketches & designs of the artist. It is more simple & primitive growth. As if for ages sand and clay might have thus flowed into the forms of foliage—before plants were produced to clothe the earth. The earth I tread on is not a dead inert mass. It is a body—has a spirit—is organic—and fluid to the influence of its spirit—and to whatever particle of that spirit is in me. She is not dead but sleepeth. It is more cheering than the fertility & luxuriance of vineyards—this fundamental fertility near to the principle of growth. To be sure it is somewhat foecal and stercoral—. So the poet's creative moment is when the frost is coming out in the spring. (*J* 4:230)

Attending to liquid, Thoreau discovers analogies among water, blood, sap, spirit—each of these fluids is life, nourishing the earth, invigorating the poet. Looking up from the sandy foliage, he notices the mist hanging in the woods, a white background from which lichens vividly emerge, appearing, in concert with the fog, "more loose-flowing—expanded—flattened out— the colors brighter." Suddenly, as if animated by the ubiquitous moisture, the lichens come to life, swell to "eclipse the trees they cover." Water is everywhere: thrusting mud, enlivening fungus, flowing in veins. The gnosis: "True as Thales said—The world was made out of water—that is the principle of all things" (4:231-2).

On the eve of a new year, after three bright days, Thoreau experiences an aqueous epiphany, an Easter in the depth of winter. Observing his environment with the precision of the scientist, he enjoys the vision of the saint, feels the muse of the poet. He apprehends a potent principle of life and art, an aqueous unity sustaining the sloshing many. All is changed. A few days after, Thoreau commences a fourth draft of *Walden* and works unceasingly on successive drafts until the book finds print some two years later. He pushes the book toward spring, culminating its quest for life in the famous thawing sequence in the "Spring" chapter, where the deep cut becomes a congregation of water, word, world—a *hydrologos. True as Thales said—The world was made out of water—that is the principle of all things.*

This December journal description and the ensuing revision of it into the remarkable passage in "Spring" reveal an important and overlooked current in the two books Thoreau published while alive, *A Week on the Concord and Merrimack Rivers* (1849) and *Walden* (1854). This neglected tendency springs from Thales, the sixth-century B.C.E. Ionian hailed as the first Western philosopher and famous for claiming that water is the fundamental principle of the cosmos. Like Thales, whom he studied in the early 1840s, Thoreau in *A Week* and *Walden* focuses on water, speculating on its diffusions through nature. In both books, he wonders if water—not spirit, not idea—may indeed be the principle of life, the nourishment of nature. Returning to the original thinker of the West, Thoreau goes to the source of everything—the watery abyss boiling before Plato inscribed his clean laws in the sky.

Living in water—meandering down the Merrimack River, fishing in Walden Pond—Thoreau turns. He turns in a polarized *kosmos*, where order is not superior to turbulence but its complementary opposite, where enduring shapes, rivers and ponds, are created by transient currents. Revolving in the fluid sources of the world, Thoreau metamorphoses into a fish, becomes a mud snake. In an aqueous cosmos one should practice, he admonishes, a buoyant *ethos*—elastic, flexible, fluxional, able to float, to wiggle in the muck. Moreover, turning in water—as a being of the living and forgotten cosmos, as a human trying to model his behavior on vexed eddies—Thoreau the poet tropes his liquid insights into flowing texts. He attempts to write a river in *A Week on the Concord and Merrimack Rivers*, to create a pond in *Walden*: his books essay *to be* what they are about, to pattern the cosmos with *logos*.

Accordingly, a primary purpose of this chapter is to chart how Thales's aqueous drifts flow through Thoreau's textual landscapes. This Thalesian stream is clearly important in Thoreau's oeuvre, for it allows us to understand more deeply Thoreau's theory of life—his sense of its origin, its processes, it accessibility.

Looking backward to this ancient effort to locate life in a physical principle, Thoreau also participates in the biological thinking of his own age. While musing on water, Thoreau was also reading Goethe, who approached nature—as we know—in a Thalesian mood, attempting to locate life—the whole sustaining the parts—in *physis* as much as *pneuma*. This concurrence of Goethean biology and Thalesian cosmology in Thoreau's *A Week* and *Walden*, then, is a second key subject of this chapter. Examining this coincidence of Goethe and Thales illuminates Thoreau's efforts to discover life not so much in spirit, soul, or God as in sap, mud, ponds, and rivers.

Like Goethe, Thoreau translated the processes of nature into directions for writing. He wished to embody in words the pulsations of the world. This is a third focus of this chapter: the ways in which Thoreau transmutes the turnings of water into key tropes in his books. Viewing water as one of nature's pervasive forces and believing that powerful writing is wild like nature, Thoreau in *A Week* and *Walden* diffuses liquid through his textual landscape by the agency of his tropes. In both books, certain tropes become principles of distribution, metamorphosing Thoreau's literary world into liquid, making it buoyant and elastic, like mud in the deep cut. To be sure, the imagery in Thoreau's books often lolls in the sun or breathes in the leaves, but his figures are never far from the water that may have made the world.

Thales and the Nile

In 1840, eleven years before his aqueous epiphany, fresh out of Harvard, his journal only three years old, Thoreau was prompted by Thales's thoughts on the soul to observe: "What the first philosopher taught the last will have to repeat—The *world* makes no progress" (*J* 1:123). In Thoreau's day it did indeed seem that philosophy had come full circle. The insights of the first Greek philosopher, Thales, were being explored in the laboratories and studies of early nineteenth-century scientists and philosophers. First and last were both in search of a primal and pervasive principle of life, not in a heavenly creator but in biological creatures.

In 1840, Thoreau also attended to the nature of philosophy. He spent this year perusing Ralph Cudworth's *True Intellectual System of the Universe* (1678), Francois Fenelon's *Abrege de la vie des plus illustres philosophes de l'antiquitie* (ca. 1700), and Baron Joseph de Gerando's *Histoire comparee des systemes de philosophie* (1822-3).[1] While in Cudworth's fervent attack on atheism Thoreau learned of the endeavors of noble philosophers, pagan and Christian, to ascertain the principle cause of the cosmos, it was in the French historians of thought that he found Thales revealed.[2] In those texts he found the core of the first Greek thinker in the three statements attributed to him by Aristotle. In the *Metaphysics* (ca. 340 B.C.E.), Aristotle reports that Thales believed that "[t]he earth rests upon water," and that the "first-principle" is "water"; in *De Anima* (ca. 350 B.C.E.), Aristotle further records the following statement of his predecessor: "All things are full of gods," for which reason "the magnetic stone has soul in it" that "sets a piece of iron in motion."[3] Gerando and Fenelon, following Aristotle, explicate the first two statements. If water is the primary cause of everything, then the earth is water in a highly condensed state, and the air is constituted by extremely rarefied liquid. All things change perpetually from one to the other, earth rarefying into air, air condensing into earth, both ultimately resolving themselves back to the primal water. The entire universe is continually replenished by this unceasing surge, a force patterning all visible phenomena.[4] In Fenelon's mind, Thales's apothegm on magnetism is a parable for his water philosophy: the effects of the magnet reinforce the idea that a primal sympathy exists among things, all of which are animated by the same principle, call it water, life, or gods.[5]

Of the many legends that attached themselves to Thales, ranging from his prophetic skills in predicting eclipses to his entrepreneurial ones in cornering the olive market, one relates specifically to his knowledge of water, his theory of the inundation of the Nile.[6] According to several later commentators, Fenelon included, Thales believed that the summer rising and winter falling of this great river were caused by the Estesian winds, whose strong currents controlled the water's flow.[7] It makes sense that Thales would be very familiar with the rhythms of water. He could only have reached his ontology of liquid by closely attending to evaporation, rain, dew, mists, and springs, attuned to metamorphoses of solid to liquid to gas and back again. His philosophy grounded itself in science, his theory in practice. Though Thales may have been, as the French historians report and as Thoreau records in his journal, "the first of the Greeks who taught that souls are immortal," he relied firmly on natural process in reaching his conclusions, a point that Gerando emphasizes repeatedly.[8] It is one that Thoreau makes as well, noting that Thales thought that "'virtue consists in leading a life conformable to nature'" (*J* 1:123, 178).

Indeed, as Philip Wheelwright has explained, rehearsing the arguments of Gerando, Thales and the Milesian thinkers who followed after him (Anaximander, Anaximenes) are scientific more than religious in spirit. First, they account for nature in terms of nature, deciphering first causes in water, the unlimited (Anaximander), air (Anaximenes), refusing to invoke supernatural powers or to rely merely on speculation. When Thales uses the words "soul" or "gods," he clearly does not have in mind mythological gods, but *psyche* and *theos* as physical potencies, like water, magnetism, and electricity. Likewise, Thales and his successors keep their insights free of esoteric, hermetic haze; anyone who wishes to observe physical phenomena with rigor can understand their conclusions. Their philosophy, like scientific data, is democratic. Finally, these early scientists apprehend relationships between parts and the whole, never seeing an event as purely isolated, but as a result of a larger cause, a synecdoche of a greater process.[9]

Goethe's Urstoff

Proving Thoreau's aphorism on the coincidence of the first and last philosophy, Thalesian cosmology persists in the transcendental anatomy flourishing in late eighteenth- and early nineteenth-century scientific environs. Often called "romantic science" or "transcendental biology," transcendental anatomy—as we have seen—sprang from Goethe's searches for the *Urpflanze* and the *Urtier*, ideal archetypes of the plant and animal realms.[10] Again, the basic assumption of the transcendentalist biologist is this: certain archetypes (the leaf, the vertebra)—deep physical structures—organize the surges of life into coherent flora and fauna. (These archetypes, it should be clear, *correspond* to—are *analogous* to, not *equal* to—Thales's aqueous patterns. While Goethe shares with Thales two hypotheses—the source of life is likely physical and this origin manifests itself by way of metamorphosis [the changes of water into solid and gas, the transformations of archetype into organic parts]—the German thinker is certainly more scientifically sophisticated than the Greek one and more concerned with specific relationships between structures and functions.)

As Thoreau was well aware, Goethe went to Italy in 1786 in search of the primal plant form, curious about its generation and sustenance of botanical diversity.[11] Reading the *Italian Journey* in 1837, Thoreau would have learned—as did Emerson and Fuller—of Goethe's botanical gnosis. Strolling through the flora in the heat of the July sun, Goethe, as we know, saw "in a flash" that in the leaf is the primal vegetable form, the seed of botany.[12] As the leaf in the plant, so the vertebra in the animal: both *Urtypen* are centripetal forces, harvesting the "unknown center" and "unknowable periphery" of life into palpable forms—marigolds and opossums, oaks and elephants. If Thales's aqueous *Urstoff* is grasped through its undulations and evaporations (the rhythms of the Nile), Goethe's water of life is known through its sprigs and blooms, sinews and bones. In both cases, convoluted shapes gesture toward a boundless whole.

In the early 1850s, right around the time of his watery epiphany, Thoreau was studying other scientific thinkers in the Goethean tradition, Alexander von Humboldt and Coleridge. Both of these figures, like Goethe, searched for a holistic physical power animating the beings of the cosmos. Their work likely complemented Goethe's in Thoreau's mind, for each, in varying degrees of intensity (Humboldt more, Coleridge less), strained to look through the leaf, the fish, the bird to the energy shaping veins, bones, brain. (Of course, during this time Thoreau was also under the influence of another scientist in the Goethean line, Louis Agassiz, who studied under Goethe's disciple Lorenz Oken before coming to America from Switzerland in 1846. Given the Thalesian context in which I'm considering Thoreau, Agassiz merits less attention than Humboldt and Coleridge, for Agassiz, a natural theologian, was finally more interested in scripture and spirit than in nature and matter—a fact that increasingly dampened Thoreau's interest in the Swiss scientist as the '50s wore on.[13])

In the spring of 1850, Thoreau was supplementing his reading of Goethe with the biological cosmology of Humboldt, a German-born friend of Goethe. Traveling in Cuba, Mexico, and South America in the first years of the nineteenth century, Humboldt found that the study of plants led not only to the discovery of new facts, but also, and more importantly, to connections among facts, insights into the relations among plants, geography, and cosmos.[14] Humboldt recorded his conclusions on botanical relations in several scientific works, two of which were read by Thoreau, *Views of Nature; or Contemplations on the Sublime Phenomenon of Creation* (1808) in 1850 and *Personal Narrative of Travels to the Equinoctial Regions of America, during the Years* 1799-1804 (1807-34) in 1852. But Humboldt's most Thalesian effort remains his *Cosmos: A Sketch of a Physical Description of the Universe* (1843-1862), the early volumes of which were perused by Thoreau in the spring of 1850.[15] In this five-volume book, Humboldt brings his capacious knowledge of physical fact to bear on the following thesis: "Nature . . . is a unity in diversity of phenomena; a harmony, blending together all created things, however dissimilar in form and attributes; one great whole . . . animated by the breath of life." To prove this thesis, Humboldt surveys a bewildering diversity of particular facts. He draws from biology, physics, geography, botany, galvanism and other sciences while ranging from the "remotest nebulae" to the "minutest organisms of animal creation." This expansive attention yields not a mere catalogue of isolated facts but a representation of "a Cosmos, or [a] harmoniously ordered whole"[16]—an insight, as he observes elsewhere, into the "universal diffusion of life over the whole surface of the Earth."[17]

Also around 1850, in further preparation for his watery epiphany on December 1851, Thoreau was reading yet another recent avatar of Thales, Coleridge, whose own cosmological endeavor, *Hints Toward the Formation of a More Comprehensive Theory of Life* (1816; published 1848), was stimulated by Schelling and Henrik Steffens, enthusiastic students of Goethe.[18] In this book, Coleridge sets out, with recent scientific discoveries in chemistry and biology as his guide, to fathom life, its definition and morphology. Life, he declares, is "the *power* which discloses itself from within as a principle of *unity* in the *many*." In other words, "life [is] the *principle of individuation*, or the power which unites a given *all* into a *whole* that is presupposed by all its parts." Each individual organism is a condensed pattern of the whole, transforming the energy of the all into its own parts. The primary law of life is polarity, Coleridge's principle of metamorphosis. Like Thales and Goethe before him, he believes that specimens are mergings of whole and part, syntheses of thesis and antithesis. These poles are manifested not only as assimilations of universal into particular, but also as chemical combinations of magnetism (attraction) and electricity (repulsion) into chemical affinity (cohesion of opposites) as well as correspondent biological fusions of reproduction and irritability into sensibility.[19] The extensive notes Thoreau made on Coleridge's book in the 1850s proved part of his own compounding of ancient and modern into a sensitivity for the whole, preparation for his vision of holy water rolling through mud-formed leaves in the Massachusetts spring.[20]

The Actual is the Rarest Poetry

Fittingly, just as he begins a discussion of Goethe's *Italian Journey* in *A Week on the Concord and Merrimack Rivers*, Thoreau records the following observation: "A true account of the actual is the rarest poetry" (*WC* 325). He goes on to praise Goethe for his excellence in "giving an exact description of things as they appeared to him, and their effect upon him" (326). While Thoreau—surprisingly—does not mention Goethe's search for the *Urpflanze* and even criticizes Goethe for lacking the "unconscious" genius of the true poet (Goethe remains a mere, measured "Artist" in Thoreau's mind [327]), he nonetheless reveals his profound affinity with Goethe on the issue of observation. Like Goethe, Thoreau believes that close attention to the palpable is the true muse of poetry, for this immediate gaze can vouchsafe an experience of *life*. Seeing nature with the eyes of the poet—not with the instruments of the positivistic scientist—one can overcome alienating, deadening gaps between subject and object, part and whole, and finds one's place in the flow.

Thoreau, like Goethe, is clear about the limitations of positivism. As he writes in his journal in 1851, some months after his New Year's gnosis in the deep cut, "[e]ven the facts of science may dust the mind by their dryness—unless they are in a sense effaced each morning or rather rendered fertile by the dews of fresh & living truth" (*J* 3: 291). The discrete fact alone is dead. Yet, seen in connection to life, it thrives. Thoreau set down a similar meditation in 1850:

> The scientific startling & successful as it is, is always some thing less than the vague poetic—it is that of it which subsides—it is the sun shorn of its beams a mere disk—the sun indeed—but—no longer phospher—light bringer or giver . . . Science applies a finite rule to the infinite.— & is what you can weigh and measure and bring away. Its sun no longer dazzles us and fills the universe with light. (3:44)

While the Newtonian would separate the sun from its energies and view it as a circle of atoms held in empty space by gravity, the poetic scientist would see the sun only in connection to life and light.

(Here recall Blake on the sun, in his commentary on his lost painting *The Vision of the Last Judgment*: "What it will be Questioned When the Sun rises do you not see a round Disk of fire somewhat like a Guinea O no no I see an Innumerable company of the Heavenly host crying Holy Holy Holy is the Lord God Almighty I question not my corporeal or Vegetative Eye any more than I would Question a Window concerning a Sight I look thro it & not with it."[21])

Thoreau practices this poetic science—learned from Coleridge and Humboldt as much as from Goethe—in both of his books. For instance, he opens *A Week* by announcing his primary motivation for taking a river journey: to find enduring patterns in the fretting waters. "As yesterday and the historical ages are past, as the work of to-day is present, so some flitting perspectives and demi-experiences of the life that is in nature are, in time, veritably future, or rather outside to time, perennial, young, divine, in the wind and rain which never die" (*WC* 8). In the flux of past, present, and future (the river of time) momentarily flash quick revelations of durable life, "perennial, young, divine," in physical processes that never die. Some pages later, he elaborates: he desires to view the river as a part of the original and ubiquitous whole, as "an emblem of all progress, following the same law with the system, with time, and all that is made" (12). Later in *A Week*, Thoreau experiences such a Goethean vision: "As we [he and his brother John] sailed under this canopy of leaves we saw the sky through its chinks, and, as it were, the meaning and idea of the tree stamped in a thousand hieroglyphs on the heavens. The universe is so aptly fitted to our organization that the eye wanders and reposes at the same time" (159). Without mentioning Goethe, Thoreau nonetheless gains the German poet's primary vision. Correctly seen, through intuitive perception, each leaf is an expression of a deeper sap; to cast one's gaze over the many is likewise to peer into the one. After several such gnostic moments (the content of which I shall explore deeply in a moment) in *A Week*, Thoreau concludes with a paean to the knowledge of the senses: "We need pray for no higher heaven than the pure senses can furnish, a *purely* sensuous life. . . . May we not *see* God? . . . Is not Nature, rightly read, that of which she is commonly taken to be a symbol merely?" (382). The senses, he continues, can surely "penetrate the spaces of the real" if we can "hesitate to trust [our] calculations" and instead try to see through the visible types to the invisible mysteries animating them. The "astronomers" who have achieved such palpable visions of life are not necessarily Newton and Laplace, positivists, but seers such as Zoroaster, Socrates, Christ, Shakespeare, and Swedenborg (386). Ultimately, these and other poetic "scientists" have apprehended the "Silence" out of which all sounds emerge, the "universal refuge," the "balm to our every chagrin," "waves" beyond interpretation (391-3)—the primal void that speaks and is the cosmos.

Merging his senses and his sensibility, his objective gaze and his subjective desire for the whole, his Understanding and his Reason, Thoreau studies the waves and gains a world. Carrying out this method, he practices a more empirical version of what Laura Dassow Walls has called Emerson's rational holism.[22] According to Walls, while Emerson tends to begin with a theory of the whole and then apply it to the part, Thoreau generally starts with the part and finds in it the whole. While this distinction may not always hold—for Emerson gazes hard at parts on the common and Thoreau wants to overlook nature to spirit in the "Higher Laws" chapter of *Walden*—it is important, for it highlights Thoreau's observational rigor. While Emerson was content to read about the scientific theories of others and apply them to his scene, Thoreau went to nature himself, with his pencil and notebook, recording the rhythms of the seasons, the turns of the animals, and the dispersions of seeds. To learn about rivers, he took a journey down the Concord and Merrimack, researching their natural history, registering their flows. To understand the flora and fauna of Concord, he planted at Walden Pond, where he actually measured the depth of the pond at the same time he meditated on the foundation of life. Yet, in the end, Thoreau, like Emerson (and Fuller and Ishmael), always used positivistic science as a means to a greater end, summed up powerfully in "Walking" (1851; 1862):

> My desire for knowledge [positivistic information] is intermittent, but my desire to bathe my head in atmospheres unknown to my feet is perennial and constant. The highest that we can attain to is not Knowledge, but Sympathy with Intelligence. I do not know that this higher knowledge amounts to anything more definite than a novel and grand surprise on a sudden revelation of the insufficiency of all that we called Knowledge before,—a discovery that there are more things in heaven and earth than are dreamed of in our philosophy. It is the lighting up of the mist by the sun. Man cannot *know* in any higher sense than this.[23]

The Fish Principle

In *A Week*, Thoreau combines his method of knowing—the poetry of fact—and his reading in Thales and Goethe to search for the origin of the cosmos in two rivers.

Even before his gnosis in 1851 of an aqueous principle in the deep cut, Thoreau was meditating on diffusions of water, conjecturing that water is where we live.[24] As early as 1840, fresh from his actual 1839 week-long voyage down the Concord and Merrimack Rivers (he would not write about this experience until about six years later), he proposed that all of us are beings of water, fishy: "I fancy I am amphibious and swim in all the brooks and pools in the neighborhood, with the perch and bream, or doze under the pads of our river amid the winding aisles and corridors formed by their stems, with the stately pickerel" (*J* 1:109). Some two years later, still before planting himself at Walden, he elaborated: "I have not yet met with the philosopher who could in a quite conclusive undoubtful way—show me *the* and if not *the* then how *any*—difference, between man and a fish. We are so much alike" (2:108). While sojourning at the Pond, he began in 1845 to channel such thoughts into *A Week*.

The first page of the book suggests parallels between the Concord River, formerly called the Musketaquid, and the original flows of civilization. Though probably not as old as the Nile or Euphrates, the Concord did, like its fluviatile ancestors, become the source of civilization, attracting English settlers to its banks in 1635 (*WC* 5). These thoughts of first rivers—and of rivers in general as origins—prompt Thoreau a few pages later to declare that waves "agitated by the wind" keep "nature fresh" (7). Continuing to draw from physical data—the facts of history and science—Thoreau, still in the brief introductory chapter called "Concord River," observes that trees are patterns of water: the river bank "is skirted with maples, alders, and other fluviatile trees, overrun with the grape vine" (10). This sense of water pervading even the groves, making them exuberant with grape, leads him to return to huge, primal rivers, the Mississippi, Ganges, Nile, to consider them as links connecting the world: "They are the natural highways of all nations, not only levelling the ground, and removing obstacles from the path of the traveller, quenching his thirst, and bearing him on their bosoms, but conducting him through . . . the globe" (12). These ubiquitous arteries, carrying nourishment throughout the planet, correspond to all rivers, each of which, including the Concord, is, as we have seen, "an emblem of all progress, following the same law with the system, with time, and all that is made" (12). Finding a principle of development in rivers inspires Thoreau to suggest, through an extended trope, that the aquatic and terrestrial worlds are little different, that they perhaps overlap. Thinking of the Concord, he remarks that he is interested in "the weeds at the bottom gently bending down the stream, shaken by the watery wind, still planted where their seeds had sunk, but ere long to die and go down likewise" (12-3). Water and wind, seaweeds and earthplants are analogous. Perhaps wind is but a form of water, rarefied liquid. Maybe humans and leaves alike breathe water.

Thoreau has gleaned that water is perhaps a primeval and pervasive source of nourishment, that the entire atmosphere may be aqueous. This small spring he *spreads* throughout the book, quickly turning water into other specimens in the first chapter, "Saturday." Extending his merging of water and wind, he says that a worthy boat should be "a sort of amphibious animal . . . related by one half its structure to some swift and shapely fish, and by the other to some strong-winged and graceful bird" (*WC* 16). While floating and flying down river—part man, part fish, part bird—Thoreau suddenly experiences a major gnosis, similar to Emerson's on the common, Goethe's in the gardens. His observations and meditations thus far in the book suddenly coalesce into a vision of a primal pattern of life—an *Urbild*.

> Whether we live by the sea-side, or by the lakes and rivers, or on the prairie, it concerns us to attend to the nature of fishes, since they are not phenomena confined to certain localities only, but forms and phases of the life in nature universally dispersed. The countless shoals which annually coast the shores of Europe and America, are not so

interesting to the student of nature, as the more fertile law itself, which deposits their spawn on the tops of mountains, and on the interior plains; the fish principle in nature, from which it results that they may be found in water in so many places, in greater or less numbers. . . . The seeds of the life of fishes are every where disseminated, whether the winds waft them, or the waters float them, or the deep earth holds them; wherever a pond is dug, straightway it is stocked with this vivacious race. . . . There are fishes wherever there is a fluid medium, and even in clouds and in melted metals we detect their semblance. (25-6)

This remarkable passage details a key figure for water in *A Week*, a primary vehicle of distribution: *fish*. Having observed rivers, fish, and boats thus far in the book, Thoreau has concluded that water is everywhere—the very atmosphere is liquid; that it animates nature, keeps it fresh; and that it is the whole animating parts—underlying liquid, solid, gas (river, earth, air), conflating each creature into land animal, fish, and fowl. The fish principle, like Goethe's leaf and Emerson's currents, is a pervasive structure of this aqueous font of life. This fishy pattern coheres life into "forms and phases" that disperse themselves throughout the cosmos; it condenses pervasive life into discrete "seeds" that are disseminated through the whole; it is ubiquitous, extant in winds, waters, and earth. A new Thales, Thoreau has observed water in everything; Goethe *redivivus*, he has found a persistent form, an archetype, in which this principle of life manifests itself. His gnosis: we are descendants of Leviathan, the unruly whale. Moby-Dick swims in our veins.

Immediately after his vision of the fish principle, Thoreau indirectly details it further by cataloguing the virtues of various fish: buoyancy, balance, unity in diversity. His first specimen, aptly, is the sun fish, the first principle of the Neoplatonists sunk into fins. These fish generally hang stationary in the water, though keeping "up a constant sculling or waving motion with their fins, which is exceedingly graceful, and expressive of their humble happiness" (*WC* 27). Calm in flux (still and still moving), balanced in their habitat (negotiating between part and whole), these fish gather disparate elements into a heterogeneous pattern. Indeed, as Thoreau adds, each harvests different colors, the rays of the sun, and the reflections of pebbles into a beautiful mosaic (28). Thoreau discovers similar excellence in other fish: the Perch, Shiner, and Alewife (28-38). At the end of his catalog, he concludes that fish are exemplars of virtue (both virility—life—and ethics), cleverly punning on "fish": "Away with the super*fic*ial and selfish phil-

anthropy of men,—who knows what admirable virtue of fishes may be below low-water mark, bearing up against a hard destiny, not admired by that fellow creature who alone can appreciate it" (37; italics mine).[25]

Buoyancy

These fish exemplify the fish principle, the rhythm of life. As such, they not only reveal and embody the living waters but also constitute ethical paradigms. The human who can live like a fish—be buoyant, balanced, polar—is alive, healthy, good. Later, in "Tuesday," Thoreau is clear about his ethics of buoyancy. Observing boats, man-made fish, Thoreau moralizes: "They [boats, and by connection, fish] suggested how few circumstances are necessary to the well-being and serenity of man, how indifferent all employments are, and that any may seem noble and poetic to the eyes of men, if pursued with sufficient buoyancy and freedom" (*WC* 209). A few paragraphs later, he continues to speculate on floating, adding that the "the prevalence of the law of buoyancy" gives him "confidence" (212). Thinking still of floating, he concludes two days later, in "Thursday," that "All the world reposes in beauty to him who preserves equipoise in his life, and moves serenely on his path without secret violence; as he who sails down a stream, he has only to steer, keeping his bark in the middle, and carry it round the falls" (317). Preserving equipoise, the drifter takes on the qualities of "Silence," the abysmal undercurrent from which phenomena bubble upward, the "Unnamed" origin of everything: "[b]uoyancy, freedom, flexibility, variety, possibility" (136).

Gathered in these passages are Thoreau's buoyant versions of Emerson's middle way, Fuller's vagrancy, Melville's spiraling. To float well—to behave like a fish, to swim or sail efficiently—one must negotiate between control and insecurity. If one fights the water—moves against its current—one risks drowning; if one merely flows with the current, one hazards being slammed against rocks, taken out to sea. The trick is to move with the water, slightly redirecting its flow—with a rudder, with the breast stroke—to gain a modicum of control over direction and velocity. Translating the skills of effective floating to directions for the *bona vita*, Thoreau would be mobile, flexible and adaptable in the unpredictable waves of the world: changes of mind, alterations of weather, revolution. If we try too hard to map and control the shifting landscape—to settle it—we remove ourselves from salubrious currents, become brittle, moribund. Yet, if we merely give into whim, with no controlling technologies like rudders or words, then we become mere sensualists, bits blown helplessly in the winds. The middle way is best: negotiating the terrain successfully without stifling its invigorating strife.

Waves and Words

Like Goethe and Coleridge, Thoreau wanted not only to decipher the hieroglyphs of nature to unleash a life in which he could flourish. He also wished
to use nature's diaphanous graphs as models for his own sacred writing—a
buoyant style. As his midwinter epiphany at the deep cut revealed, organic
and artistic creativity are one, both processes of assimilating the energy of
the whole into living parts. Goethe's *Faust* is modeled on the plant;
Coleridge never tired of praising Shakespeare's organic forms. In a similar
way, Thoreau tries in *A Week* and *Walden* to create landscapes in words, in *A
Week* often fashioning words into fish meandering through a watery week,
in *Walden*, sometimes rooting his elements in the condensed sap of earth.

Indeed, throughout his life, Thoreau, like Emerson, equated good writing with natural elements, searching for the *logos* of *hydros*, tropes to *distrib-
ute* through his words the animating forces of the woods. Only three weeks
after his December vision of ubiquitous water, he observed that writing is a
channeling of sap: "If thou are a writer, write as if thy time were short. . . .
The spring will not last forever. These fertile & expanding seasons of thy
life—when the rain reaches thy root—when thy vigor shoots when thy
flower is budding, shall be fewer & farther between" (*J* 4:281). Transforming
rain into linguistic vigor, the writer will express sentences in which "every
word is rooted in the soil, is indeed flowery and verduous. . . . as blooming as
wreaths of evergreen and flowers" (1:386). These vegetable sentences will
comprise a "[t]ruly good book," one "as wildly natural and primitive—mysterious & marvellous ambrosial & fertile—as a fungus or a lichen" (3:141).

In shaping the worlds of *A Week* and *Walden*, Thoreau faces a problem of
distribution. If the writer discovers an animating principle—be it water, leaf,
or bone—then he will desire to spread its nourishing virtues throughout his
book. He requires a principle of metamorphosis, morphology. Both Milesian thinker and Romantic biologist glimpsed an agent of distribution, a
vehicle by which the abyss percolates through the many. Thales found it in
condensation and rarefication; Goethe in metamorphosis, of leaf and vertebra into stalk and spine; Coleridge in polarity; Humboldt in diffusion. In
both of his books, Thoreau likewise uncovers holistic powers, boundless
waters—wavering through fins, leaves, and breezes. Observing fish, wind,
and leaves, he often sees water behind them, spreading through the creatures
it sustains. These living parts, he realizes, translate—turn, trope—the energy
of this aqueous whole into their individual powers. Essaying to write nature,
Thoreau in his texts must create his own agents of diffusion, vehicles to dis-
tribute the nourishment of the whole—in this case, the wealth of water—
through his pages. These agents are his tropes. In *A Week* and *Walden*, he

early experiences a watery epiphany—similar to the one by the deep cut—that inspires him to translate this ubiquitous liquid throughout the diversity of his linguistic world.[26]

After his gnosis of the fish principle, Thoreau merges *kosmos, ethos,* and *logos* through the remainder of *A Week.* His tropes, like fish, *swim.* Indeed, he structures his very book on swimming. Meandering leisurely through a week, going with the flow of the river, Thoreau swims, albeit in his boat, letting the current take him where it will. He becomes increasingly awed by nature's grandeur, calmly meditating with the current, moving his thoughts with the water, ranging on subjects as varied as the eddies: history, mythology, poetry, local folklore, natural philosophy, friendship, music. When critics complain of the absence of form in this book, when Thoreau's contemporaries neglected to purchase it (leaving him with one of the larger libraries in Concord when he was forced to reclaim nine hundred unsold copies), they are rejecting his "fishy" behavior.[27]

Through words, *A Week* becomes a water world in which everything becomes everything else. The early troping, by which Thoreau blends water and wind, bird and fish, man and fish, is continued throughout the book. The opening "Concord" chapter establishes water as the primary principle; the following section, "Saturday," condenses water into the fish principle; the next chapter, "Sunday," diffuses it through the cosmos, opening with mist: "In the morning the river and adjacent country were covered with a dense fog, through which the smoke of our fire curled up like a still subtiler mist; but before we had rowed many rods, the sun arose and the fog rapidly dispersed, leaving a slight steam only to curl along the surface of the water" (*WC* 43). Reinforcing earlier diffusions, Thoreau figuratively states that air is water, all creatures are fish. Trees are water as well, fluviatile, we learn again some paragraphs later; the water willow, for example, is "wedded to the water" (44-5). Air and tree are water, transparent; fish and bird swim through its currents. As Thoreau observes of the Sunday atmosphere: "both air and water [are] so transparent, that the flight of the kingfisher or robin over the river was as distinctly seen reflected in the water below as in the air above. . . . We were uncertain whether the water floated the land, or the land held the water in its bosom" (45). Three pages later, Thoreau more overtly declares these coalescings. "Two men in a skiff" floating on the river are like a feather in the air or a leaf on the current. Floating on water/air, they are "in their element," following "natural laws." Just as they beautifully float—practicing a "natural philosophy"—so birds fly and fish swim. Men of water, fishy humans, bird-like beings, they merge harmoniously with the watery whole, blending water, air, and earth (48-9).

In the wake of these equivalences, the rest of *A Week* is flooded: everything is at the same time both itself and everything else. Good men are wet, ignoble ones dry (69-70); sand is water on which one can walk (199); the man in equipoise, like a fish floating in water, experiences beauty (317-8); powerful art exudes the superfluity, the overflowing, of nature (318); the "hardest material obeys the same law with the most fluid," "trees are but rivers of sap," the heavens "rivers of stars and milky ways," rocks and thoughts flow and circulate (331); sky, rarefied liquid, is an aqueous text revealing the truths of the mind (358-9); sailing is flying is plowing (360-1); a good book is a stone on which "the waves of Silence may break" (393).

Time Is But the Stream

While in *A Week* Thoreau *swims* with the river, in *Walden* he *sinks* into (sounds) the pond. Influenced by his environment, where he will settle more than sail, Thoreau replaces horizontal movement with vertical. His principle of distribution, his primary trope, is shaped by his environment. Remaining in one place, watching trees and plants inhabit their ecological niche and drink the earth's sap, Thoreau in *Walden* trades fish for plant.

While Thoreau changes his disposition at Walden, he continues to fathom Thales's aqueous insight. Like the flows of the Concord and Merrimack, the water of Walden Pond seems primeval. It preexists Eden. It is the true Castalian Fountain, the liquid of Ovid's Golden Age, "a gem of the first water" (*W* 179). Prior to time, it seems everlasting, mirroring the heavens while windowing earth, partaking equally of temporal and eternal, intermediate "between land and sky" (176-7, 188-9). Thoreau can tap the virtues of this water by unveiling its fish principle, by fishing: dropping his line down into the pond, he angles in the sky, sounding for literal fish with rod and reel, for the fish principle with mind:

> It was very queer, especially [fishing] in dark nights, when your thoughts had wandered to vast and cosmogonal themes in other spheres, to feel this faint jerk, which came to interrupt your dreams and link you to Nature again. It seemed as if I might next cast my line upward into the air, as well as downward into this element which was scarcely more dense. Thus I caught two fishes as it were with one hook. (175)

Descent and ascent, Thoreau finds, are the same: the contemplative fisherman sinks his hook into water to catch the sky just as the plant hugs the earth to rise and the pond dweller digs a foundation to erect a house. This vertical choreography of fishing becomes a pattern of key tropes in *Walden*: the plant and planting. These contradictory movements—fishing in water and sky at the same time, descending roots and rising stalks—structure what is perhaps the most dense passage in the book, an early gnostic sequence analogous to the "fish principle" paragraph in *A Week*. Thoreau ends his second chapter "Where I Lived, What I Lived For" thus:

> Time is but the stream I go a-fishing in. I drink at it; but while I drink I see the sandy bottom and detect how shallow it is. Its thin current slides away, but eternity remains. I would drink deeper; fish in the sky, whose bottom is pebbly with stars. I cannot count one. I know not the first letter of the alphabet. I have always been regretting that I was not as wise as the day I was born. The intellect is a clever; it discerns and rifts its way into the secret of things. I do not wish to be any more busy with my hands than is necessary. My head is hands and feet. I feel all my best faculties concentrated in it. My instinct tells me that my head is an organ for burrowing, as some creatures use their snout and fore-paws, and with it I would mine and burrow my way through these hills. I think that the richest vein is somewhere hereabouts; so by the divining rod and thin rising vapors I judge; and here I will begin to mine. (*W* 98)

Time, the finite world, is here rendered as water. Searching for its nature, its nourishment, its fish principle, requires fishing. Fishing attentively in water proper inspires "detection" (uncovering, unveiling, revelation) of an eternal principle of which the temporal water partakes. The nature of this principle could be aqueous itself: it is the bed of a stream, soaked by liquid, muddy. Descending into this muck, Thoreau understands it is a source of the cosmos, out of which even the stars arose and still arise. There, Thoreau himself momentarily returns to an original, infantile state, his mind revolving backward to a state of pure potential. He dreams of being this wise always. Yet, suddenly, out of the formless chaos of his infantile mind, forms begin to arise: he is enacting the birth of the universe. No longer nebulous, the mind organizes itself into "intellect," which is a "cleaver" capable of discerning and rifting its way into the secret of things, able to make differentiations within the soup. Indeed, his mind organizes itself into an organizing principle, a technology, a tool capable of classifying, shaping, and partially solving the currents of nature. This instrumental mind is flexible, however, ready for several different labors: it is not only a cleaver but also a spade, hands and feet, a mining tool, a divining rod. Drawing energy from the formless forces from which it arises, this tool remains nebulous, protean, heterogeneous—not too rigid, not too flaccid. Thoreau's mind is like a plant, a supple, coherent form arising from the mire: he descends and ascends (rooting into dark earth, rising to the sun); draws nourishment from above and below (drinking from the stream bed and the stars); is passive, taking in carbon dioxide and light (no more busy with his hands and feet than necessary) and active, sending forth oxygen to alter the atmosphere (like a mining tool changes the earth).

In this remarkable passage—a parable of cosmogony and much else—Thoreau turns from the fish principle to the primal leaf. Influenced by his forest environment at Walden, in his second book he spreads the world's water not through the figure of the fin but through that of the root, frequently transforming his second book into sappy leaves, more stationary forms of water. *Walden* is indeed Thoreau's own quest for the *Urpflanze,* water condensed into fronds of chlorophyll. In his masterpiece, he fulfills a youthful dream of leaves, recorded in his journal in the early 1840s:

> I have seen where the mildew on a jar had taken the form of perfect leaves—thick—downy—and luxuriant. What an impulse was given some time or other to vegetation that now nothing can stay it. Some one has said he could write an epic to be called the leaf—and this would seem to have been the theme of the creator himself. The leaf either . . . fluid or crystalline—is natures constant cypher. (*J* 2:80)

If *A Week* is the saga of fish, *Walden* is this epic of leaf.

Early in the book, in the "Economy" chapter, Thoreau indirectly proclaims his desire to become a plant, a more stationary pattern of water: "Why has man rooted himself thus firmly in the earth, but that he may rise in the same proportions to the heavens above?"—for the "nobler plants are valued for the fruit they bear at last in the air and light" (*W* 15). He yearns for universal vegetation, wishing each man to absorb and cultivate the rarefied liquid of air: "I want the flower and fruit of a man; that some fragrance be wafted over from him to me" (77). In becoming simple and natural, partaking of the archetype, we must photosynthesize, take in air and light: to be "as simple and well as Nature ourselves," we should "dispel the clouds which hang over our own brows, and take up a little life into our pores" (78-9). Thoreau cultivates this strain in later chapters where he equates his life at Walden Pond with planting (83-84); grows, during meditation, like "corn in the night" (111); feels a breath taking sympathy with "the fluttering alder and poplar leaves" (129); believes that we are made healthy by "Nature's universal, vegetable, botanic medicines" (138); plants beans to apprehend the "kindredship [that] is in Nature" (159, 164); declares his desire to eat only vegetables, not meat, to open to God's breath, to flower, photosynthetically (215, 219-20); sees, fittingly, the fisherman's boat as a "floating leaf" (297).

Higher Laws: A Jarring Digression

Yet, right in the middle of *Walden*, in "Higher Laws," Thoreau turns against the sensual and aspires toward the spiritual. He becomes a dualist (like Ahab), claiming that he is split between a spiritual and savage instinct (*W* 210), that the spiritual impulse is higher and better (218-20).

Many would read this central chapter as a discourse on Thoreau's true transcendentalist philosophy. The typical transcendentalist reading states: all of Thoreau's physical observing, recording, and working are merely symbolic, earthly activities that will ultimately be rewarded by a vision of heaven. Certainly, there is good reason for such a reading. Like Emerson and Fuller, Thoreau was brought up in philosophical and religious traditions that believed that "Nature . . . must be overcome" because it is "unclean" (*W* 219,221). Indeed, Thoreau cut his philosophical teeth, recall, on Cudworth's *True Intellectual System of the Universe*: while he was sinking into Thales's deeps in the 1840s, he was also ascending to Cudworth's Neoplatonic One.

Like his contemporaries Emerson, Fuller, and Melville, even Thoreau must struggle between the transcendental impulses of his traditions and his own love of the earth. However, to be sure, Thoreau labors less than Emerson and Fuller, likely because he spent more time out of doors, in the mud and huckleberries, than his bookish colleagues. As we know, Laura Dassow Walls has shown that Thoreau indeed differentiated himself from Emerson in practicing an empirical holism instead of a rational one.[28] This distinction is helpful and interprets accurately Emerson's own assessment of his primary difference from Thoreau. In his rather ambiguous eulogy on Thoreau (Thoreau possessed "genius" and was the truest American but was "chilling" in social settings and lacked ambition [*EW* 10:421-52]), Emerson, perhaps unwittingly, reveals Thoreau's ecological sensibility to be more profound than his own. Here's Emerson describing what it was like to walk with Thoreau:

> It was a pleasure and a privilege to walk with him. He knew the country like a fox or a bird, and passed through it freely by paths of his own. He knew every track in the snow or on the ground, and what creature had taken this path before him. One must submit abjectly to such a

guide, and the reward was great. Under his arm he carried an old music-book to press plants; in his pocket, his diary and pencil, a spy-glass for birds, microscope, jack-knife, and twine. He wore straw hat, stout shoes, strong gray trousers, to brave shrub-oaks and smilax, and to climb a tree for a hawk's or a squirrel's nest. He waded into the pool for the water-plants, and his strong legs were no insignificant part of his armor. On the day I speak of he looked for the Menyanthes [genus of bog plants], detected it across the wide pool, and, on examination of the florets, decided that it had been in flower five days. He drew out of his breast-pocket his diary, and read the names of all the plants that should bloom on this day, whereof he kept account as a banker when his notes fall due. . . . Presently he heard a note which he called that of the night-warbler, a bird he had never identified, had been in search of for twelve years, which always, when he saw it, was in the act of diving down into a tree or bush, and which it was vain to seek; the only bird that sings indifferently by night or by day. I told him he must beware of finding and booking it, lest life should have nothing more to show him. He said, "What you seek in vain for, half your life, one day you come full upon all the family at dinner. You seek it like a dream, and as soon as you find it you become its prey." (10:437-8)

Emerson admits that Thoreau's observations of nature are much deeper and more precise than his own: Thoreau approaches nature like a biologist—recording, classifying, predicting. For him, watching nature is not a leisurely pastime but a rigorous practice. Emerson realizes this and admonishes his younger acquaintance not to reduce life to a catalogue of facts. Not quite grasping Thoreau's science, Waldo fears that Henry uses only his Understanding to perceive parts and not his Reason to apprehend the whole. Yet, Thoreau (allegedly) retorts: attending closely to facts one's entire life will one day yield gnosis. Unpredictably, overwhelmingly, one will suddenly see his place in the web of the whole, "prey" to nature's living processes. Saying this to his older companion, Thoreau suggests that it is Emerson who needs to question his way of seeing. Perhaps, Thoreau intimates, in worrying more about theory than fact, whole than part, Emerson risks missing out on such a profound revelation. Whether or not Emerson's gnosis on the common—less empirical than Thoreau's—is as deep as Thoreau's is of course not the point. The point is that Thoreau, as Walls has argued and as Emerson has here suggested, embraces *physis* more vigorously and concretely than his more philosophical contemporaries.

With these meditations on Thoreau's naturalism in mind, we can now return to the jarring "Higher Laws" chapter and read it not so much as a remnant of an adolescent Christianity or a collegiate Platonism as a dramatization of a way of seeing that is ultimately renounced in *Walden*—a step in a difficult journey toward ecological gnosis. While Thoreau degrades the wild as polluted and brutish in this chapter right in the middle of the book, he exuberantly praises this same wilderness in the end. He concludes his book by claiming that wilderness is life—"We need the tonic of wildness"; "We can never have enough of nature" (*W* 318)—and that extravagance is the way to live—"I fear chiefly lest my expression may not be *extra-vagant* enough" (324). These conclusions, intoned in the wake of another powerful gnosis in the muddy deep cut (to which I shall turn in a few sentences), resolve Thoreau's potential *agon* between spirit and matter, suggesting that Thoreau in the end overcomes his metaphysical yearning and finds his place in the turbulence.

Seen this way, Thoreau's *Walden* constitutes a more felicitous grasp of ecology than we have seen so far in Emerson, Fuller, and Melville. Published in 1854, these unbridled paeans to the wild are transitional, pushing gnostic ecology away from the intense struggles of the three writers we have so far studied and toward the more robust materialism of the 1855 Whitman. Again, Thoreau and Whitman are not different in kind from their more theoretical—and troubled—contemporaries; rather, they are different in degree—less likely to theorize and Platonize, more likely to grasp the hard fact in the glare of time.

Sporting on the Bank

Aside from his brief descent into spiritual idealism, throughout *Walden* Thoreau cultivates his early botanical insight that descent and ascent are part of the same organic process. The open-ended structure of *A Week*, modeled on swimming in endless rivers, indeed gives way to a more organic form in *Walden*, in which an early epiphany is, like a seed, fertilized to fruition in the penultimate "Spring" chapter. In this famous sequence, Thoreau retells his New Year's Eve epiphany before the deep cut. Gazing through the thawing earth, he sees liquid coalesce into leaves, forgets higher laws to play in the muck.

> Innumerable little streams overlap and interlace one with another, exhibiting a sort of hybrid product, which obeys half way the law of currents, and half way that of vegetation. As it flows it takes the forms of sappy leaves or vines, making heaps of pulpy sprays a foot or more in depth, and resembling . . . the laciniated lobed and imbricated thal-

luses of some lichens; or you are reminded of coral, of leopards' paws or birds' feet, of brains or lungs or bowels, and excrements of all kinds. . . .

When I see on the one side the inert bank . . . and on the other this luxuriant foliage, the creation of an hour, I am affected as if in a peculiar sense I stood in the laboratory of the Artist who made the world and me,—had come to where he was still at work, sporting on this bank, and with excess of energy strewing his fresh designs about. I feel as if I were nearer to the vitals of the globe, for this sandy overflow is something such a foliaceous mass as the vitals of the animal body. You find thus in the very sands an anticipation of the vegetable leaf. (*W* 305-6)

Thoreau here sees more clearly what he enacted when he fished in the stream of time: the origin and process of the cosmos. Out of the flowing mud, a figure of the first watery chaos, coherent shapes organize themselves into leaves, lobes, feet. The "Artist" melding these patterns is not a rational demiurge; rather, he is a reveler, "sporting" on the bank, "strewing" his overabundant energy into fresh beings. The primary form arising from the ooze is the leaf, Goethe's *Urbild* churning sloppy life into discrete forms.

Watching microcosms emerge from the chaos, Thoreau thinks of language—how each palpable leafy pattern is a symbol of the whole, a word of the abyss: leaf is *logos*, word frond, water made flesh. Internally, this archetypal leaf is liquid, elastic, plastic, potential (the unformed abyss, a centrifugal energy). It is a "lobe," a word embodying in sound, materially, its properties. "[L]*obe*", Thoreau writes, is "especially applicable to the liver and lungs and the *leaves* of fat, (λειβω, *labor, lapsus*, to flow or slip downward, a lapsing; λοβοζ, *globus*, lobe, globe; also lap, flap, and many other words)." This intrinsic sap presses into a more stable material form (a balance of centrifugal and centripetal forces), rendered linguistically by the liquid "B" stiffening into the more solid "F" or "V." Externally, the lobe forms "a dry thin *leaf*, even as the *f* and *v* are a pressed and dried *b* . . . with a liquid *l* behind it pressing it forward" (306). Magically, the natural process by which water takes the shape of the leaf is enacted by the word "leaf." The word "leaf," like a biological leaf, bears the content, form, and sound of nature. It is a synecdoche for an organic principle (nature's "constant cypher," an outward form of a pervasive energy, like water); it embodies both formless energy, fluid (figured by "l" pushing into the "b"), and evolving form (represented by "f" and "v"); and it intones the rhythms of creation (liquid "l," alveolar sonorant, flowing into bilabial voiced stop "b," forming into labiodental voiceless spirant "f").

Experiencing this process, Thoreau understands the cosmos to be an epic of the leaf, a vast poem he rewrites into his own textual universe of words and water, linguistic sap and leaf. The *world* (Walden Pond and *Walden* the book) is a vast, protean *word*, resolving into definite *leaf*, dissolving to liquid *lobe*, vacillating between *b* and *f*, *dynamis* (potential) and *entelecheia* (actuality), endlessly metamorphosing into water, leaf, fish, bird: "The feathers and wings of birds are still drier and thinner leaves. . . . The very globe continually transcends and translates itself. . . . The whole tree itself is but one leaf, and rivers are still vaster leaves whose pulp is intervening earth, and towns and cities are the ova of insects in their axils" (*W* 307).

"Transcendence" and "translation" are yet more general tropes for the diffusion of water, subsuming "swimming" and "planting" into a more global process. The world's water, its sap, turns (tropes, metamorphoses) itself, patterning its liquid energies into leaves of varying dryness, ranging from soggy lobes to moist fins to crisp wings. Aptly, the movement is double, up and down: translation details the process by which roots, grasping downward to earth, transform wet soil into nutriment, turn water to sap. This process of course results in transcendence, the rise of leaves toward the sun, the exhalation of oxygen, which is the sustenance of the atmosphere, liquid air. It is this double movement that Thoreau enacts at Walden Pond, both in living and writing. As a dweller, he translates earth's energy into his own in planting beans, building fires, and catching fish. This translation is the condition of his transcendence, his comprehension of laws, of ubiquitous principles, like water. In writing his book, he translates natural process into the structure of his book, troping his discrete textual world into a moist organic habitat, a huge leaf; this linguistic practice makes the book an instance of transcendent, ubiquitous law: *True as Thales said—The world was made out of water—that is the principle of all things.*

Laura Dassow Walls has beautifully summed up Thoreau's primary *Walden* vision. He "opened his eyes and saw, in the streets, fields, and forests, chaos: not the ancient void out of which man created pristine order, but a new insight into the imbrication of all order with disorder, disorder with the emergence of order, the *self*-organizing power of a chaotic nature quite apart from human desire of even presence."[29] Immediately after experiencing the sliding ooze organize itself into tenuous orders, Thoreau indeed sings a hymn to wildness, to the creative powers of chaos beyond human desires:

> Our village life would stagnate if it were not for the unexplored forests
> and meadows which surround it. We need the tonic of wildness. . . .
> We can never have enough of nature. We must be refreshed by the

117 <<< *Thoreau Over the Deep*

sight of inexhaustible vigor, vast and titanic features, the sea-coast
with its wrecks, the wilderness with its living and its decaying trees,
the thunder-cloud, the rain which lasts three weeks and produces
freshets. We need to witness our own limits transgressed, and some
life pasturing freely where we never wander. (*W* 317-8)

Following his own imperative, Thoreau concludes *Walden* by transgress-
ing his own rut, leaving the pond because he had worn a path from the door
of his hut to the shore. Like the water he finds bubbling and stewing
throughout the cosmos ("[t]he life in us is like the water in a river" [*W* 332]),
Thoreau flows over boundaries, endlessly seeking new forms of life (having
other "lives to live [323]). After swimming like a fish in *A Week*, after growing
like a plant in *Walden*, he revolves to other patterns, as seasons roll into summer, spending his last years roaming around the trunks of trees, locating life
and faith in seeds, attending to their dispersals.[30]
     In this constant flux, Thoreau carries out his most persistent advice, pith-
ily recorded around the same time he saw the deep cut dissolve into cosmic
water. In "Walking," first published in 1862 but growing from a lecture deliv-
ered in April of 1851, Thoreau asserts that "all good things are wild and free."
This essay stands as a powerful summation of Thoreau's thinking, a coda to
a life lived without principle. Fittingly, in that piece, Thoreau embraces yet
another figure of the first water: the swamp—a procreative confusion from
which temporary orders (fungi, frogs, and fables) arise.[31] Fish, leaf, seed,
swamp. Thoreau swimming, planting, dispersing, baptizing in a bog. Eddies
sloshing on the first waves in dawn. The world is made out of water. Word is
made out of world.

5 >>>
Whitman's Atoms

Ferrying

Loving journey more than destination, Whitman would often spend his summer evenings during the 1840s and '50s riding the Brooklyn ferry back and forth between his home borough and Manhattan. During the same period, in less aqueous moods, he would do the same on the horse-drawn buses in the city, moving up and down Broadway, often sitting up top with the driver (*SD* 16-9). These twilight excursions allowed Whitman to indulge in a favorite activity: moving with no end in mind, taking pleasure in merely circulating. Favoring the potential as much as the actual, the nomadic poet could open himself to possibility, never knowing what the next block would offer, always expectant, hoping for a glimpse of radiance, a sympathetic glance. These revolutions against stasis kept before Whitman's gaze a steady stream of particulars, randomly moving in and out of assemblages, coalescing into vaguely defined flocks, only to disintegrate again into unique units.

Wishing to apprehend concrete, living parts free of an abstract, stultifying principle, Whitman the bus driver, Whitman the ferryman, revolts against two primary and related world pictures of his day: Platonism (transcendent ideas are real; mundane particulars, illusory) and pantheistic organism (immanent spirit is being; particular organisms are its vehicles). Whitman found the former embodied all around him, in American Christians and Swedenborgians as well as in—at times (as we have seen)—Emerson, Fuller, and Thoreau. The latter Whitman also discovered in Emerson and his circle, who occasionally drew from the pantheistic passages in Wordsworth and Coleridge. While Whitman of course was influenced by both of these traditions (he was always drawn to Quakerism; he was brought to a boil by Emerson), he very often found them stifling: unworldly barriers against free movement. The Platonist (and Christian) would degrade the particular to a mere cipher of the universal; the pantheist would reduce individual organisms to modes of spirit. The impetuous Whitman, however, would hold evanescent, tumultuous parts free from a transcendent, orderly principle. He would see parts and particles as circulations of a capricious whole, an abysmal whim. Anything can happen, and it usually does.

Disposed to drift, Whitman in the 1850s swerved from Plato and pantheism to Lucretius, who in *De Rerum Natura* (ca. 94-55 B.C.E.) argues that things are not reflections of a timeless universal or patterns of immanent spirit but rather temporary gatherings of heterogeneous atoms, shifting multiplicities, random conglomerations. Fresh from Lucretius when writing his first, 1855 version of *Leaves of Grass*, Whitman in this iconoclastic book looks at grass and sees not unity or spirit but rather specks whirling perpetually on a boundless current of life, gathering periodically into ripples of green. In turning against such transcendentalist philosophies in his 1855 edition of *Leaves*, especially in the poem later to be titled "Song of Myself," Whitman pushes ancient atomism toward the recent nomadology of Gilles Deleuze and Felix Guattari. Inflecting Lucretius's atomism through his desire for motion, Whitman in his first version of "Song of Myself" uproots the radicle symbols of Platonism and pantheism—plant, leaf, tree, parts controlled by an orderly whole—and replaces them with Deleuze and Guattari's radical rhizomes: unstable gatherings of free parts moving in an unfettered whole.

Whitman's poem, in content and form, is literally a rhizomatic, nomadic field of grass, a sprawling, evolving ecosystem in which parts and whole enter into perpetual and unpredictable conversation. Its parts (cells and organs; tropes and figures) suddenly swerve into new combinations that alter the living currents of the whole (the abyss of life; the overall composition); this fresh whole in turn affects the dispositions of the parts, forcing them to leap into further novel forms that will again change the whole. And so on. Rhizomes (systems of endlessly branching horizontal roots, fields of grass, improvisational poems, gatherings of burgeoning cells, the living cosmos) never stop. With no stable origin (no single, discernible seed), no clear *telos* (no unalterable purpose), they move like Whitman on the boat or the bus, open always to the shifting lay of the land, ready to combine with whatever vibrates with life.

Reading the Whitman of the 1855 "Song of Myself" in light of this curious conjunction of Lucretius and Deleuze and Guattari shows that the early Whitman's persistent invocations of cosmic unity are not his efforts, as D. H. Lawrence once claimed, to conquer the many with the All or his endeavors, as Quentin Anderson has argued, to impose an imperial self onto the world.[1] While Whitman certainly spent many lines pushing for philosophical wholeness and political unity at the expense of parts and diversity, he never let go of an opposing desire to see the whole in revolving parts, to sense parts in a fluctuating whole. Certainly this tension between hierarchy and polarity, as Kerry C. Larson and David S. Reynolds have respectively shown, beset Whitman most of his life.[2] Yet, in 1855, Whitman, fresh from Lucretius and restless to circulate, emphatically extols the particular without reducing it to the whole, grasps a whole never separate from parts. His first poem stands as a manifesto of nomadic thought, a restless text that forces us to reassess his later paeans to the universal. Perhaps we will come to see Whitman's cosmos, early and late, not as a stable unity organizing unruly diversity; but rather as a boundless abyss in which atoms move in and out of temporary federations.

Indeed, we find in Whitman's 1855 "Song of Myself" something we have not yet seen in Emerson, Fuller, Melville, or even Thoreau: a *blithe, untroubled* embrace of turbulence as the primary throb of life. Unlike his predecessors, Whitman in this poem does not struggle to overcome metaphysical desire (as Nietzsche and Heidegger define it). Rather, he felicitously and persistently claims that body and soul are not separate and hierarchical but rather interdependent and polarized; that "materialism" and "positive science" must be embraced before one can apprehend the unfathomable "dimness" that breeds life. While this unclogged celebration of physical tumult may have waned in other poems, "Song of Myself" remains a full-bodied exemplar of gnostic ecology, of Romantic turbulence, a poem erotically craving the force of life.

Rhizome and Nomad

"Rhizome" is the primary trope of the nomadic thought of Deleuze and Guattari, who proffer a perpetually mobile philosophy moving on the margins of Western traditions. In *A Thousand Plateaus* (1987), Deleuze and Guattari contrast the stable tree and the errant rhizome. The tree, as imagined in traditional thought, is an unequal marriage of unity and diversity, a one controlling the many. From the root, the one, multiplicity emerges and returns: from the Platonic forms, issue particulars; from Coleridge's spirit grow plants and animals. Particulars never escape their roots. According to Deleuze and Guattari, even Modernist revisions of classical thought can partake of the same arborescent paradigm. They believe, for instance, that while Joyce's *Finnegans Wake* abandons a principal root and engrafts onto secondary, multiple roots, the novel still presupposes primal unity, to be remembered in the past, realized in the future, embraced as potentiality. Even though Joyce's words are wildly heterogeneous and mobile, shifting like kaleidoscopic images in a dream, they still assume a hidden, cyclical unity: Shem and Shaun, Humphrey Chimpden Earwicker and Anna Livia Plurabell.[3] While I would certainly disagree with this placing of Joyce in the "aborescent" tradition (he's in the gnostic line: his "unity," an abyss; his words, diaphanous echoes of soundless undercurrents), I nonetheless believe that Deleuze and Guattari's characterization of "classical" thought, including Platonism and pantheism, creates a valuable foil for Whitman's revisions.

Deleuze and Guattari replace the tree, the classical image of world and book, with the rhizome, a subterranean, horizontal stem possessing no central root, growing several directions at once. Emerging from no stable unity, rhizomes are intense multiplicities. They can be concentrated (bulbs and tubers) or distributed (weeds and crabgrass). They do not have to be botanical but can be any assemblage featuring the following principles: *connection* and *heterogeneity*, or the ability to connect to most anything other, to agglomerate—not unify—diverse elements; *multiplicity*, or the power to preclude one element from taking precedence and submitting the remainder to order; *asignifying rupture*, or the ability to start up again after being broken, to engraft with foreign elements in order to survive, like ants that won't be killed or nomadic tribes; *cartography* and *decalcomania*, or the capacity to construct tentative, revisable, open-ended patterns (maps) capable of negotiating changing terrains.[4]

In other words, the rhizome is the living image of the living world. Correctly seen, through the eyes of the nomadic thinker—the gnostic ecologist—organic processes are not stable, harmonious systems with central origins and clear purposes. Rather, they are turbulent and uncertain as much as patterned and predictable. Even the tree and the plant are really rhizomatic if they are viewed not as orderly unfoldings of a fixed, spiritual seed but as agitated outgrowths of the living abyss, as imbrications of chaos and order. For a seed or a human or an ecosystem to thrive, each must exhibit the characteristics of the rhizome. Each must be able to connect to—adapt to—heterogeneous energies and influences; must retain a balance of parts, precluding one element from submitting the rest to unmoving order; must be able to engraft with foreign elements, healing itself when sick with outside substances; must be open to new terrains, able to assimilate changes in weather, alterations in environment. Yet, and I think this is one of Deleuze and Guattari's primary and important points, most Western thinkers—pilgrims, not nomads—have ignored, consciously or not, the rhizomatic features of the cosmos and instead have reduced the universe to an unalterable system, an organism that really behaves like a machine.

Aptly, for Deleuze and Guattari, the rhizome is the primary *imago mundi* for the nomadic thinker. This peripatetic philosopher espouses rhizomatic energies that cannot be "overcoded," or reduced to predictability. He does not ground his ideas on transcendent laws from above or immanent harmonies from within. Rather, he lives with and explores what Deleuze and Guattari call the "abstract line," the shape of becoming, "abstract" because not rooted to one place. This line is "the line of flight or deterritorialization according to which they [nomads and rhizomes] change in nature and connect with other multiplicities."[5] In their effort to counter traditional ideas of energy—as transcendent or immanent spirit—Deleuze and Guattari actually associate this placeless power with mechanical force. Yet, this denomination is inaccurate, for this line is really the turbulent force of life, organic not in the pantheistic sense but in the gnostic one. The line wiggles physical energies into living beings: it is a "streaming, spiraling, zigzagging, snaking, feverish line of variation," liberating "a power of life that human beings had rectified and organisms confined, and which matter now expresses as the trait, flow, or impulse traversing it."[6] Indeed, this nomadic line, as Deleuze claims in "Nomad Thought" (1977), always counters the "administrative machines" of scientists and philosophers who attempt to reduce the world to a closed system. As a rhizomatic force, the nomadic principle is open and mobile, a decodifying surge, a principle of "embarkation" floating toward "icy subterranean streams—or toward torrid rivers," living perpetually in a "period of drifting, of 'deterritorialization,'" "beyond law, contract, or institution."[7]

These rhizomatic, nomadic shapes are always polarized without being unified. They are zig-zags; they are spirals; they are streams and rivers. Think of a nomadic tribe, ordered and unpredictable. It is organized by the shape of the land—the terrain, the location of water; yet, at the same time, it is unstable, unbound by strict code, always ready for greener pastures, ever on the verge of fragmenting into splinter groups.

For Deleuze and Guattari, America—unified and plural—is potentially the most nomadic nation, often taking the shape of the rhizome. Much of what is interesting—according to Deleuze and Guattari's canons of taste—on American soil takes the "route" of the rhizome: "the beatniks, the underground, bands and gangs, successive lateral offshoots in immediate connection with an outside." The vigor of America is the nomadic "West," with "its shifting and displaced frontier." Rejecting stable tree and steady root, America spreads outward into the grassy plains, in its better moments producing rhizomatic texts to counter the arborescent ones of Europe, growing, Deleuze and Guattari remind us, *Leaves of Grass*, a book whose first edition is literally covered with figures of grass, the weed that can thrive and spread in any terrain.[8]

Specks Dancing in a Sunbeam

Whitman opens the 1855 poem that would later be called "Song of Myself" by invoking three vehicles of his mobile poetry: "atom," "soul," "grass":

I celebrate myself,
And what I assume you shall assume,
For every atom belonging to me as good belongs to you.

I loafe and invite my soul,
I lean and loafe at my ease . . . . observing a spear of summer grass.
(*SM* 1:1-5)

As Gay Wilson Allen reminds us, when Whitman began writing this
poem, he had just come from reading *De Rerum Natura* with great interest.
In his notebook, Whitman notes that the first book of Lucretius's poem contains an "Apostrophe to Venus as the reproductive power," the second
explains "Atomic theory," and the third shows that "Body & Soul are one."[9]
Significantly, Whitman learned that atoms are nomadic: always in motion,
unbounded, moving in multiplicities. The universe is comprised of an
unlimited void and indestructible, peripatetic atoms: "[N]o rest is given to
the atoms, because there is no bottom where they can accumulate and
makeup their abode. Things go on happening all the time through ceaseless
movement in every direction; and atoms of matter bouncing up from below
are supplied out of the infinite." These atoms never achieve stable unity but
move in and out of assemblages, traveling with one group for a while only to
engraft with another later. Atoms "shed by one thing lessen it by their depar-
ture but enlarge another by their coming; here they bring decay, there full
bloom, but they do not linger there. So the sum of things is perpetually
renewed. Mortals live by mutual interchange."[10]
These atoms are not moved by a transcendent or immanent spirit.
Rather, they move "of themselves," sporadically, randomly, like the specks
dancing in a sunbeam. They are a "multitude of tiny particles mingling in
a multitude of ways in empty space within the light of the beam, as
though contending in everlasting conflict, rushing into battle rank upon
rank with never a moment's pause in rapid sequence of unions and dis-
unions." While atoms often tend to travel downward in a straight line,
they sometimes unpredictably "swerve." This swerve is creative, for it
causes the atoms to collide, the result of which is temporary agglomera-
tion into a body.

When atoms are traveling straight down through empty space by their
own weight, at quite indeterminate times and places they swerve ever so
little from their course. . . . If it were not for this swerve, everything
would fall downwards like rain drops . . . No collision would take

place and no impact of atom on atom would be created. Thus nature would never have created anything.[11]

As Michel Serres claims, this swerve, or *clinamen*, creates a turbulence in linear order, forming polarized spirals that gather atoms into ephemeral federations, living things. The *clinamen* he associates with Venus, muse of the rhizome, mother of turbulent congregations, matrix of life born from the sea. She counters, like a nomad, the laws of the linear fall, which Serres ties to Mars, upholder of the values of traditional Western thought: unity, predictability, stasis—figures of death.[12] (Indeed, Deleuze and Guattari invoke Serres's work on Lucretius to illuminate what they call "nomad science," a science that attends to rhizomatic vortices over predictable lines and circles.)[13]

It is from Lucretius that Whitman may have learned his love of motion, recognizing that nature itself exists by virtue of the nomadic principle, that organs—plants, trees, people—are really rhizomes: torsions of perpetually moving atoms. Not only bodies, but also invisible powers, like souls, are material federations of atoms. As Lucretius explains in book three, "Body & Soul are one," to use Whitman's own words. Whitman clearly has in mind Lucretius's argument that "the mind, which we often call the intellect, the seat of guidance and control of life, *is part of a man*, no less than hand or foot or eyes are parts of a whole living creature." Likewise, our vital spirit is not part of some pre-established harmony or unity but very fine atoms diffused through the body. Indeed, "*mind and spirit are interconnected* and compose between them a single substance," a material force generating the assemblages we call thought and life.[14] Whitman translates this notion into "Song of Myself," where body and soul are both material, two federations of atoms that merge into a living being. For Whitman, soul is not part of transcendent spirit, a synecdoche of Plato's forms; nor is it an agent of spiritual immanence. Rather, it is a highly active, powerfully mobile natural force, always hungry to merge with other patterns. Whitman is the poet, after all, of "materialism first and last imbuing" (*SM* 23:487).

Whitman's distinction between body and soul is not a dualistic separation of matter and mind. Rather, his distinction is between the actual and potential, the concrete body and the placeless line of becoming, the atom and the creative, connective, *clinamen*. For Whitman, body and soul are not different in kind—both are material processes, congregations of restless atoms—but in tendency—the body tends to remain separate and discrete, the soul generally dissolves and merges. Each constitutes a slightly different function in the same process, a distinct drift in the dynamic, diverse system known as "Walt Whitman." The loafing Whitman at the beginning of the poem is actual—a real, visible, concrete body—but at the same time, he is potential, a principle of mobility capable of connecting with most any other confederation of atoms. And it is Whitman's soul that is this power of connection, the creative swerve, a power that distributes Whitman's body through other confederations, meshes it with other rhizomes. Through the agency of his soul, he ceases to be, as Donald Pease claims, a "subjective identity and becomes instead a democratic relation," a process of connection.[15] His body (his ponderous atoms) loafing, he activates his soul (his imponderable atoms), inviting it; immediately, he observes a blade of grass, a gathering of atoms with which he merges, as a goose joins its flock. This gang of soul and grass atoms distributes Whitman throughout the universe.

Early in the poem, grass always appears immediately after Whitman's body and soul act in concert. Right after the opening quoted above, right after he invites his soul and looks to the grass, he embarks on a nomadic journey through other beings. After observing the grass, the moves to and joins the atmosphere:

> It is for my mouth forever . . . I am in love with it,
> I will go to the bank by the wood and become undisguised and naked,
> I am mad for it to be in contact with me. (*SM* 2:10-2)

From grass to atmosphere, he migrates to his own breath, his entire respiratory system, heart, blood, and lungs. From there, he moves to his sense of smell, and the scent of leaves, shore, rocks, hay. Then he goes to his ears, hearing the words of his voice, these words "loosed to eddies of the wind." Then to touch: "[a] few light kisses. . . . a few embraces. . . . a reaching of arms" (2:12-2).

The same congeries of body, soul, and grass occurs a few sections later, in the famous part five in which Whitman's body and soul amorously intertwine. Returning to his initial loafing after a journey through a rich world of particulars—air, hay, rocks, he again invokes his soul, this time to an assignation. His soul opens his shirt, plunges its tongue into his "barestript heart." Penetrated by soul, Whitman's body again expands, feels its potential to be connected to other congregations: he spreads with peace and joy and knowledge, relating to God as older brother, men likewise as brothers, woman as sisters, the creative love of the universe, the limitless leaves in the fields, the brown ants under earth, the "mossy scabs of the wormfence, and heaped stones, and elder and mullen and pokeweed" (*SM* 5:75-89). After this expansion, Whitman immediately returns to the grass in the beginning of the next section, picturing a child coming to him to ask, "What is the grass?" This question prompts yet further migrations; indeed, it could be said to fuel the mobile form and content of the remainder of the poem.

As F. O. Matthiessen has noted, in the opening pages of his first notebook, Whitman proclaims that the grass frustrates the rational tendencies of traditional forms of knowledge: "Bring all the art and science of the world, and baffle and humble it with one spear of grass."[16] Throughout "Song of Myself," grass is Whitman's figure for the body fully realizing its soul—for the actual, the concrete, being endlessly transported by the potential. The grass, in other words, is one of Whitman's primary tropes for the rhizome. Grass, like Deleuze and Guattari's rhizome, is almost always thought of in the plural, as in *leaves* of grass. (Indeed, Deleuze and Guattari associate the rhizome with grass.[17]) A field of grass growing wild is diverse, fecund and dynamic gathering, comprised of several different strains, exploding in the sun and spreading seeds in the breeze. Each blade retains its particularity while blending with the whole field; the entire field changes with the ripple of each spear. This field can connect to most any other grouping, sprouting indiscriminately in forests, deserts, beaches, between the cracks of a city sidewalk.

Ubiquitous, restless, vigorous, grass is an unsettling figure. Soon after his body and soul become fully aware of one another in their moment of sexual unity, Whitman describes the agitated relationship among body, soul, and grass: "I guess it must be the flag of my disposition, out of hopeful green stuff woven" (*SM* 6:92). Grass as a flag is both an emblem and a vanguard; it symbolizes as well as leads the charge, standing at the prow. It is avant-garde, always forward looking, advancing over unknown plans. It is the standard of the nomad. It is offered as the image, importantly, of Whitman's "disposition," an apt word for detailing his rhizomatic self. First, obviously, Whitman's disposition is his mood or temperament, his habitual way of thinking, speaking, acting. At the same time, his disposition is his arrangement or distribution—in this case, his atoms and their potential to swerve and to connect, his federation of body and soul. Of course, this arrangement is never self-contained or submissive to an external or internal harmony; indeed, disposition derives from the Latin *dis* (apart) and *ponere* (to put). Whitman's atoms are held apart, as repulsive as they are attractive, as likely to merge with other groups of atoms as to stay with Whitman's own federation. The etymology reminds us that "disposition" is a version of the verb "dispose," which means, among other things, "to transfer or to part with." Whitman exists in transferring himself, like grass, over infinite terrains, itinerantly parting with one congregation to join the next.

Void and Plenitude

Here I briefly pause on the atom. Are Whitman's atoms, like Newton's, discrete, massy, impenetrable bits moving and combining in a void? Or, on the contrary, are they—more like Faraday's—"spherules of force," unique, whirling patterns of a plenitude of energy? We might look to Lucretius for an answer. Certainly Lucretius claims, like Newton, that only two components make up the cosmos—atoms and the void. Yet, Lucretius also believes, closer to Faraday, that an oceanic power, figured by Venus who rises from the sea, pervades, animates, and combines these atoms. Serres, Lucretius's great disciple, also sees Lucretius in both lights: he realizes that for Lucretius "[b]odies are made of atoms and void" but invariably discusses Lucretius's atomic theory in terms of currents, flows, eddies, and waves.[18]

Void or plenitude? Atoms as corpuscles or spherules?

On the surface, it seems that Whitman himself will not help us answer this question: in section forty-four of the 1855 "Song of Myself," he refers to eternity as both a plenitude of "bottomless reservoirs" (*SM* 44:1136-7) and a void, a "huge first Nothing" (44:1158). Yet, as Joseph Beaver has suggested, while Whitman knew of the corpuscular theory of atoms and occasionally described atoms as if they were solid and discrete, he more often endorsed the theory of Faraday, Richard Owen (the American geologist, not the British anatomist), and James Clerk Maxwell: atoms are unique vibrations of a plenary force.[19] As Beaver notes, Whitman in *Specimen Days* (1882) invokes this latter theory. Meditating on a "cherish'd" theme for a "never-achieved poem" on "creation's incessant unrest" (which he likens to "exfoliation" and "Darwin's evolution"), Whitman quotes the following, from an undesignated scientific source, in a footnote:

The misty nebulae are moving, and besides are whirling around in great spirals, some one way, some another. Every molecule of matter in the whole universe is swinging to and fro; every particle of ether which fills space is in jelly-like vibration. Light is one kind of motion, heat another, electricity another, magnetism another, sound another. Every human sense is the result of motion; every perception, every thought is but motion of the molecules of the brain translated by that incomprehensible thing we call mind. The processes of growth, of existence, of decay, whether in worlds, or in the minutest organisms, are but motion.[20] (*SD* 289)

According to Beaver, this unidentified passage closely resembles a sequence from Owen's *Key to the Geology of the Globe* (1857). Close to Faraday, Owen believed that the sun, the source of life, is an electrical force and the source of all motion. Hence, all other forces issue from the dynamic energy of the sun:

> The phenomena of heat, light, and electricity, (the latter in all its forms,) may result from modifications of motion, (vibratory or undulatory, disturbed equilibrium, etc.,) and many facts point to a similarity or connection between volcanic, electrical, and nervous agency.[21]

These two passages suggest that the cosmos is a boundless force, likely electrical, perpetually spiraling into torsions. Indeed, as Beaver further observes, Whitman consistently refers to life as an electrical force thriving by centrifugal leaps and centripetal landings.[22] In "Song of Myself," for instance, Whitman claims that he is a pattern and conductor of electrical energy: "Mine no callous shell, / I have instant conductors all over me" (*SM* 27: 614-3); "Through me the afflatus surging and surging. . . . through me the current and index" (24: 506). Likewise, in "I Sing the Body Electric," Whitman compares the soul to an electrical charge (*LG* 121-32); he likens the sun to electricity, concluding that "Electric life [is] forever at the centre," in "From Far Dakota's Canons" (654). As forms of electricity, every atom and every combination of atoms is polarized. In "Song of Myself," Whitman is "One of that centripetal and centrifugal gang" (43:1107); he is an "eddy" who "drift[s] in lacy jags" (52:1328). Moreover, he celebrates an "unseen force centripetal, centrifugal, through space's spread" in "You Tides with Ceaseless Swell" (*LG* 705); in "A Song of the Rolling Earth," he likens the stars to "centripetal and centrifugal sisters" (268).

Whitman's atoms, then, are spherules of a boundless plenitude—Whitman "loafing" on the grass discovers the same cosmos as Emerson walking across the common. For both gnostic ecologists, atoms are discrete and distributed, concrete bodies and swellings of soul, solid and nebulous. Moreover, these atoms pattern both a plenitude *and* a void; that is, they are whirlings of an abyss that is everything and nothing—a fullness of life that is empty to reason. Whitman, as I mentioned, refers to this abyss as both an oceanic reservoir and a nothing. He also calls it "the dimness" out of which "opposite equals advance" in the "breed of life" (*SM* 3:39).

As Whitman, so Serres. Just as Whitman inflects Lucretius through the science of this day to sound the first unruly currents, so Serres in *Genesis* (1982) draws on the ancient atomist and Ilya Prigogine to rewrite biblical cosmogony. For Serres, the primal abyss (monster of chaos, unruly ocean) is not defeated and vanquished by divine light. Rather, chaos energizes order as much as order organizes chaos. The result of this relation is not the *fiat lux* but *la belle noiseuse*, the Venus of Lucretius rising turbulent from the sea, a vortex mediating between unruly drifts and balanced coherences. She— not Yahweh—is the source of being, churning the oceanic cosmos into vortices that hum. These turbulences comprise phenomena, organs and things, which, like Venus their mother, emerge from this generative ooze as beautiful noises: cacophonies harmonized, aleatory compositions. In the beginning was turbulence, "the first form": "One must imagine Venus turbulent, above the noise of the sea."[23]

Imagining Venus, we now see Whitman achieving what Serres claims for many great poets, including Lucretius: discovering scientific truth long before scientists get around to it.[24]

Experiments in Language

Whitman once referred to *Leaves of Grass* as a "language experiment."[25] Drawing from the language of science, he suggests in this phrase that his words are an attempt, a trial, an essay (like Emerson's description of design, like Thoreau's biological experiment at Walden Pond) intended to substantiate an insight. Certainly Whitman's words in "Song of Myself" do just this: they embody in form the "jelly like vibrations" and the oscillatory swings of the cosmos apprehended by Whitman as he lay on the grass.

Whitman's pages are leaves of grass, reckless shoots. As Mark Bauerlein argues, Whitman's poetic language often does not cohere into an organic form (the "organic form" of the pantheists—spiritual whole controlling parts) but rather "disintegrates" into a "plurality" of ambiguous meanings, fugitive drifts (the organic flux of the gnostic ecologist—parts and whole in a tumultuous dance).[26] The first six sections of "Song" notably substantiate this argument, resisting unity, sending the readers on their own excursions.

The "atoms," "soul," and "grass" of the first five lines are an overgrown field.

I celebrate myself,
And what I assume you shall assume,
For every atom belonging to me as good belongs to you.

I loafe and invite my soul,
I lean and loafe at my ease . . . . observing a spear of summer grass.

The poem opens with an affirmation of a unique self, an unabashed autobiographical proclamation. But who is this self? Whitman, remember, did not put a title on his first edition of the poem; only in 1881 did he call the poem "Song of Myself," after entitling it "Poem of Walt Whitman, An American" in '56 and "Walt Whitman" in the editions of the '60s and '70s. Not only does the 1855 version of the poem bear no title; it comes packaged in an anonymously published collection. From 1856 onward, Whitman published *Leaves* under his name, but not in 1855. The "self" in this first version could be anyone. "Myself" here is "everybody," an extremely plural site. The verb "celebrate" further undercuts the noun's denotative capacities. To celebrate not only means to praise or to honor; it also means to perform, as in "to celebrate a mass." "Myself," then, is both an object to be extolled and a part to be performed, a role to be acted. Its ontological status is dubious. While it is an object—a direct object—to be praised, it is also a prefabricated role, a ritualized fiction. This "self" is specific and vague, unique and plural, real and artificial.

The second proclamation of this "self" is equally unstable: "And what I assume you shall assume." Curiously, this Protean self makes what seems an authoritative command; indeed, the sentence feels more imperative than indicative. Is Whitman suggesting that we shall make his assumptions in the future or commanding that we make them right now? On what grounds can such an ill-defined self make such a claim? This "self" proclaims that we "assume" what he does. (Again the statement works on two levels, the indicative, which points to the future, and the imperative, which here refers to the present.) This proclamation suggests that we share mental presuppositions ("assumptions") and physical consumptions ("assume" derives from the Latin *assumere*, to take in) with this "self." We think the same thoughts, breathe the same air. However, "assume" expresses other meanings that uproot these significations. The word also means to put on or don, as in "to assume the mantle," and to feign or affect, as in "to assume an attitude of anger." We do not necessarily share, then, actual conditions, like thoughts and bodily processes; we could also have in common artificial coverings and deceptive acts. We share fictions, potential states, as much as the real, the actual. We are as much uprooted, roving from role to role, as grounded, moored in common opinions and biology.

In the midst of these skittish semantics, Whitman suddenly calls the law. Or so it seems. He counters the paratactical structure and vague regions of the first two lines with hypotaxis, strict logic, in the third: "For every atom belonging to me as good belongs to you." While the first two lines share no logical connection, the second and third are tightly linked. The logic goes:

You shall assume what I assume because we share the same atoms. Yet, again, this authority is dubious. Notably, Whitman does not claim that "every atom that belongs to me belongs to you" but offers the more vague construction: "every atom belonging to me *as good* belongs to you" (italics mine). This means: "My atoms might as well as belong to you; they don't really, but they could." This implies: "My atoms might not belong to you; if so, then you have no reason to assume what I assume." Whitman undercuts his own logic, his own authority. His lines are further destabilized by the pun on "atom." Certainly, an "atom" is, as we have seen, a Lucretian element. But it also echoes "Adam," the mythical common ancestor who bequeathed to us severely limited knowledge and meagre authority. If this "self" is made of "Adam," then the universal validity of his statements is highly dubious. Moreover, "atom" faintly echoes "etym," the root of "etymology," the *true* sense of a word. If these three lines have demonstrated anything, it is that words rarely possess a single, authentic meaning.

The next two lines do not unify this multivalence. Rather, they take readers further afield. In one of the more bizarre transitions in the history of poetry, Whitman suddenly leaves his aggressive proclamations and logical rigor behind to become passive and loose: "I loafe and invite my soul / I lean and loafe at my ease. . . ." What has caused this active self to become abruptly passive? What has caused him to shift from scientific terminology—"atoms"—to religious or mystical: "soul." His transition is unpredictable, certainly beyond law, as is his misspelling of "loafe."

But even this abrupt shift does not prepare readers for what follows after the ellipses: "I lean and loafe at my ease. . . . observing a spear of summer grass." Nothing has prepared readers for this transition. What does the concrete, highly specific blade of grass have to do with the vague meandering of the first three lines? Whitman's use of ellipses make his invocation of grass seem entirely improvisational. He quite literally seems to be making his poem up as he goes along, freely associating, using words to map the sporadic pulses of his mind.

These abrupt shifts define the first six sections of the poem and, indeed, the entire piece. For example, after pointing to the grass, Whitman immediately shifts to perfume, then the atmosphere, then his breath, then his heart, and so on. He does not return to the grass until section six, after exhibiting through four sections a random assortment of images and thoughts. Throughout these sections and the entire poem, Whitman generously inserts ellipses in his lines. These mark the hesitations of a mind groping for the next word, image, or idea, not really knowing what is coming next, finding joy in his own performances.

Curious Lurking Something

Reading Whitman's 1855 poem is surreal. Its words metamorphose into waving grass, which in turn dissolves into an unbounded sea. Perusing this verse is to descend into the disturbed realm of dreams—of Whitman's fancies, his boyhood reveries. As he recalls in *Specimen Days*:

> Even as a boy, I had the fancy, the wish, to write a piece, perhaps a poem, about the seashore—that suggesting, dividing line, contact junction, the solid marrying the liquid—that curious, lurking something (as doubtless every objective form finally becomes to the subjective spirit) which means far more than its mere first sight, grand as that is—blending the real and ideal, and each made a portion of the other. (*SD* 138-9)

In his 1855 "Song," Whitman figures this shifting seashore with the grass—both the image and his own words. While the seashore is an "objective form," a concrete, actual assemblage, when viewed by the "subjective spirit"—which seems a synonym for the "soul"—it is transformed to potential, a multiplicity to which he can connect. Under the gaze of the nomadic poet, all objects take on the qualities of the shore: they become heterogeneous regions, permeable to other elements, sites where opposites (solid and liquid, real and ideal) merge, where potential (suggestion, that curious lurking something) blurs and fringes the actual. The "subjective spirit" is here a solvent: it dissolves solid objects into liquid possibilities, softening connections among atoms; it opens gatherings to other groups, transforms unities into rhizomes.

Similarly, Whitman's oceanic language instructs readers to activate their souls, to merge with his lines, to transform his words into wandering bands. As he writes a few sentences later in *Specimen Days*, to live is to merge with others, to meet and fuse, to absorb each other (*SD* 139). Mutual absorption is the process of the world as rhizome. Whitman's soul, the readers' hermeneutic spirits, are principles of dissolution and connection, capable of merging with most any object—his body, the grass, a text, the shore, the atmosphere, the president, a prostitute, a beetle rolling a ball of dung. Any object or word, if seen as a region of potential, can be turned into a rhizome. It is all in the seeing.

The Gnosis of Loafing

Whitman's mode of seeing—like Goethe's, Emerson's, Fuller's, Melville's, and Thoreau's—blends the rigor of positivistic science with the play of poetry. As with these forebears, Whitman always holds hard to the palpable, to the fact of the scientist:

A word of reality . . . . materialism first and last imbuing

Hurrah for positive science! Long live exact demonstration!

Gentlemen, I receive you, and attach and clasp hands with you,
The facts are useful and real . . . (*SM* 23:487-8, 93-4)

Yet, though the data of the scientist are essential, they are not the ultimate but rather transitions to the beyond. As Whitman continues, these facts "are not my dwelling . . . I enter by then to an area of the dwelling" (23:494-5).

This poetic science is clearly rendered by Whitman's famous lyric "When I Heard the Learn'd Astronomer" (1865). In this brief poem, Whitman emphasizes the limitations of mere positivism. When he goes to hear an astronomer lecture about the heavens with the help of figures and charts and diagrams, he recoils when he feels that the stars are reduced to mere proof for a scientific theory:

How soon unaccountable I became tired and sick,
Till rising and gliding out I wander'd off by myself,
In the mystical moist night-air, and from time to time,
Look'd up in perfect silence at the stars. (*LG* 483)

While this piece is often used "as a piece of evidence showing Whitman's impatience with science,"[27] it is actually a precise description of Whitman's own scientific (gnostic) method. That Whitman attends the lecture proves that he is interested in positive science; he becomes tired and sick only when he thinks that scientific theories are being overemphasized as the sole registers of the real. He then leaves the institutes of positivism and enters his dwelling: gnostic science. Inspired by "unaccountable"—immeasurable—impulses, he "wanders" in the groundless dark, randomly glancing upward, finding no words to convey his experience. Like Virgil to Dante, positivistic science leads him to the paradise of the abyss but there stops short, leaving him to sound alone the undulations of the watery night air.

Whitman's playful wandering—his openness to what the landscape might yield, his sporadic glances at what captures his attention—is of a piece with his "loafing" in "Song of Myself." For Whitman, neither of these practices is mere laziness, a simple waste of time. Rather, both are *gnostic* modes requiring great discipline. As James S. Hans has shown, Whitman's loafing is not an instance of lesser attention but of "different attention," a "loosened" form of seeing that is actually more difficult than conventional modes of observation. According to Hans, most would associate attention with work. To achieve some sort of quantifiable result—the solution to a problem, new information—one must strain and hold one's gaze toward a certain object or event. Yet, as Hans further suggests, attention as work is often connected to self-interest: one tries to see something that relates to one's own ego and thus blocks out whatever does not relate.[28] Attention as work is clearly an example of conventional Western modes of observation, ranging from scientific method to philosophical theorizing. These modes always run the risk of subjecting the world to the procrustean grids of egotistical, or in this case, metaphysical desire: the rage for order.

Attention as loafing and wandering, however, tends to de-emphasize the ego. If one merely circulates and is open to whatever the landscape will reveal, one is more likely to perceive more, in both scope and depth. Think of Goethe and Emerson walking through regions of fauna, Fuller meandering around the waterfalls of Niagara, Ishmael whirling around the whale, Thoreau sailing and fishing. In each case, the observer is not looking for anything in particular, not attempting to filter the world through *self*-consciousness. Rather, each visionary is simply attempting to be *conscious* of the cosmos, relaxing philosophical and scientific agendas, merely trying to see immediately everything as it is. Of course, this requires extreme discipline. Just as Zen Buddhists must sit (practice *zazen*) for years before seeing the universe simply as it is (*satori*), so the gnostic ecologist must often wander and loaf for long periods of time before he or she can drop "mean egotism," become "nothing" to see "all."[29]

Though Whitman seems to sing of himself, he really expresses the cosmos: he is not a self-conscious ego so much as a consciousness through whose perspective we see the world fare forward. Whether he is loafing before the grass or wandering by the ocean or in the night, he reveals the universe in the light of his soul, his subjective spirit, embracing the palpable facts of the scientists only to dissolve them back into the dimness from which they came and still come.

The Open Road

Whitman's meditations on atoms, soul, and grass in the first six sections of his poem—which have inspired excursions on seeing and loafing—constitute a primer for nomadic writing and reading. After his journey in these sections—fueled by his gnosis while leaning and lounging—Whitman can claim with confidence at the end of section six that the drift of the world is constant: "all goes onward and outward. . . . and nothing collapses / And to die is different from what anyone supposed, and luckier" (*SM* 6:120-1). All is revolving, merging: death is not cessation but redistribution of atoms, connections with new groups. He elaborates, saying of "manifold objects" that "no two [are] alike, and every one good / The earth good, and the stars good, and their adjuncts all good" (7:125-6). Each particular experience is new, a fresh step in a precipitous journey. One cannot, to accelerate Heraclitus, step in the same river *once*.

These early mental excursions set the pattern for the entire 1855 "Song of Myself," a poem structured by the rhythm of travel interspersed with rests of varying length. Whitman's famous catalogues are perpetual motion, the soul connecting with as many particulars as possible; the general philosophical reflections are rest stops, some brief (a line or two in the midst of a catalogue) others longer, a night's rest (sustained sections between catalogues). Whitman's general conclusions, then, are not static claims or foundations for cities: they are fuel for further agitations. Right after Whitman's second rest ("All goes onward and outward"), he embarks, becoming, again, the grass. This time his journey is long and incredibly diverse, spreading like seeds over space. He begins by merging with a baby, staying long enough to brush flies from its face; he then moves to a "youngster and redfaced girl"; quickly, he goes to a suicide victim, the "blab of the pave," buses, sleighs, hurrahs, enemies, oaths, and duels. Then there is a brief rest, speculating on the materiality of the soul: "The souls moving along. . . . are they invisible while the least atom of the stones is visible?" Then back to the trail, to groans of "overfed or half-starved," exclamations of women giving birth, vibrating speech, and arrests of criminals (*SM* 8:140-59). He then continues, cataloging particulars for the next seven sections (nine through sixteen), ranging over almost every imaginable scene—barns, butchers, bathers, the "pure contralto"—with short rests from time to time. He only pauses for a longer rest in section seventeen, where he tries to gather a general impression from his journey so far. Realizing fully that he can "resist anything better than [his] own diversity," Whitman speculates that every particular, figured by the grass and air, is equally diverse and mobile: "This [the collection of particulars through which he has traveled] is the grass that grows wherever the land and water is, / This is the common air that bathes the globe" (17:358-9).

Rough Kosmos
Several readers of Whitman, most notably D. H. Lawrence and Quentin Anderson, have viewed his quest for the common—grass, air, atoms—as a

desire for an ordering principle that reduces diversity to unity.[30] There is a good reason for this. Right in the middle of his poem, Whitman seems to translate his observations of common atomic composition into a vision of cosmic harmony. In section twenty-four, Whitman ostensibly invokes something like the Platonic universal or pantheistic spirit, suggesting that his particularity partakes of this principle: "Walt Whitman, an American, one of the roughs, a kosmos" (*SM* 4:499). "Kosmos" can mean, of course, a harmonious whole. Is Whitman, for all his celebration of turbulence, returning to Plato or mimicking Coleridge?

If we look at the lines following his cosmic nomination and invocation of the "whole" elsewhere, we understand that he is not. Following the pronouncement of his cosmic name, Whitman claims that he has not meshed with a stable whole; rather, he remains "[d]isorderly fleshly and sensual. . . . eating drinking and breeding / No sentimentalist. . . . no stander above men and women or part from them. . . . no more modest than immodest" (*SM* 24: 500-2). (Indeed, in later editions, Whitman uses "turbulent" instead of "disorderly.") He is not controlled by invisible spirit but rather flows along with the spontaneous ("disorderly") swerves of physical ("fleshly," "sensual") atoms. He is biological, eating and drinking, made of the same stuff as other men and women.

Indeed, this whole is far from fixed. It, like the eddies that comprise it, is radically plural, comprised of centrifugal as well as centripetal forces—a huge rhizome: "I take part. . . . I see and hear the whole, / The cries and curses and roar. . . . the plaudits for well aimed shots, / The ambulanza slowly passing and trailing its red drip" (*SM* 33:856-8). Aptly, Whitman invokes the "whole" in the context of war: a multiplicity of conflicting atoms moving in the abyss, sometimes entering into temporary federations, other times bouncing off one another. The cosmos is, like Whitman himself, full of contradictions, containing "multitudes" (51:1314-6).

Whitman's early rhizomatic cosmos perhaps did not persist in his later poetry. The rhizome certainly seems banished from poems like "Passage to India" (1871), "Song of the Universal," (1874) or "Eidolons" (1876). Perhaps after the Civil War, Whitman feared free-floating particulars. However, after reading the 1855 "Song of Myself" in light of the rhizome, we wonder if Whitman's earlier, pre-Civil War invocations of unity are more Lucretian than Platonic, more celebrations of itinerant congregations than proclamations of universal laws. Perhaps "Song of the Open Road" (1856), "Crossing Brooklyn Ferry" (1856), "Out of the Cradle Endlessly Rocking" (1859), "As I Ebb'd with the Ocean of Life" (1859), "Children of Adam" (1860), and "Calamus" (1860) merit reassessment.

Reinstatement of the Vague

We realize that Whitman's nomadic thought flows not only through his own texts but through the works of later circulatory thinkers. We might think here of William James, a deep reader and admirer of Whitman, who claims in *Principles of Psychology* (1890) that consciousness is an open-ended, ever moving condition, structured as much by transitives, "places of flight," as substantives, "the resting places" (127). If we examine the workings of the mind, we realize that consciousness is not comprised of discrete bits of perceptions or thoughts, that it is not a "chain" or "train"; rather, the consciousness is "nothing jointed; it flows. A 'river' or a 'stream' are the metaphors by which it is most naturally described" (126). This stream never stops but only occasionally slows:

> Like a bird's life, it seems to be made of an alternation of flights and perchings. The rhythm of language expresses this, where every thought is expressed in a sentence, and every sentence is closed by a period. The resting-places are usually occupied by sensorial imaginations of some sort, whose peculiarity is that they can be held before the mind for an indefinite time, and contemplated without changing; the places of flight are filled with thoughts of relations, static or dynamic, that for the most part obtain between the matters contemplated in the periods of comparative rest.[31]

James laments that most philosophers, in both Lockean empirical and Kantian idealist schools, focus only on the resting places, believing the consciousness to be comprised of static links or bits logically connected to each other. However, James shows that mental substantives are temporary rests in the onward, dynamic flow of thought. The static "ideas," percepts or concepts, so valued by the philosophers are illusions. We never have the same idea twice; consciousness moves and changes as quickly as time:

> [e]very thought we have of a given fact is, strictly speaking, unique, and only bears resemblance of kind with our other thoughts of the same fact. When the identical fact recurs, we *must* think of it in a fresh manner, see it under a somewhat different angle, apprehend it in different relations from those in which it last appeared.[32]

Not only are substantives never identical; they are never definite or discrete. Objects or ideas before the mind, if we are open to the stream, always exhibit a "fringe." Any substantive idea—say, of the sky or an apple—completes a transition that has come before it and anticipates one to follow. These transitions are ever altering, based on moods, thoughts, and levels of energy. The apple we look at after reading the early chapters of Genesis will not be the same one we focus on after apple picking; a thunder clap that unexpectedly breaks into our hearing differs markedly from one we expect. In all cases, the objects or thoughts become "fringed" once they enter the consciousness, surrounded by a "halo" or "penumbra" of relations. As James observes:

> [e]very definite image in the mind is steeped and dyed in the water that flows around it. With it goes the sense of its relations, near and remote, the dying echo of whence it came to us, the dawning sense of whither it is to lead. The significance, the value, of the image is all in this halo or penumbra that surrounds and escorts it.[33]

Images in the mind are quite literally dissolved, spread backward to the sensations before them, stretched forward to the ones to follow. They are transitive and substantive, actual and potential, nouns and verbs, "vague," thresholds between past and future (130).

Writing some fifty years earlier, Whitman also wishes to emphasize mental transitions, the vagaries of flux. "Song of Myself" is structured by the rhythms of transitive and substantive; it spends section after section cataloging particulars as if they are temporary eddies in a rushing stream. Most elements in his catalogues are not substantive at all; they are pure transitions, moving Whitman from one perception to the next. Others on which he lingers longer are more durable eddies, like the woman watching the bathers (section eleven) or the fall of the Alamo (section thirty-four), yet they are still transitions, albeit longer ones, to other destinations. What we might call Whitman's substantives are his resting places, times when he pauses to reflect on a general impression, to offer a tentative conclusion.

James, like Whitman, suggests that consciousness, viewed as a stream, turns objects and thoughts into vague regions with permeable, undefined boundaries. Under the gaze of the active, dissolving consciousness (Whitman's "soul" or "subjective spirit") objects and thoughts are seen for what they really are: eddies of varying duration in the stream of time.

Drifting in Eddies

Further predicting James, Whitman continually describes atoms, his body and others, as *flows, streams, eddies in the drift*. Leaves of grass are ripples in the current.

In one of his reflective substantives, Whitman, feeling himself interpenetrating a multitude, proclaims that "To me the converging objects of the universe perpetually flow" (*SM* 20:404). Each object is like a stream with which his own stream of thought momentarily merges. As he writes a few sections later, "[t]hrough me the afflatus surging and surging. . . . through me the current and index" (24:506-7). This "afflatus"—electricity (as we have seen) as much as water or air—is the billows of the abyss whirling Whitman into his own unique current. To revolve blithely in its torsions, Whitman relinquishes "mean egotism," opening to the surge: "Mine is no callous shell / I have instant conductors all over me whether I pass or stop" (27:613-5).

Becoming permeable and interpenetrated by the flows of other objects, Whitman the eddy can become distributed throughout the universe, become a nineteenth-century space traveler. He can "rise extatic through all, and sweep with the true gravitation, / The whirling and whirling is elemental within me" (*SM* 37:953-4); he can effuse his "flesh in eddies" and drift in "lacy jags" (52:1327-8). He can become both a site through which diverse currents flow and a line of flight, revolving forward with the stream. He can know his place in the whole.

Let's think more closely about the eddy than we have before. All the water upstream flows into the eddy, converges into it to render it visible, to give it existence; the water leaving the vortex, flowing downstream, has been through the torsion, has had its current altered. The eddy is dependent on the entire flow for its existence while at the same time it alters the entire flow. The eddy is not autonomous, self-contained; it is distributed throughout the whole stream.

As Hugh Kenner, meditating on Pound's vortices (Pound on Whitman in "A Pact": "We have one sap and one root— / Let there be commerce between us."), has observed, a vortex, an eddy, is a "pattern of energy," an "integrity" shaped and made visible by the energies flowing through it. Just as a vortex is turned by the pervasive water, so iron filings are figured by the magnet, so a man:

> Imagine . . . the metabolic flow that passes through a man and is not the man: some hundred tons of solids, liquids and gases serving to render a single man corporeal during the seventy years he persists, a patterned integrity, a knot through which pass the swift strands of simultaneous ecological cycles, recycling transformations of solar energy.[34]

Seen this way, a human being, indeed any form, becomes a vortex, a relatively stable, durable pattern through which the different forces of the solar system rush—sustaining, nourishing, decaying. The stream of consciousness is ontology as much as psychology.

Destroying the Teacher

The Whitmanian eddy is of course another rhizomatic form, like grass, his own words and lines, the seashore, the flow. Fashioning himself and his poem a vortex, Whitman and his words open to the world, gathering food, sun, love, and thoughts into unique yet distributed assemblages. Opening to the currents of his words, readers themselves can likewise become numinous spirals, nomadic exegetes—readers who do not stop to make sense of Whitman so much as turn with his verse.

Whitman likely had such an ideal reader in mind at the end of his poem, which aptly concludes with an admonishment to travel. Whitman, himself tramping "a perpetual journey" (*SM* 46:1198), leaves his readers not with a comforting moral or a controlling theme—"chair . . . church [or] philosophy"—but rather with a "rain-proof coat and good shoes and a staff cut from the woods" (46:1199-1202). His final gesture: to lead his readers to a knoll and point to vast landscapes and long roads (46:1200-6). His last prescription: do not settle in this poem; leave it behind—"[h]e most honors my style who learn[s] under it to destroy the teacher" (46:1231-3).

To honor Whitman's style is to avoid imposing hermeneutic closure on its linguistic distributions, to understand its lines as directions for intellectual excursions. In this chapter (in this entire book), I have tried to honor this ethic by pointing to tendencies and potentialities rather than conceptualizing structures and evidence. In other words, I hope I have suggested more than argued, urged more than demonstrated. Where I have not, I have lapsed, unable to move with Whitman's quick parts. For Whitman would put his readers on ferries and omnibuses, with one-way tickets. His best readers—James in the stream, Pound deep in a *periplous*—have taken this lesson, gone on the road, set keel to breaker, swerved and circulated with the grass-green waves.

Conclusion
Clouds Over the Ocean

In part of a discarded draft of *Ecce Homo* (1888-9), Nietzsche had the following to say of Emerson:

> Emerson with his essays has been a good friend and cheered me up even in black periods: he contains so much skepsis, so many possibilities that even virtue achieves esprit in his writings. A unique case! Even as a boy I enjoyed listening to him.[1]

Skepsis and *esprit*: these are the qualities Nietzsche locates in Emerson, from whom, we now know, he learned the gay science and much else.[2] Emerson's mobile, fluxional philosophy—skeptical of absolute truth and psychic security—indeed vouchsafes a vision of spirit: not the idealist ghost in the organ but rather physical drifts—a nebulous cosmos in varying degrees of turbulence. For the gnostic ecologist—also a Romantic skeptic—revelation does not unveil a world that begins and ends with light—light dividing waters, light parting the clouds. Rather, the apocalypse is a matter of mist, of cumulus and cirrus. The Alpha is a noisy ocean; the Omega, a wandering cloud.

So a word on clouds, and clocks. In his 1965 Compton Memorial Lecture *Of Clouds and Clocks*, Sir Karl Popper says this of C. S. Peirce:

> Among the few dissenters [to physical determinism—the doctrine that all clouds are clocks] was Charles Sanders Peirce, the great American mathematician and physicist and, I believe, one of the greatest philosophers of all time . . . So far as I know Peirce was the first post-Newtonian physicist and philosopher who thus dared to adopt the view that to some degree all clocks are clouds; or in other words, that only clouds exist, though clouds of very different degrees of cloudiness.[3]

Long before Prigogine and Stengers meditated on stochastic processes in *Order Out of Chaos* (1984), Peirce proposed the following hypothesis in "The Architecture of Theories" (1891):

Now the only possible way of accounting for the laws of nature and for uniformity in general is to suppose them results of evolution. This supposes them not to be absolute, not to be obeyed precisely. It makes an element of indeterminacy, spontaneity, or absolute chance in nature. Just as, when we attempt to verify any physical law, we find our observations cannot be satisfied by it, and rightly attribute the discrepancy to errors of observation, so we must suppose far more minute discrepancies to exist owing to the imperfect cogency of the law itself, to a certain swerving of the facts from any definite formula.[4]

Facts minutely "swerve" from definite laws: the Lucretian *clinamen* is afoot. For Peirce, the "indeterminacy, spontaneity, and absolute chance in nature"—nature's inherent cloudiness—is not a state to be lamented. To be sure, the scientist can never figure out nature once and for all, but this is a good thing, for chance is the principle of diversification, variation, complexity—that is, of life. Predicting Prigogine and Stengers, Peirce believes that if it were not for chance, the second law of thermodynamics would run the universe down to heat death. As he observes in "The Doctrine of Necessity" (1892), in a passage that Prigogine and Stengers themselves favorably cite:

> You have all heard of the dissipation of energy [caused by entropy]. It is found that in all transformations of energy a part is converted into heat and heat is always tending to equalize its temperature. The consequence is that the energy of the universe is tending by virtue of its necessary laws toward a death of the universe in which there shall be no force but heat and the temperature everywhere the same.
>
> But although no force can counteract this tendency, chance may and will have the opposite influence. Force is in the long run dissipative; chance is in the long run concentrative. The dissipation of energy by the regular laws of nature is by these very laws accompanied by circumstances more and more favorable to its reconcentration by chance. There must therefore be a point at which the two tendencies are balanced and that is no doubt the actual condition of the whole universe at the present time.[5]

Physics is a study of law and chance, of the regularity of clouds but also of the irregularity of clocks. Biology focuses on similar mergings. As Peirce reminds us (and as Gregory Bateson emphasizes), evolutionary variations, though chosen by the law of natural selection, are products of chance, results of stochastic process.[6] Clouds are just as important as clocks, for a clock without the swerves of clouds will inevitably run down and die.

The redemption of clouds: the *esprit* (gas, mist, steam) of *skepsis*. It should not surprise us that Peirce's friend William James also discovered salvation in the clouds. Indeed, James's explorations of indeterminacy probably surpassed Peirce's, for Peirce the mathematician was out to plot chance numerically. James makes no such attempt but rather wishes, as he claims in his *Principles of Psychology* (1890), to reinstate "the vague to its proper place in our mental life."[7] As William Joseph Gavin makes clear in *William James and the Reinstatement of the Vague* (1992), this sort of statement is not unique in James's volumes, as this brief sampling of quotes suggests. From "Will to Believe": "In the great boarding-house of nature, the cakes and butter and the syrup seldom come out . . . even and leave the plates . . . clean. Indeed, we should view them with suspicion if they did"; from *Pragmatism*: "Profusion, not economy, may after all be reality's key-note" and "May there not after all be a possible ambiguity in truth"; and from *Essays in Radical Empiricism*: "[O]ur experiences, taken all togther, [are] a quasi-chaos."[8]

As we have already seen in our meditation on Whitman, James emphasizes the cloudy portions of consciousness that most philosophers and scientists have ignored. James knows that definite feelings, perceptions, and thoughts are semi-stable turbulences in the stream of consciousness, phenomena pervaded by and steeped in penumbra, fringes, and mysterious forms.[9] He develops these psychological insights philosophically in *A Pluralistic Universe* (1909), where he writes that:

[r]eality, life, experience, concreteness, immediacy, exceeds our logic, overflows and surrounds it. If you like to employ words eulogistically, as most men do, and so encourage confusion, you may say that reality obeys a higher logic, or enjoys a higher rationality. But I think that even eulogistic words should be used rather to distinguish than to commingle meanings, so I prefer bluntly to call reality if not irrational then at least non-rational in its constitution,—and by reality here I mean reality where things *happen*, all temporal reality without exception. I myself find no good warrant for even suspecting the existence of any reality of a higher denomination than that distributed and strung along and flowing sort of reality which we finite beings swim in. That is the sort of reality given us, and that is the sort with which logic is so incommensurable.[10]

James's senses of incommensurability are not, we should remember, mere exercises in deconstruction or extreme skepticism. They are meant, like Peirce's take on chance, to describe accurately the constitution of the cosmos. Moreover, in James's case, vagueness, as Richard Poirier shows in his *Poetry and Pragmatism* (1992) (in a chapter aptly titled "The Reinstatement of the Vague"), is the space in which significant toil occurs. It is in the indeterminate regions, in language and thought, that the pragmatist acts, the poet creates, the scientist discovers, the political reformer thrives. If the world were determinate, fixed once and for all, then these actions would be meaningless, mere apings of a pre-fabricated script.[11] The vague is the cumulus of cultivation, culture.

The clouds persist: it is in the nebulous atmospheres that John Dewey finds his antifoundational muse, Richard Rorty, his own edifying *daimon*. As in the case of James, both of these self-styled pragmatists blur in order to blow and to bloom: to breathe the spirit of health. James, Dewey, and Rorty, for all of their differences, take, consciously or not, the risky cosmos of Pierce as their *point de depart*: nature creates in the clouds (random mutation, entropic complexity, rain from above), so should we.

This is a legacy—a perpetual drift—of American Romanticism, its turbulent ecology and its agitated vision. It runs not only through the Dionysian *skepsis* and *esprit* of Nietzsche and his twentieth-century followers (Heidegger, Serres, Deleuze). It is also the tutelary spirit of American pragmatism, which continues to bequeath to us, to quote Poirier, a skepticism, linguistic or otherwise, that "point[s] to something beyond skepticism, to possibilities of personal and cultural renewal."[12] If pragmatism is the genius of American thought, then America remains a Romantic nation.

Clouds, in other words, need not be gloomy grammarians. They can return to one of their first uses: pillars leading nomads across the desert, veils to reveal and conceal the mystery of the divine. Think of the crepuscular cloudy sky in which Emerson becomes transparent; the mists roiling over Fuller's cataracts; the steam rising from Ishmael's head as he composes a little treatise on metaphysics; Thoreau's hazy lichens; Whitman's dissolutions into the atmosphere.

We end, as we begin, with the sublime, bottomless abyss, huge drifts suffused with light. For the sublime is precisely this: sublimation, the abrupt transformation of a solid into a gas, earth into the clouds that sustain it, the roar of the *agora* into quiet cirrus.

Notes

PREFACE

1. For Bedford's story, see "Still Frozen After All These Years," *New York Times Magazine* (Jan. 12, 1997), 7:2. For a detailed account of cryonics, see K. Eric Drexler, *Engines of Creation* (Garden City, NJ: Anchor Press/Doubleday, 1986).

2. Max Weber, "Science as Vocation," *From Max Weber: Essays in Sociology*, trans., ed., intro. H. H. Gerth and C. Wright Mills (Oxford: Oxford Univ. Press, 1946), 139.

3. Weber, *The Religion of China: Confucianism and Taoism*, trans. and ed. Hans H. Gerth, intro. C. K. Yang (New York and London: Macmillan, 1951), 247-9.

4. Weber, *The Protestant Ethic and the Spirit of Capitalism*, trans. Talcott Parsons, intro. Anthony Giddens (London and New York: Routledge, 1992), 1, 64-5, 70-5, 117-25, 180-5.

5. Martin Heidegger, *The Question Concerning Technology and Other Essays*, trans. and intro. William Lovitt (New York: Harper and Row, 1977); Herbert Marcuse, *One Dimensional Man: Studies in the Ideology of Advanced Industrial Society* (Boston: Beacon, 1966); Evelyn Fox Keller, *Reflections on Gender and Science* (New Haven and London: Yale Univ. Press, 1985); Jean-Francois Lyotard, *The Postmodern Condition: A Report on Knowledge*, trans. Geoff Bennington and Brian Massumi, fore. Frederic Jameson (Minneapolis: Univ. of Minnesota Press, 1984); Ken Wilber, *The Marriage of Sense and Soul* (New York: Random House, 1998). These and other twentieth-century critiques of "disenchantment" overtly grow out of Nietzsche or Marx but also have their roots in Romantic critiques of the Enlightenment.

6. The term "chaosmos" comes from James Joyce's *Finnegans Wake*. Philip Kuberski uses the word in his brilliant study of literature, science, and theory to describe "a unitary and yet untotalized, a chiasmic concept of the world as a field of mutual and simultaneous interference and convergence, an interanimation of the subjective and the objective, an endless realm of chance which nevertheless displays a persistent tendency toward pattern and order" (*Chaosmos: Literature, Science, Theory* [Albany: State Univ. of New York Press, 1994], 3). See also Umberto Eco's *Aesthetics of Chaosmos: The Middle Ages of James Joyce*, trans. Ellen Esrock (Tulsa: Tulsa Univ. Press, 1982).

7. Morse Peckham, "Romanticism: The Present State of Theory," *The Triumph of Romanticism: Collected Essays by Morse Peckham* (Columbia: Univ. of South Carolina Press, 1970), 76-8; *Man's Rage for Chaos: Biology, Behavior, the Arts* (Philadelphia: Chilton Books, 1965), 291-4, 314-5.

8. A. O. Lovejoy, "On the Discrimination of Romanticisms," *English Romantic Poets*, ed. M. H. Abrams (Oxford and New York: Oxford Univ. Press, 1975), 3-24.

9. Jacques Barzun, *Romanticism and the Modern Ego* (Boston: Little, Brown, 1961); René Wellek, "The Concept of Romanticism in Literary Scholarship," *Comparative Literature* 1 (1949), 1-23; 147-72; Mario Praz, *The Romantic Agony*, trans. Angus Davidson (New

York: Meridian, 1956); Peckham, "Romanticism: The Present State of the Theory";
M. H. Abrams, *Natural Supernaturalism: Tradition and Revolution in Romantic Literature* (New York: Norton, 1971); Karl Kroeber, *Ecological Literary Criticism: Romantic
Imagining and the Biology of Mind* (New York: Columbia Univ. Press, 1994); Jonathan
Bate, *Romantic Ecology: Wordsworth and the Environmental Tradition* (London: Routledge, 1991). For purposes of length, I am admittedly simplifying the complex, rich
arguments of these important critics to their primary conclusions.

10. F.O. Matthiessen, *The American Renaissance: Art and Expression in the Age of Emerson
and Whitman* (New York and Oxford: Oxford Univ. Press, 1941); John T. Irwin, *Ameri-
can Hieroglyphics: The Symbol of Egyptian Hieroglyphics in the American Renaissance*
(Baltimore and London: Johns Hopkins Univ. Press, 1983); Richard Poirier, *Poetry and
Pragmatism* (Cambridge, Mass., and London: Harvard Univ. Press, 1992); Stanley
Cavell, *In Quest of the Ordinary: Lines of Skepticism and Romanticism* (London and
Chicago: Chicago Univ. Press, 1988); Lawrence Buell, *The Environmental Imagination:
Thoreau, Nature Writing, and the Formation of American Culture* (Cambridge, Mass.:
The Belknap Press of Harvard Univ. Press, 1995); Laura Dassow Walls, *Seeing New
Worlds: Henry David Thoreau and Nineteenth-Century Natural Science* (Madison:
Univ. of Wisconsin Press, 1995); Lee Rust Brown, *The Emerson Museum: Practical
Romanticism and the Pursuit of the Whole* (Cambridge, Mass., and London: Harvard
Univ. Press, 1997); Michael Lopez, *Emerson and Power: Creative Antagonism in the
Nineteenth Century* (Dekalb: Northern Illinois Univ. Press, 1996).

11. See, for instance, Betty Jo Teeter Dobb's *The Janus Faces of Genius: The Role and
Alchemy in Newton's Thought* (Cambridge and New York: Cambridge Univ. Press,
1991); Carl Grabo's *Newton Among Poets: Shelley's Use of Science in Prometheus
Unbound* (Chapel Hill: Univ. of North Carolina Press, 1930); Shanta Kadambi, "The
Newtonian Wordsworth," Diss. Yale Univ., 1970.

12. Camille Paglia, *Sexual Personae: Art and Decadence from Nefertiti to Emily Dickinson*
(New Haven and London: Yale Univ. Press, 1990), 623-74; Joanne Feit Diehl, *Dickinson
and the Romantic Imagination* (Princeton: Princeton Univ. Press, 1981); Margaret
Homans, *Women Writers and Poetic Identity: Dorothy Wordsworth, Emily Bronte, and
Emily Dickinson* (Princeton: Princeton Univ. Press, 1980), 162-214.

13. Daniel J. Orsini, "Emily Dickinson and the Romantic Use of Science," *Massachusetts
Studies in English* 7:4/8:1 (1981), 57-69; Richard B. Sewall, *The Life of Emily Dickinson*
(Cambridge, Mass.: Harvard Univ. Press, 1974), 342-57; Eric Wilson, "Dickinson's
Chemistry of Death," *ATQ* 12:1 (March 1998), 27-44.

14. For the relationship between Emerson and Melville, see John B. Williams, *White Fire:
The Influence of Emerson on Melville* (Long Beach, CA: California State Univ. Press,
1991).

15. Christina Zwarg has lucidly discussed the complex relationship between Emerson and
Fuller in *Feminist Conversations: Fuller, Emerson, and the Play of Reading* (Ithaca and
London: Cornell Univ. Press, 1995), 1-58.

16. For connections between Emerson and Whitman, see Jerome Loving, *Emerson, Whit-
man, and the American Muse* (Chapel Hill: Univ. of North Carolina Press, 1982). Two
studies of Whitman that illuminate him in a decidedly "non-Emersonian" light are M.
Jimmie Killingsworth's *Whitman's Poetry of the Body: Sexuality, Politics, Texts* (Chapel
Hill: Univ. of North Carolina Press, 1989) and Harold Aspiz's *Walt Whitman and the
Body Beautiful* (Urbana: Univ. of Illinois Press, 1980). In my opinion, the best study of
Thoreau's intellectual divergence from Emerson is Walls' *Seeing New Worlds*.

INTRODUCTION

1. For a full account of Emerson's inflections of Faraday, see Eric Wilson, *Emerson's Sublime Science* (London and New York: Macmillan/St. Martin's, 1999), 76-97, and "Emerson and Electromagnetism," *ESQ* 42:2 (1996), 93-124.

2. Hans Jonas, *The Gnostic Religion: The Message of the Alien God and the Beginnings of Christianity* (Boston: Beacon Press, 1958), 322-3.

3. Ilya Prigogine and Isabelle Stengers, *Order Out of Chaos: Man's New Dialogue with Nature* (New York: Bantam, 1984), 3.

4. Bentley Layton, "Introduction to *The Secret Book According to John*," *The Gnostic Scriptures*, trans. and intro. Bentley Layton (Garden City, NY: Doubleday, 1987), 23.

5. Layton, *The Secret Book According to John*, *The Gnostic Scriptures*, trans. and intro. Bentley Layton (Garden City, NY: Doubleday, 1987), 32-3.

6. Jonas, 49-54; Kurt Rudolph, *Gnosis: The Nature and History of Gnosticism* (San Francisco: Harper San Francisco, 1987), 58-79; Jacques Lacarriere, *The Gnostics*, trans. Nina Rootes, fore. Lawrence Durrell (New York: Dutton, 1977), 18-9.

7. Jonas, 62-5; Rudolph, 78-84; Lacarriere, 20.

8. Layton, *Secret Book According to John*, 36-38.

9. Jonas, 74-91; Rudolph 113-34; Lacarriere, 19.

10. *Secret Book According to John*, 47-51.

11. Prigogine and Stengers, *Order Out of Chaos*, 2.

12. Prigogine and Stengers, *Order Out of Chaos*, 9-12; 147-85; 213-90.

13. Prigogine and Stengers, *Order Out of Chaos*, 291-307; 307-13.

14. J. A. Simpson and E. S. C. Weiner, et al., *Oxford English Dictionary* (Oxford and New York: Clarendon Press of Oxford Univ. Press, 1989).

15. The best general studies of Boehme remain Alexandre Koyre's *Philosophie de Jacob Boehme* (Paris: Librairie Philosophique, J. Vrin, 1929) and Hans L. Martensen's *Jacob Boehme (1575-1624): Studies in his Life and Teachings*, trans. T. Rhys Evans (London: Rockliff, 1949). See also Andrew Weeks, *Jacob Boehme: An Intellectual Biography of the Seventeenth-Century Philosopher and Mystic* (Albany: State Univ. of New York Press, 1991), 98-126; John Joseph Stoudt, *Jacob Boehme: His Life and Thought*, fore. Paul Tillich (New York: Seabury, 1968), 195-218; Nicholas Berdyaev, "Unground and Freedom," intro. *Six Theosophic Points and Other Writings*, by Jacob Boehme, trans. John Rolleston Earle (Ann Arbor: Univ. of Michigan Press, 1958), v-xxxvii. The influence of Boehme on Romantic thought is profound and probably not yet fully fathomed. Some good preliminary studies include Ronald Gray's *Goethe the Alchemist: A Study of Alchemical Symbolism in Goethe's Literary and Scientific Works* (Cambridge: Cambridge Univ. Press, 1952), 1-52; Thomas McFarland, *Coleridge and the Pantheist Tradition* (Oxford: Clarendon Press of Oxford Univ. Press, 1969), 325-32; Newton P. Stallknecht, *Strange Seas of Thought: Studies in Wordsworth's Philosophy of Man and Nature* (Westport, Conn.: Greenwood, 1977), 101-34; Kathleen Raine, *Blake and Tradition* (Princeton: Princeton Univ. Press, 1968), 360-71.

16. Three studies of Nietzsche have ably explored his conflations of chaos and order: Stanley Rosen's "Nietzsche's Image of Chaos," *International Philosophical Quarterly* 20 (March 1980), 3-23; Michel Haar's "Nietzsche and Metaphysical Language," *The New Nietzsche*, ed. and intro. David B. Allison (Cambridge, Mass., and London: MIT Press, 1985), 5-36; and Jean Granier's "Nietzsche's Conception of Chaos," *The New Nietzsche*, ed. and intro. David B. Allison (Cambridge, Mass., and London: MIT Press, 1985), 135-41. For Nietzsche's "biological" inflections of organic strife, see Alfred I. Tauber, "A Typology of Niet-

zsche's Biology," *Biology and Philosophy* 9:1 (Jan. 1994), 25-44. See also Alistar Moles, *Nietzsche's Philosophy of Nature and Cosmology* (New York: Peter Lang, 1990). Nietzsche's relationship to Romanticism is problematic and complex. While Nietzsche consistently critiques a certain "transcendentalist" version of Romanticism, he nonetheless shares major affinities with key Romantic thinkers, especially Emerson and Whitman. See, for instance, Michael Lopez, *Emerson and Power: Creative Antagonism in the Nineteenth Century* (Dekalb: Northern Illinois Univ. Press, 1996); George J. Stack, *Emerson and Nietzsche: An Elective Affinity* (Athens: Ohio Univ. Press, 1992); Stanley Cavell, *Conditions Handsome and Unhandsome: The Constitution of Emersonian Perfectionism* (Chicago: Univ. of Chicago Press, 1990), 33-63; C. N. Stavrou, *Whitman and Nietzsche: A Comparative Study of Their Thought* (Chapel Hill: Univ. of North Carolina Press, 1969); Adrian Del Caro, "Kingdom of This World: Whitman and Nietzsche Compared," *Walt Whitman: Here and Now* (Westport, Conn.: Greenwood, 1985), 193-215.

17. Anna Bramwell, *Ecology in the Twentieth Century: A History* (New Haven and London: Yale Univ. Press, 1989), 4-5.

18. Ernst Haeckel, *Generelle Morphologie der Organismen*, quoted in Bramwell, 40.

19. Bramwell, 61-3; Roderick Nash, *Wilderness and the American Mind* (New Haven and London: Yale Univ. Press, 1973), 44-66; Max Oelschlaeger, *The Idea of Wilderness: From Prehistory to the Age of Ecology* (New Haven and London: Yale Univ. Press, 1991), 110-2, 132-50.

20. Karl Kroeber, *Ecological Literary Criticism: Romantic Imagining and the Biology of Mind* (New York: Columbia Univ. Press, 1994); Jonathan Bate, *Romantic Ecology: Wordsworth and the Environmental Tradition* (London: Routledge, 1991); Lawrence Buell, *The Environmental Imagination: Thoreau, Nature Writing, and the Formation of American Culture* (Cambridge, Mass.: The Belknap Press of Harvard Univ. Press, 1995); Laura Dassow Walls, *Seeing New Worlds: Henry David Thoreau and Nineteenth-Century Natural Science* (Madison: Univ. of Wisconsin Press, 1995). For a helpful overview of Romantic ecology, see Tony Pinkney, "Romantic Ecology," *A Companion to Romanticism*, ed. Duncan Wu (Oxford and Malden, Mass.: Blackwell, 1998), 411-19.

21. F. W. J. Schelling, *Of Human Freedom*, trans. and intro. James Gutman (Chicago: Open Court, 1936):

> Following the eternal act of self-revelation, the world as we now behold it, is all rule, order and form; but the unruly lies ever in the depths as though it might break through, and order and form nowhere appear to have been original, but it seems as though what had initially been unruly had been brought to order. This is the incomprehensible basis of reality in things, the irreducible remainder which cannot be resolved into reason by the greatest exertion but always remains in the depths. Out of this which is unreasonable, reason in the true sense is born. (34)

For insightful discussions of Schelling's Boehmean belief in an original "Ungrund" that perpetually overflows order with chaos, see James Gutmann, "Introduction," *Of Human Freedom*, by F. W. J. Schelling, trans. James Gutmann (Chicago: Open Court, 1936), xxii-xxxiii; and Slavoj Zizek, "The Abyss of Freedom," intro. *Ages of the World*, by F. W. J. Schelling, trans. Judith Norman (Ann Arbor: Univ. of Michigan Press, 1997), 5-20.

22. See, for instance, Schelling's *Of Human Freedom*, 50: "[E]very nature can be revealed only in its opposite—love in hatred, unity in strife. If there were no division of the principles, then unity could not manifest its omnipotence; if there was no conflict then love could not become real."

23. See Schelling's "On the Relation of the Plastic Arts to Nature" (1807), trans. J. E. Cabot, *Critical Theory Since Plato*, ed. Hazard Adams (New York: Harcourt, Brace, Jovanovich, 1971), 448:

> The sublimest arithmetic and geometry are innate in the stars, and unconsciously displayed by them in their motions. More distinctly, but still beyond their grasp, the living cognition appears in animals; and thus we see them, though wandering about without reflection, bring about innumerable results far more excellent than themselves: the bird that, intoxicated with music transcends itself in soullike tones; the little artistic creature, that, without practice or instruction, accomplishes light works of architecture; but all directed by an overpowering spirit, that lightens in them already with single flashes of knowledge, but as yet appears nowhere as the full sun, as in man.

24. In 1829, Goethe had this to say about Romanticism of the French variation.

> I call the classic *healthy*, the romantic *sickly*. In this sense, the "Nibelungenlied" is as classic as the "Iliad," for both are vigorous and healthy. More modern productions are romantic, not because they are new, but because they are weak, morbid, and sickly; the antique is classic, not because it is old, but because it is strong, joyous, and healthy. (*Conversations of Goethe with Eckermann and Soret*, trans. John Oxenford [London: G. Bell, 1892], 380).

Of course, we know that this view is not representative, for Goethe shared major affinities with the leading Romantic theorists of his day, like Schiller, Schelling, and the Schlegels. See Ernst Behler, *German Romantic Literary Theory* (Cambridge: Cambridge Univ. Press, 1993), 1-53, 95-109, 165-80.

25. James Gleick, *Chaos: Making a New Science* (New York: Penguin, 1987), 164-7; Nicholas Vazsonyi, "Searching for 'The Order of Things': Does Goethe's *Faust II* Suffer from the 'Fatal Conceit'?," *Monatshefte* 88:1 (1996), 83; Herbert Rowland, "Chaos and Art in Goethe's *Novelle*," *Goethe Yearbook* 8 (1996), 95.

26. Gleick, 196-7; Rowland, 94.

27. Rowland, 96-7; Vazsonyi, 26.

28. Gray, *Goethe the Alchemist: A Study of Alchemical Symbolism in Goethe's Literary and Scientific Works* (Cambridge: Cambridge Univ. Press, 1952), 1-52; Adolf Portmann, "Goethe and the Concept of Metamorphosis," *Goethe and the Sciences: A Reappraisal*, eds. Frederick Amrine, Francis J. Zucker, and Harvey Wheeler (Dordecht and Boston: D. Reidel Publishing, 1987), 137-45.

29. Philip F. Rehbok, "Transcendental Anatomy," *Romanticism and the Sciences*, eds. Andrew Cunningham and Nichalos Jardine (Cambridge and New York: Cambridge Univ. Press, 1990), 144-5.

30. Goethe, *Italian Journey*, trans. W. H. Auden and Elizabeth Mayer (New York: Penguin, 1970), 366-8.

31. Karl Vietor, *Goethe the Thinker* (Cambridge, MA: Harvard Univ. Press, 1950), 19.

32. Goethe, Letter to H. W. Wackenroder, January 21, 1832, quoted in Vietor, 19.

33. Frederick Burwick, *The Damnation of Newton: Goethe's Color Theory and Romantic Perception* (Berlin and New York: Walter de Gruyter, 1986), 9; Rudolph Magnus, *Goethe as a Scientist*, fore. Gunther Schmid, trans. Heinz Norden (New York: Henry Schuman, 1949), 233.

34. Dennis L. Sepper, *Goethe Contra Newton: Polemics and the Project for a New Science of Color* (Cambridge: Cambridge Univ. Press, 1988), 45.

35. Arthur G. Zajonc, "Facts as Theory: Aspects of Goethe's Philosophy of Science," *Goethe*

and the Sciences: A Reappraisal, eds. Frederick Amrine, Francis J. Zucker, and Harvery Wheeler (Dordecht and Boston: D. Reidel Publishing, 1987), 242; Nigel Hoffman, "The Unity of Science and Art: Goethean Phenomenology as a New Ecological Discipline," *Goethe's Way of Science*, eds. David Seamon and Arthur Zajonc (Albany: State Univ. of New York Press, 1998), 166-7.

36. Alfred North Whitehead, *Science and the Modern World* (New York and Toronto: Mentor, 1925), 57-8.
37. John G. Rudy, *Wordsworth and the Zen Mind: The Poetry of Self-Emptying* (Albany: State Univ. of New York Press, 1996), 14-5.
38. Masao Abe, "The Problem of Self-Centeredness as the Root-Source of Human Suffering," quoted in Rudy, 15.
39. Quoted in Douglas Miller, "Introduction," *Scientific Studies, Goethe: The Collected Works*, vol. 12, by Johann Wolfgang von Goethe (Princeton: Princeton Univ. Press, 1988), xxi.
40. Peter Salm, *Poem as Plant: A Biological View of Goethe's Faust* (Cleveland: Press of Case Western Reserve Univ., 1971), 43-140.
41. Goethe, *Maxims and Reflections*, quoted in Max L. Baeumer, "The Criteria of Modern Criticism on Goethe as Critic," *Goethe as Critic of Literature*, eds. Karl J. Fink and Max L. Baeumer (New York and London: Univ. Press of America, 1984), 10.
42. Friedrich Schlegel, *Philosophical Fragments*, trans. Peter Firchow, fore. Rodolphe Gashé (London and Minneapolis: Univ. of Minnesota Press, 1991), 14.
43. Eric Wilson, *Emerson's Sublime Science* (New York and London: Macmillan/St. Martin's, 1999), 19-28.
44. William Herschel, "The Construction of the Heavens," quoted in Michael A. Hoskins, *William Herschel and the Construction of the Heavens* (New York: Norton, 1963), 115.
45. James Hutton, *Theory of the Earth*, quoted in A. Wolf, *A History of Science, Technology, and Philosophy in the 18th Century*, rev. D. Mckie, vol. 1 (New York: Harper, 1961), 405-7.
46. Humphry Davy, *Elements of Chemical Philosophy*, *The Collected Works of Sir Humphry Davy*, ed. John Davy, vol. 4 (London: Smith, 1839-40), 38-40.
47. Michael Faraday, *Experimental Researches in Electricity*, vol. 45, *Great Books of the Western World*, eds. Robert Maynard Hutchens, et al. (Chicago: Encyclopedia Britannica, 1952), 26-30, 220-38; "A Speculation Touching Electrical Conduction and the Nature of Matter," *Great Books of the Western World*, eds. Robert Maynard Hutchens, et al. (Chicago: Encyclopedia Britannica, 1952), 855.
48. Jean-Baptiste Lamarck, *Philosophical Zoology*, trans. Hugh Elliot (London: Macmillan, 1914). For my sense of Lamarck, I largely follow Ernst Mayr, *The Growth of Biological Thought: Diversity, Evolution, and Inheritance* (Cambridge, Mass., and London: The Belknap Press of Harvard Univ. Press, 1982), 345-58.
49. Marilyn Gaull, "Coleridge and the Kingdoms of the World," *Wordsworth Circle* 22:1 (Winter 1991), 47.
50. Whitehead, 90-105.
51. Karl Menges, "Romantic Anti-Foundationalism and the Theory of Chaos," *Romanticism and Beyond: A Festschrift for John F. Fetzer*, eds. Clifford A. Bernd, Ingeborg Henderson, and Winder McConnell (New York: Peter Lang, 1996), 45. Menges follows directly Dietrich Mathy, *Poesie und Chaos: Zur anarchistischen Komponente der fruhromantiischen Asthetik* (Munich: Weixler, 1984), and indirectly Morse Peckham, *Man's Rage for Chaos: Biology, Behavior, the Arts* (Philadelphia: Chilton Books, 1965). For a recent, provocative study of British Romanticism and postmodern indeterminacy, see

Ira Livingston, *The Arrow of Chaos: Romanticism and Postmodernity* (Minneapolis: Univ. of Minnesota Press, 1997).

52. Quoted in Menges, 45 (translation mine); Menges 45-7; 46-8; 46.

53. Lori Wagner, "Chaos and Logos in Friedrich Schlegel's Concept of Romantic Poetry and the 'Roman' Form," *European Romantic Review* 5:1 (Summer 1994), 16; Joyce S. Walker, "Romantic Chaos: The Dynamic Paradigm in Novalis's *Heinrich von Ofterdingen* and Contemporary Science," *The German Quarterly* 66:1 (Winter 1993), 43.

54. Schelling, *Of Human Freedom*, 34-5; Zizek, 5-20.

55. For Blake's concept of "Eternity"—a gnostic one—see his *Book of Urizen* (1794), 2.3.36-9; *Milton* (1804; 1809-10), 2.30.19-20, and *Jerusalem* (1804; 1818-20), 2.38.31-2, 41-2. His most famous statement on polarity ("progression" through "contraries") can be found in *The Marriage of Heaven and Hell* (1790; 1793), 4.9-11, 3.6-8 (*The Complete Poetry and Prose of William Blake*, ed. David Erdman, comm. Harold Bloom [New York: Doubleday, 1988]). For a reading of Blake, chaos, and polarity, from a Jungian perspective, see Christine Gallant, *Blake and the Assimilation of Chaos* (Princeton: Princeton Univ. Press, 1978). Hazard Adams's *Blake and Yeats: The Contrary Vision* (New York: Russell and Russell, 1968), 22-56, remains an excellent analysis of Blake's polarized vision.

56. Eric Wilson, "Coleridge's Conversing," *Southern Humanities Review* 32:1 (Winter 1998), 1-21.

57. Samuel Taylor Coleridge, *Hints Toward the Formation of a More Comprehensive Theory of Life*, *The Collected Works of Samuel Taylor Coleridge*, gen. ed. Kathleen Coburn, vol. 11 (Princeton: Princeton Univ. Press, 1969-), 510, 518-9; *Collected Letters of Samuel Taylor Coleridge*, ed. Earl Leslie Griggs, vol. 4 (Oxford: Clarendon Press of Oxford Univ. Press, 1959), 807.

58. Stallknecht, 101-40; E. D. Hirsch, *Wordsworth and Schelling: A Typological Study of Romanticism* (New Haven and London: Yale Univ. Press, 1960). See William Wordsworth, *The Fourteen-Book Prelude*, ed. W. J. B. Owen (Ithaca and London: Cornell Univ. Press, 1985), 6.593-617; "Lines Written a Few Miles Above Tintern Abbey, On Revisiting the Banks of the Wye during a Tour, July 13, 1798," 94-112, *Lyrical Ballads, and Other Poems, 1797-1800*, eds. James Butler and Karen Green (Ithaca and London: Cornell Univ. Press, 1992).

59. Henry James, *Hawthorne*, ed. Tony Tanner (London and New York: Macmillan/St. Martin's, 1968), 55-6.

60. Perry Miller, *Nature's Nation* (Cambridge, Mass.: Harvard Univ. Press, 1967), 11.

61. Richard Poirier, *Poetry and Pragmatism* (Cambridge, Mass., and London: Harvard Univ. Press, 1992), 11; 12.

62. Leo Marx, "The Full Thoreau," rev. of *The Environmental Imagination: Thoreau, Nature Writing, and the Formation of American Culture*, by Lawrence Buell, and *Seeing New Worlds: Henry David Thoreau and Nineteenth-Century Natural Science*, by Laura Dassow Walls, *New York Review of Books* 46:12 (July 15, 1999), 45.

63. Marx, *The Machine in the Garden: Technology and the Pastoral in America* (Oxford and New York: Oxford Univ. Press, 1964); R. W. B. Lewis, *The American Adam: Innocence, Tragedy, Tradition in the Nineteenth Century* (Chicago and London: Univ. of Chicago Press, 1968).

CHAPTER ONE

1. M. H. Abrams, *Natural Supernaturalism: Tradition and Revolution in Romantic Literature* (London and New York: Norton, 1971), 97-117; Thomas Weiskel, *The Romantic*

Sublime: Studies in the Structure and Psychology of the Transcendent (London and Baltimore: Johns Hopkins Univ. Press, 1976), 1-33; Raimonda Modiano, *Coleridge and the Concept of Nature* (London: Macmillan, 1985), 113-16; Albert O. Wlecke, *Wordsworth and the Sublime* (Berkeley: Univ. of California Press, 1973), 1-19.

2. Immanuel Kant, *Critique of Judgment*, trans. James Creed Meredith (Oxford: Clarendon, 1952), 90-2; Edmund Burke, *A Philosophical Enquiry into the Origins of Our Ideas of the Sublime and the Beautiful*, ed. and intro. Adam Phillips (Oxford and New York: Oxford Univ. Press, 1990), 36, 53, 113-4, 121-2.

3. Jean-Francois Lyotard, *The Postmodern Condition: A Report on Knowledge*, trans. Geoff Bennington and Brian Massumi (Minneapolis: Univ. of Minnesota Press, 1984), xxiii-xxv; 77-82.

4. Harold Bloom, *Poetry and Repression: Revisionism from Blake to Stevens* (New Haven and London: Yale Univ. Press, 1976), 235-48; Rob Wilson, *The American Sublime: The Genealogy of a Poetic Genre* (Madison: Univ. of Wisconsin Press, 1991), 5; Joanne Feit Diehl, "In the Twilight of the Gods: Woman Poets and the American Sublime," *The American Sublime*, ed. Mary Arensberg (Albany: State Univ. of New York Press, 1986), 174.

5. As I have shown in a recent review essay ("From Metaphysical Poverty to Practical Power: Emerson's Embrace of the Physical World," *ESQ* 43:1-4 [1997], 295-322), several scholars during the last decade have worked to shatter the image of the optimistic, overly idealistic Emerson. The major texts of this revisionary trend are Lee Rust Brown, *The Emerson Museum: Practical Romanticism and the Pursuit of the Whole* (Cambridge, Mass., and London: Harvard Univ. Press, 1997); Michael Lopez, *Emerson and Power: Creative Antagonism in the Nineteenth Century* (Dekalb: Northern Illinios Univ. Press, 1996); Stanley Cavell, *Philosophical Passages: Wittgenstein, Emerson, Austin, Derrida* (Oxford: Blackwell, 1995), 12-41, 91-103; David Jacobson, *Emerson's Pragmatic Vision* (University Park: Pennsylvania State Univ. Press, 1993); Richard Poirier, *Poetry and Pragmatism* (Cambridge, Mass., and London: Harvard Univ. Press, 1992); George J. Stack, *Emerson and Nietzsche: An Elective Affinity* (Athens: Ohio Univ. Press, 1992). I hope this chapter on Emerson deepens and extends this prior work.

6. James B. Twitchell, *Romantic Horizons: Aspects of the Sublime in English Poetry and Painting, 1770-1850* (Columbia: Univ. of Missouri Press, 1983), 198.

7. Bloom, *Agon: Towards a Theory of Revision* (Oxford and New York: Oxford Univ. Press, 1982), 158.

8. Eric Wilson, *Emerson's Sublime Science* (London and New York: Macmillan/St. Martin's, 1999), 40-4.

9. For an excellent meditation on Emerson's "poetic" scientific method, see Laura Dassow Walls, "The Anatomy of Truth: Emerson's Poetic Science," *Configurations* 5:3 (Fall 1997), 425-462.

10. Lopez, 4-5.

11. Wilson, *Emerson's Sublime Science*, 77-81; Eric Wilson, "Emerson and Electromagnetism," *ESQ* 42:2 (1996), 93-124.

12. Humphry Davy, *Elements of Chemical Philosophy*, Collected Works of Sir Humphry Davy, ed. John Davy, vol. 4 (London: Smith, 1839-40), 39; 132; 164.

13. Wilson, *Emerson's Sublime Science*, 83-7, 91-6; Wilson, "Emerson and Electromagnetism," 103-7.

14. Michael Faraday, *Experimental Researches in Electricity*, vol. 45, Great Books of the Western World, eds. Robert Maynard Hutchins, et al. (Chicago: Encyclopedia Britannica,

1952), 269; Barbara Giusti Doran, "Origins and Consolidation of Field Theory in Nineteenth-Century Britain: From the Mechanical to the Electromagnetic View of Nature," vol. 6, *Historical Studies in Physical Sciences*, ed. Russell McCormmach, (Princeton: Princeton Univ. Press, 1975), 134; Mary B. Hesse, *Forces and Fields: The Concept of Action at a Distance in the History of Physics* (London: Thomas Nelson and Sons, 1961), 218.

15. Faraday, "A Speculation Touching Electrical Conduction and the Nature of Matter," vol. 45, *Great Books of the Western World*. Eds. Robert Maynard Hutchins, et al (Chicago: Encyclopedia Britannica, 1952), 854-5.

16. Alfred North Whitehead, *Science and the Modern World* (New York and Toronto: Mentor, 1925), 96.

17. Karl Popper, "The Rationality of Scientific Revolutions," *Scientific Revolutions*, ed. Ian Hacking (Oxford: Oxford Univ. Press, 1981), 101.

18. Albert Einstein and Leopold Infeld, *The Evolution of Physics: The Growth of Ideas from Early Concepts to Relativity and Quanta* (New York: Simon and Schuster, 1961), 129; Werner Heisenberg, *Physics and Philosophy: The Revolution in Modern Science* (New York: Harper Torchbooks, 1958), 95.

19. There have been other studies that have developed Emerson's disruptive style from other angles. See B. L. Packer, *Emerson's Fall: A New Interpretation of the Major Essays* (New York: Continuum, 1982); Alan Hodder, *Emerson's Rhetoric of Revelation: Nature, the Readers, and the Apocalypse Within* (University Park and London: Pennsylvania State Univ. Press, 1989); Julie Ellison, *Emerson's Romantic Style* (Princeton: Princeton Univ. Press, 1984); Eric Cheyfitz, *The Transparent: Sexual Politics in the Language of Emerson* (Baltimore and London: Johns Hopkins Univ. Press, 1981).

20. Wilson, *Emerson's Sublime Science*, 160-2; Eric Wilson, "Weaving: Breathing: Thinking: The Poetics of Emerson's *Nature*," *ATQ* 10:1 (March 1996), 5-24.

21. Michel Serres, *Feux et signaux de brume, Zola* (Paris: Grasset, 1975), 17-8.

22. Serres, "Lucretius: Religion and Science," *Hermes: Literature, Science, Philosophy*, eds. Josue V. Harari and David F. Bell (Baltimore and London: Johns Hopkins Univ. Press, 1982), 98-9.

23. Sir William Thomson (Lord Kelvin), *Mathematical and Physical Papers*, vol. 1 (Cambridge: Cambridge Univ. Press, 1881), 514; Ilya Prigogine and Isabelle Stengers, *Order Out of Chaos: Man's New Dialogue with Nature* (New York: Bantam, 1984); Ilya Prigogine and G. Nicolis, *Self-Organization in Nonequilibrium Systems: From Dissipative Structures to Order Through Fluctuations* (New York: Wiley, 1977); Katherine Hayles, "Introduction: Complex Dynamics in Literature and Science," *Chaos and Disorder: Complex Dynamics in Literature and Science*, ed. Katherine Hayles (Univ. of Chicago Press, 1991), 12-4.

24. William Paulson, "Literature, Complexity, Interdisciplinarity," *Chaos and Order: Complex Dynamics in Literature and Science*, ed. Katherine Hayles (Chicago and London: Univ. of Chicago Press, 1991), 38-40.

25. Serres, "The Origin of Language: Biology, Information Theory, and Thermodynamics," *Hermes: Literature, Science, Philosophy*, eds. Josue V. Harari and David F. Bell (Baltimore and London: Johns Hopkins Univ. Press, 1982), 74.

26. Gregory Bateson, *Mind and Nature: A Necessary Unity* (New York: E. P. Dutton, 1979), 11.

27. David Bohm, *Wholeness and the Implicate Order* (London and New York: Ark Paperbacks, 1983), 11; xii.

28. James Gleick, *Chaos: Making a New Science* (New York: Penguin, 1987), 8.

29. Wilson, "Weaving: Breathing: Thinking," 18-20; Wilson, *Emerson's Sublime Science*, 159-62.

30. Lyotard, 80.

31. Philip Kuberski, *Chaosmos: Literature, Science, and Theory* (Albany: State Univ. of New York Press, 1994), 3. For a brilliant and germane discussion of the "chaosmic" possibilities of the shell, as object and trope, see also Kuberski's "The Metaphor of the Shell," *The Persistence of Memory: Organism, Myth, Text* (Berkeley: Univ. of California Press, 1992, S-93.

32. Walls, "The Anatomy of Truth"; Brown.

CHAPTER TWO

1. Margaret Fuller, "Autobiographical Sketch," *The Portable Margaret Fuller*, ed. Mary Kelley (New York: Penguin, 1994), 6-7.

2. Fuller, "Autobiographical Sketch," 8-9.

3. Christina Zwarg, *Feminist Conversations: Fuller, Emerson, and the Play of Reading* (Ithaca and London: Cornell Univ. Press, 1995), 167-73, 184-5. See also Annette Kolodny, "Inventing a Feminist Discourse: Rhetoric and Resistance in Margaret Fuller's *Woman in the Nineteenth Century*." *New Literary History* 25 (1994), 355-82; and Jeffrey Steele, "Margaret Fuller's Rhetoric of Transformation," *Woman in the Nineteenth Century: A Norton Critical Edition*, ed. Larry J. Reynolds (New York and London: Norton, 1998), 278-98.

4. Ovid, *The Metamorphoses of Ovid*, trans. Allen Mandelbaum (San Diego, New York, and London: Harcourt Brace, 1993), 3.

5. Ovid, 3-4.

6. Ovid, 5.

7. Ovid, 5.

8. Ovid, 5-8.

9. Ovid, 18-9.

10. Ovid, 20-5; 25-33; 50.

11. Plato, *The Symposium*, trans. Michael Joyce, *The Collected Dialogues of Plato*, eds. Edith Hamilton and Huntington Cairns (Princeton: Princeton Univ. Press, 1961), 189d-193c.

12. Plato, *Symposium*, 201d-212b.

13. Friedrich Nietzsche, *Will to Power*, trans. Walter Kaufmann and R. J. Hollingdale, ed. Walter Kaufmann (New York: Vintage, 1967), 309-10.

14. Frederick Augustus Braun, *Margaret Fuller and Goethe: The Development of a Remarkable Personality, Her Religion and Philosophy, and Her Relationship to Emerson, J. F. Clarke, and Transcendentalism* (Folcroft, Pa.: Folcroft, 1971), 62-70; Perry Miller, ed., *Margaret Fuller: American Romantic: A Selection from Her Writings and Correspondence* (Ithaca: Cornell Univ. Press, 1963), 77-8.

15. Margaret Fuller, "Goethe," *Margaret Fuller: American Romantic: A Selection from Her Writings and Correspondence*, ed. and intro. Perry Miller (Ithaca: Cornell Univ. Press, 1963), 91.

16. Mary-Jo Haronian, "Margaret Fuller's Visions," *ESQ* 44:1-2 (1998), 35-59.

17. Ernst Mayr, *The Growth of Biological Thought: Diversity, Evolution, and Inheritance* (Cambridge, Mass., and London: The Belknap Press of Harvard Univ. Press, 1982), 457.

18. As several scholars have noted, Goethe was significantly influenced by Plotinus and other Neoplatonists. See Karl Vietor, *Goethe the Thinker* (Cambridge, Mass.: Harvard Univ. Press, 1950), 61-4.

19. Goethe, *Italian Journey*, trans. W. H. Auden and Elizabeth Mayer (New York: Penguin, 1970), 366.

20. Allen Mandelbaum, "Afterword," *The Metamorphoses of Ovid*, trans. Allen Mandelbaum (San Diego, New York, and London: Harcourt Brace, 1993), 557.

21. Kolodny, 356-8; Urbanski, 128-30; Steele, 287.

22. Charles Capper, *Margaret Fuller: An American Romantic Life: The Private Years* (New York and Oxford: Oxford Univ. Press, 1992), 195-200.

23. *The Letters of Margaret Fuller*, 2:104, ed. Robert N. Hudspeth, quoted in Capper, 296.

24. Fuller said this during the introductory lecture to her first conversation, according to a transcript by Elizabeth Palmer Peabody, quoted in Capper, 296.

25. Zwarg, 165-7.

26. "'The Impulses of Human Nature': Margaret Fuller's Journal from June Through October 1844," eds. Martha L. Berg and Alice de V. Perry, quoted in Capper, 297.

27. Christina Zwarg, 166-7; Julie Ellison, *Delicate Subjects: Romanticism, Gender, and the Ethics of Understanding*, quoted in Zwarg, 166-7.

28. M. H. Abrams, *Natural Supernaturalism: Tradition and Revolution in Romantic Literature* (New York: Norton, 1971), 172-7, 187-92. See Fichte, *The Science of Knowledge*, ed. and trans. Peter Heath and John Lachs (New York: Meredith, 1970), 93-119; Schelling, *System of Transcendental Idealism*, trans. Peter Heath, intro. Michael Vater (Charlottesville: Univ. Press of Virginia, 1978), 5-33; Hegel, *Phenomenology of Spirit*, trans. and annot. Howard P. Kainz (University Park: Pennsylvania State Univ. Press, 1994), 50-65.

29. Friedrich von Schiller, "Letters on the Aesthetical Education of Man," *Aesthetical and Philosophical Essays*, ed. Nathan Haskell Dole (Boston: Dana Estes, 1902), 3-61.

30. Friedrich Schlegel, *Philosophical Fragments*, trans. Peter Firchow, fore. Rodolphe Gasché (Minneapolis and London: Univ. of Minnesota Press, 1991), 24.

31. Friedrich Nietzsche, *Will to Power*, 445-6; *Twilight of the Idols*, trans. R. J. Hollingdale, intro. Michael Tanner (New York: Penguin, 1990), 39-44.

32. Nietzsche, *The Birth of Tragedy Out of the Spirit of Music*, trans. Walter Kaufmann, *The Basic Writings of Nietzsche*, trans., ed., and comm. Walter Kaufmann (New York: Modern Library, 1966), 33-52; Nietzsche, *Will to Power*, 539-43; Nietzsche, *Thus Spoke Zarathustra*, trans. Walter Kaufmann, *The Portable Nietzsche*, trans., ed., and intro. Walter Kaufmann (New York: Penguin, 1982), 327-33, 340-3.

33. Martin Heidegger, *Being and Time*, trans. John Macquarrie and Edward Robinson (New York and Evanston: Harper and Row, 1962), 26-8, 49-63; Heidegger, "What is Metaphysics?" trans. David Farrell Krell, *Martin Heidegger: Basic Writings*, ed. and intro. David Farrell Krell (New York: Harper and Row, 1977), 33-52.

34. Richard Rorty, *Philosophy and the Mirror of Nature* (Princeton: Princeton Univ. Press, 1979), 8-9; 369-70.

35. For Emerson and pragmatism, see Richard Poirier, *Poetry and Pragmatism* (Cambridge, Mass., and London: Harvard Univ. Press, 1992); for Emerson and Nietzsche, see George J. Stack, *Emerson and Nietzsche: An Elective Affinity* (Athens: Ohio Univ. Press, 1992).

36. According to Capper, Fuller wasn't only enamored by Goethe (130-1, 238-9, 254-5) but also by Schiller and the Schlegels (128-30; 177-8).

37. Joan von Mehren, *Minerva and the Muse: A Life of Margaret Fuller* (Amherst: Univ. of Massachusetts Press, 1994), 178; Urbanski, "The Seeress of Prevorst: The Central Jewel in *Summer on the Lakes*," *Margaret Fuller: A Visionary of the New Age*, ed. Marie Mitchell Olesen Urbanski (Orono: Maine: Northern Lights, 1994), 156.

CHAPTER THREE

1. Nathaniel Hawthorne, *The English Notebooks, 1856-1860*, eds. Thomas Woodson and Bill Ellis, *The Centenary Edition of the Works of Nathaniel Hawthorne*, gen. eds. William Charval, et al. (Columbus, Ohio: Ohio State Univ. Press, 1997), 163.

2. Charles Feidelson, Jr., *Symbolism and American Literature* (Chicago: Univ. of Chicago Press, 1953), 32-4; Alfred Kazin, "Introduction," *Moby-Dick or, The Whale*, ed. and intro. Alfred Kazin (Boston: Houghton Mifflin, 1956), vi-ix; Robert Zoellner, *The Salt-Sea Mastodon: A Reading of Moby-Dick* (Berkeley, Los Angeles, and London: Univ. of California Press, 1973), 5-11. See also Richard H. Brodhead, *Hawthorne, Melville, and the Novel* (Chicago: Chicago Univ. Press, 1973), 151-8; Christopher Sten, *The Weaver-God, He Weaves: Melville and the Poetics of the Novel* (Kent, Ohio: Kent State Univ. Press, 1996), 164-71; Wai-Chee Dimock, *Empire for Liberty: Melville and the Poetics of Individualism* (Princeton: Princeton Univ. Press, 1989), 114-20.

3. The two texts from which I primarily draw are Gilles Deleuze and Felix Guattari, *A Thousand Plateaus: Capitalism and Schizophrenia*, trans. and fore. Brian Massumi (Minneapolis and London: Univ. of Minnesota Press, 1987), 351-423; and Deleuze, "Nomad Thought," *The New Nietzsche*, ed. David B. Allison (Cambridge, Mass., and London: MIT Press, 1985), 142-9. While I draw heavily from their concept of the "nomad," the idea of the "pilgrim" is my own, based loosely on Deleuze's notion of the "engineer" in "Nomad Thought."

4. Zoellner, 11-2.

5. Brodhead, 137.

6. The relationship between Emerson and Melville is complex. For a good overview, see John B. Williams, *White Fire: The Influence of Emerson on Melville* (Long Beach, CA: California State Univ. Press, 1991).

7. For instance, see Plato, *The Republic*, trans. Paul Shorey, *The Collected Dialogues of Plato*, eds. Edith Hamilton and Huntington Cairns (Princeton: Princeton Univ. Press, 1961), 6:509-11; 7:514-18; Descartes, *Discourse on Method and Meditations on First Philosophy*, trans. Donald E. Cress (Indianapolis, Indiana: Hackett, 1980), 57-77.

8. John Paul Wenke, *Melville's Muse: Literary Creation and the Forms of Philosophical Fiction* (Kent, Ohio: Kent State Univ. Press, 1995), 124-7.

9. Wheelwright, Philip, trans. and ed., *The Presocratics* (New York: Odyssey Press, 1966), 44-59; John Burnet, *Early Greek Philosophy* (New York: Meridian, 1957), 40-72; 130-68.

10. Friedrich Nietzsche, *Philosophy in the Tragic Age of the Greeks*, trans. and intro. Marianne Cowan (Washington, D.C.: Regnery/Gateway, 1962), 51.

11. Nietzsche, *Will to Power*, trans. Walter Kaufmann and R. J. Hollingdale, ed. Walter Kaufmann (New York: Vintage, 1968), 7-82; 310-1.

12. Nietzsche, *Thus Spoke Zarathustra, The Portable Nietzsche*, trans. and ed. Walter Kaufmann (New York: Penguin, 1982), 254-55.

13. Nietzsche, *Will to Power*, 310.

14. Martin Heidegger, "Who is Nietzsche's Zarathustra?" trans. Bernard Magnus, *Review of Metaphysics* 20:3 (March 1967), 411-31.

15. Heidegger, *On Time and Being*, trans. Joan Stambaugh (New York and San Francisco: Harper, 1972), 7-9, 57.

16. Heidegger, *Discourse on Thinking*, trans. John M. Anderson and E. Hans Freund (New York: Harper, 1966), 54-7; 68-9.

17. Heidegger, *Early Greek Thinking: The Dawn of Western Philosophy*, trans. David Farrell

Krell and Frank A. Capuzzi (San Francisco: Harper San Francisco, 1984), 70-1.

18. Heidegger, *Being and Time,* trans. John Macquarrie and Edward Robinson (New York: Harper and Row, 1962), 27-8.

19. Hans-Georg Gadamer, *Truth and Method* (New York: Seabury, 1975), 167, 236.

20. James S. Hans, *The Question of Value: Thinking Through Nietzsche, Heidegger, and Freud* (Carbondale and Edwardsville: Southern Illinois Univ. Press, 1989), 31.

21. Robert M. Greenberg, "Cetology: Center of Multiplicity and Discord in *Moby-Dick*," *ESQ* 27: 1(1981), 2; Howard P. Vincent, *The Trying-Out of* Moby-Dick (Cambridge, Mass.: Riverside, 1949), 365.

22. John Keats, *Selected Poems and Letters,* ed. Douglas Bush. (Boston: Houghton Mifflin, 1959), 261.

23. 1 *Kings* 16:33.

24. William B. Dillingham, *Melville's Later Novels* (Athens: Univ. of Georgia Press, 1986), 91-124.

25. Arthur O. Lovejoy, *The Great Chain of Being: A Study of the History of an Idea* (Cambridge, Mass., and London: Harvard Univ. Press, 1964), 144-226, 242-88.

26. Ernst Mayr, *The Growth of Biological Thought: Diversity, Evolution, and Inheritance* (Cambridge, Mass., and London: The Belknap Press of Harvard Univ. Press, 1982), 323-37, 343-57, 374.

27. Charles Darwin, "An Historical Sketch of the Progress of Opinion on the Origin of Species, previously to the Publication of This Work (1861)," *Darwin: A Norton Critical Edition,* ed. Philip Appleman (New York: Norton, 1979), 20n.

28. Karl Vietor, *Goethe as Thinker* (Cambridge, Mass.: Harvard Univ. Press, 1950), 32-8; Rudolph Magnus, *Goethe as a Scientist,* fore. Gunther Schmid, trans. Heinz Norden (New York: Henry Schuman, 1949), 116.

29. Nietzsche, *Will to Power,* 79-81.

30. Anna Bramwell, *Ecology in the Twentieth Century: A History* (New Haven and London: Yale Univ. Press, 1989), 10-1.

31. Mayr, 457; Magnus, 116-8; Vietor, 32-8; Ronald H. Brady, "The Idea in Nature: Rereading Goethe's Organics," *Goethe's Way of Science: A Phenomenology of Nature,* eds. David Seamon and Arthur J. Zajonc (Albany: State Univ. of New York Press, 1998), 95, 107.

32. Nietzsche, *Will to Power,* 343-4.

33. The best study of Melville, Darwin, and the Galapagos Islands is H. Bruce Franklin's "The Island Worlds of Darwin and Melville," *The Centennial Review of Arts and Sciences* 11 (1967), 353-70. Also see Benjamin Lease's "Two Sides of a Tortoise: Darwin and Melville in the Pacific," *Personalist* 49 (Autumn 1968), 535-7 and Mark Dunphy's "Melville's Turning of the Darwinian Table in 'The Encantadas'," *Melville Society Extracts* 79 (November 1989), 14. An interesting exception to these accounts of Melville and Darwin can be found in James Duban's "Chipping with a Chisel: The Ideology of Melville's Narrators," *Texas Studies in Literature and Language* 31:3 (Fall 1989), 341-85. In this essay, Duban argues that Darwin's *Voyage on the Beagle* sheds light on *Moby-Dick* by casting doubt on Ishmael's reliability as a narrator. As Duban suggests, Darwin in his 1839 book realizes that the travel narrator is severely limited in his ability to describe each scene accurately—in short, he is unreliable. Duban claims that Melville perhaps took this hint and cast Ishmael as untrustworthy narrator, bound—in spite of his ostensible liberal sensibility—by a racist ideology. Duban is certainly correct to suggest that Ishmael sometimes undercuts his own liberality (in his comparison of King Philip to the hunted whale and in calling his shipmates savages, for instance [355-8]). How-

ever, surely we cannot dismiss all of Ishmael's utterances as unreliable ("throw out the baby with the bath water," as it were). Indeed, what narrator is not limited by an ideology, bound by the unfair biases of his or her culture? If Ishmael occasionally exhibits the racist tendencies of mid nineteenth-century America, he more frequently proves himself a political radical, breaking down racist barriers, espousing an extreme egalitarianism. In fact, as I argue, Ishmael's Darwinian dissolutions of the great chain of being unmoor the very foundations of nineteenth-century racist hierarchies. Even if Ishmael is deluding himself at times, his most persistent observations challenge conventional and often racist distinctions between civilized and savage, progressive and primitive.

34. Charles Darwin, *The Origin of Species, Darwin: A Norton Critical Edition*, ed. Philip Appleman (New York: Norton, 1979), 109-31; Mayr, 394-469; Gillian Beer, *Darwin's Plots: Evolutionary Narrative in Darwin, George Eliot, and Nineteenth-Century Fiction* (London and Boston: Routledge and Kegan Paul, 1983), 1-78, 165-70; George Levine, *Darwin and the Novelists: Patterns of Science in Victorian Fiction* (Cambridge, Mass., and London: Harvard Univ. Press, 1988), 1-55.

35. Niles Eldredge, *Reinventing Darwin: The Great Debate of the High Table of Evolutionary Theory* (New York: Wiley, 1995), 167-97; Stephen Jay Gould, "The Evolution of Life on Earth," *Scientific American* 271:4 (October 1994), 84-91.

36. Darwin, 131.

37. An excellent and definitive study of Melville's cetological sources is Howard P. Vincent's *The Trying-Out of 'Moby-Dick'* (Carbondale: Southern Illinois Univ. Press, 1949), 121-76. See also Robert K. Wallace's "Melville, Turner, and J. E. Gray's Cetology" (*Nineteenth-Century Contexts* 13:2 [1989], 151-76). For an innovative discussion of Melville's cetological chapters in relation to "epistemological fragmentation and disarray," see Robert M. Greenberg's "Cetology: Center of Multiplicity and Discord in *Moby-Dick*," *ESQ* 27:1 [1981], 1-13.

38. Etsuko Taketani, "*Moby-Dick*: Gnostic Re-writing of History," *ATQ* 8:2 (June 1994), 126-30; Dillingham, 91-124; Thomas Vargish, "Gnostic *Mythos* in *Moby-Dick*," *PMLA* 81:5 (October 1966), 274-5.

39. Vargish, 275.

40. Kurt Rudolph, *Gnosis: The Nature and History of Gnosticism*, trans. and ed. Robert McLachlan Wilson (San Francisco: Harper San Francisco, 1987), 69-70.

41. Genesis 1:1-10; Job 41:1-34; Psalms 104:26; Isaiah 27:1; Revelation 12, 13, 14, 20.

42. James Baird, *Ishmael* (Baltimore: Johns Hopkins Univ. Press, 1956), 328-32.

43. Sten, 167-8.

44. John T. Irwin, *American Hieroglyphics: The Symbol of the Egyptian Hieroglyphics in the American Renaissance* (Baltimore and London: John Hopkins Univ. Press, 1983), 292.

CHAPTER FOUR

1. Drawing from Thoreau's journal (*J* 1:121, 140-1, 156n, 180), Robert D. Richardson Jr., details Thoreau's reading of Cudworth, Gerando, and Fenelon during the spring, summer, and fall of 1840 in *Henry Thoreau: A Life of the Mind* (Berkeley: Univ. of California Press, 1986), 78, 81. See also Robert Sattelmeyer, *Thoreau's Reading: A Study in Intellectual History* (Princeton: Princeton Univ. Press, 1988), 28-9.

2. Indeed, Cudworth has nothing good to say of Thales and his Milesian followers but condemns them as atheistic materialists (Ralph Cudworth, *The True Intellectual System of the Universe*, vol. 1 [New York and London: Garland, 1978], 113-31). In Gerando, however, Thoreau found an appreciative, detailed discussion of the life and thought of

Thales. See Joseph de Gerando, *Histoire Comparee des Systemes de Philosophie, Consideres Relativement aux Principes des Conaissances Humaines*, vol. 1 (Paris: Alexis Eymery, 1822), 334-49.

3. Francois Fenelon, *Abrege de la Vie des Anciens Philosophes, Oeuvres Completes*, vol. 7 (Geneve: Slatkine Reprints, 1971), 6-7, and Gerando, 339-44. These historians render the reports of Aristotle in *Metaphysics* (983b 7) and *De Anima* (405a 19; 411a 7). See *The Basic Works of Aristotle*, ed. and intro. Richard McKeon (New York: Random House, 1941). I have used the translations of Aristotle by Philip Wheelwright, trans. and ed., *The Presocratics* (New York: Odyssey Press, 1966), 46-7. For a lucid discussion of Thales's philosophy, see John Burnet, *Early Greek Philosophy* (New York: Meridian, 1957), 40-50.

4. Fenelon, 7, and Gerando, 339-40. For Aristotle's explanation, see *Metaphysics*, 983b 7.

5. Fenelon, 7.

6. See *Placita Philosophorum*, a circa 470 A.D. compendium of opinions on the ancient philosophers, paraphrased in Burnet, 44-5. According to Herodotus, *The Persian Wars*, 1.74, Thales predicted an eclipse that affected a battle between the Medes and the Lydians. Aristotle in his *Politics*, 1259a 9, reports that after people began mocking Thales for his poverty, he used his knowledge of the heavenly bodies to foresee a large olive crop, bought all available olive presses cheaply during the winter, and then sold them for a great profit when a huge crop of olives started to ripen during the summer.

7. Fenelon, 7.

8. Gerando, 338-9, claims that Thales was the first natural philosopher, what we would call a scientist, and compared him to Newton.

9. Wheelwright, 41-3.

10. For a good introduction to "transcendental anatomy," see Philip H. Rehbok, "Transcendental Anatomy" in *Romanticism and the Sciences*, eds. Andrew Cunningham and Nicholas Jardine (Cambridge: Cambridge Univ. Press, 1990), 144-60. Also see Philip H. Rehbok, *The Philosophical Naturalists: Themes in Early Nineteenth-Century British Biology* (Madison: Univ. of Wisconsin Press, 1983), 15-55. For discussions of Thoreau's relationship to this tradition, see Laura Dassow Walls, *Seeing New Worlds: Henry David Thoreau and Nineteenth-Century Natural Science* (Madison: Univ. of Wisconsin Press, 1995); Lawrence Buell, *The Environmental Imagination: Thoreau, Nature Writing, and the Formation of American Culture* (Cambridge, Mass: Belknap Press of Harvard Univ. Press, 1995); James McIntosh, *Thoreau as Romantic Naturalist: His Shifting Stance Toward Nature* (Ithaca and London: Cornell Univ. Press, 1974); Sattelmeyer, 26-7; Richardson, 29-30.

11. For a discussion of Thoreau's relationship to Goethe, see Walls, *Seeing New Worlds*, 34-5; Richardson, 29-30, 156-7, and Sattelmeyer, 26-7.

12. Goethe, *Italian Journey*, trans. W. H. Auden and Elizabeth Mayer (New York: Penguin, 1970), 366.

13. For accounts of Thoreau's relationship to Agassiz, see Walls, *Seeing New Worlds*, 113-5, and Walls, "Textbooks and Texts from the Brooks: Inventing Scientific Authority in America," *American Quarterly* 49:1 (March 1997), 1-25; Richardson, 365-8; and Sattelmeyer, 83-5. Walls explains that Thoreau began to move away from the abstract, natural theology of Agassiz, as well as away from the holistic tendencies of Romantic biology around 1850, and began to move toward, with the help of the work of Alexander von Humboldt, a more detailed view of the specifics of nature, ultimately sharing Charles Darwin's emphasis on diversity over unity (*Seeing* 114-30). Thoreau, I should

add, also knew of Oken, about whom he learned in 1848 from J. B. Stallo's *General Principles of the Philosophy of Nature with an Outline of Some of Its Recent Developments among the Germans, Embracing the Philosophical Systems of Schelling and Hegel and Oken's System of Nature* (Boston: Crosby and Nichols, 1848). See Sattelmeyer, 46.

14. Alexander von Humboldt, *Personal Narrative of a Journey to the Equinoctial Regions of the New Continent*, abr. and trans. Jason Wilson (New York: Penguin, 1995).

15. In *Seeing New Worlds*, Walls fully details Thoreau's reading of Humboldt, especially *Cosmos*. She argues that Humboldt's empirical attention to diversity and distribution of species led Thoreau away from the "rational holism"—her word for Romantic biology of Goethe, Coleridge, Agassiz, and Emerson—and toward a more Darwinian "empirical holism" (53-166). While certainly it is true that the post-*Walden* Thoreau was more interested in the dispersal of seeds than the ur-fluid, the ur-plant, it is equally true that during the writing of *A Week on the Concord and Merrimack Rivers* and *Walden*, Thoreau was still largely concerned with an original physical principle, the holy grail of Romantic biology or "rational holism." This fact is clearly demonstrated by Thoreau's "Spring" chapter in *Walden*, in which he, like Goethe, finds the primal leaf. For our purposes, Humboldt, it seems, would appear to the Thoreau of 1850-2 as a modern version of Thales, a Romantic biologist. Subsequently (and perhaps concurrently), however, Thoreau used Humboldt differently, as Walls shows, to help him move toward Darwin. For further discussion on Thoreau and Humboldt, see Richardson, 208-9.

16. Humboldt, *Cosmos: A Sketch of a Physical System of the Universe*, vol. 1, trans. E. C. Otte (Baltimore and London: Johns Hopkins Univ. Press, 1997), 24, 359, 24.

17. Humboldt, *Views of Nature; or Contemplations on the Sublime Phenomenon of Creation* (New York: AMS, 1970), 342.

18. For accounts of Thoreau's reading of Coleridge, see Walls, *Seeing New Worlds*, 55-60, 120; Richardson, 208-9; and Sattelmeyer, 45-7.

19. Samuel Taylor Coleridge, *Hints Toward the Formation of a More Comprehensive Theory of Life*, *The Collected Works of Samuel Taylor Coleridge*, gen. ed. Kathleen Coburn , vol. 11 (Princeton: Princeton Univ. Press 1969-), 510, 518-9.

20. As Walls, Richardson, and Sattelmeyer observe, Thoreau took extensive notes on Coleridge's *Theory of Life* at about the same time he was reading Humboldt's *Cosmos*.

21. William Blake, "A Vision of the Last Judgment," *The Complete Poetry and Prose of William Blake*, ed. David V. Erdman, comm. Harold Bloom (New York: Doubleday, 1988), 565-6.

22. Walls, *Seeing New Worlds*, 84-93. See also Joel Porte's excellent discussion of the relationship between Emerson and Thoreau in *Emerson and Thoreau: Transcendentalism in Conflict* (Middleton, Conn.: Wesleyan Univ. Press, 1966).

23. Thoreau, "Walking," *Excursions and Poems: The Writings of Henry David Thoreau* (Boston and New York: Houghton Mifflin, 1906), 245.

24. For interesting discussions of Thoreau's attraction to water, see Nina Baym's "From Metaphysics to Metaphor: The Image of Water in Emerson and Thoreau," *Studies in Romanticism* S:4 (1966), 231-234; and Joel Porte's "Henry Thoreau and the Reverend Poluphoisbois Thalassa," *The Chief Glory of Every People: Essays on Classic American Writers*, ed. Matthew J. Bruccoli (Carbondale: Southern Illinois Univ. Press), 191-210.

25. Cliff Toliver notes this pun in his article "The Re-creation of Contemplation: Walton's *Angler* and Thoreau's *Week*," *ESQ* 38:4 (1992), 293-313.

26. For an excellent discussion of Thoreau's theory of natural writing, primarily in relation

to his journal, see Sharon Cameron, *Writing Nature: Henry Thoreau's Journal* (Oxford and New York: Oxford Univ. Press, 1985).

27. As William Howarth writes in *The Book of Concord: Thoreau's Life as Writer* (New York: Viking, 1982), "The narrative line is by no means clear in *A Week*; often the digressions obscure the trip entirely" (52). However, Sherman Paul claims in *The Shores of America: Thoreau's Inward Exploration* (Urbana: Univ. of Illinois Press, 1958) that while "the expression and organization" of *A Week* "have been severely criticized," the style of the book is nonetheless "natural and organic" (197).

28. Walls, *Seeing New Worlds*, 84-93.

29. Walls, 238.

30. Thoreau, *Faith in a Seed: The Dispersion of Seeds and Other Late Natural History Writings*, ed. Bradley P. Dean, fore. Gary Paul Nabhan, intro. Robert D. Richardson, Jr. (Washington, D.C.: Island Press/Shearwater Books, 1993).

31. Thoreau, "Walking," 228, 234.

CHAPTER FIVE

1. Quentin Anderson, *The Imperial Self: An Essay in American Literary and Cultural History* (New York: Knopf, 1971), 88-165; D. H. Lawrence, "Whitman," *A Century of Whitman Criticism*, ed. Edwin Haviland Miller (Bloomington: Indiana University Press, 1969), 152-61.

2. Kerry C. Larson, *Whitman's Drama of Consensus* (Chicago and London: University of Chicago Press, 1988); David S. Reynolds, *Walt Whitman's America: A Cultural Biography* (New York: Vintage, 1996), 111-53.

3. Gilles Deleuze and Felix Guattari, *A Thousand Plateaus: Capitalism and Schizophrenia*, trans. Brian Massumi (Minneapolis: Univ. of Minnesota Press, 1987), 5-6.

4. Deleuze and Guattari, *A Thousand Plateaus*, 7-14.

5. Deleuze and Guattari, *A Thousand Plateaus*, 9.

6. Deleuze and Guattari, *A Thousand Plateaus*, 499.

7. Deleuze, "Nomad Thought," *The New Nietzsche*, ed. David B. Allison (Cambridge, Mass., and London: MIT Press, 1985), 144, 148-9.

8. Deleuze and Guattari, *A Thousand Plateaus*, 19.

9. Gay Wilson Allen, *The Solitary Singer: A Critical Biography of Walt Whitman* (New York: New York University Press, 1967), 138-40; Walt Whitman, *Notebooks and Unpublished Manuscripts*, 6 vols., ed. Edward F. Grier, *The Collected Writings of Walt Whitman*, gen. eds. Gay Wilson Allen and Sculley Bradley (New York: New York University Press, 1984), 5:1889.

10. Lucretius, *On the Nature of the Universe*, trans. R. E. Latham (New York: Penguin, 1951), 56, 62.

11. Lucretius, 63-4, 66.

12. Michel Serres, "Lucretius: Science and Religion," *Hermes: Literature, Science, Philosophy*, eds. Josue V. Harari and David F. Bell (Baltimore and London: Johns Hopkins Univ. Press, 1982), 98-103.

13. Deleuze and Guattari, *A Thousand Plateaus*, 361, 371-2.

14. Lucretius, 99, 100.

15. Donald Pease, "Blake, Whitman, Crane: The Hand of Fire," *William Blake and the Moderns*, eds. Robert J. Bertholf and Annette S. Levitt (Albany, NY: State Univ. of New York Press, 1982), 33.

16. F. O. Matthiessen, *American Renaissance: Art and Expression in the Age of Emerson and*

Whitman (New York and London:Oxford University Press, 1941), 547.

17. Deleuze and Guattari, *A Thousand Plateaus*, 18-9.

18. Serres, "Lucretius: Science and Religion," 113, 115.

19. Joseph Beaver, *Walt Whitman: A Poet of Science* (New York: Octagon, 1974), 90-1.

20. Quoted in Beaver, 91.

21. Richard Owens, *Key to the Geology of the Globe*, quoted in Beaver, 88.

22. Beaver, 85-90.

23. Serres, *Genesis*, trans. Genevieve James and James Nielson. (Ann Arbor: Univ. of Michigan Press, 1995), 121-2.

24. Serres, *Feux et signaux de brume, Zola* (Paris: Grasset, 1975), 17-8.

25. Whitman, *Walt Whitman: An American Primer*, ed. Horace Traubel (Boston: Small, Maynard, 1904), viii-ix.

26. Mark Bauerlein, *Whitman and the American Idiom* (Baton Rouge: Louisiana State Univ. Press, 1991), 9-10.

27. Beaver, 6.

28. James S. Hans, *The Mysteries of Attention* (Albany: State Univ. of New York Press, 1993), 27-33.

29. John G. Rudy's analysis of Wordsworth and Zen Buddhism is certainly just as applicable to Whitman (and perhaps to Emerson, Fuller, Ishmael, and Thoreau) as it is to Goethe. See Rudy's *Wordsworth and the Zen Mind: The Poetry of Self-Emptying* (Albany: State Univ. of New York Press, 1996), 14-5.

30. Lawrence, 152-61; Anderson, 88-165.

31. William James, *The Principles of Psychology* (New York: Dover, 1950), 243, 239, 243.

32. James, 233.

33. James, 233-48.

34. Hugh Kenner, *The Pound Era* (Berkeley: Univ. of California Press, 1971), 145-6.

CONCLUSION

1. Nietzsche, "Appendix: Variations From Nietzsche's Drafts," trans. Walter Kaufmann, *Basic Writings of Nietzsche*, trans., ed., and comm. Walter Kaufmann (New York: Modern Library, 1966), 795.

2. See George J. Stack, *Emerson and Nietzsche: An Elective Affinity* (Athens: Ohio Univ. Press, 1992); and Michael Lopez, *Emerson and Power: Creative Antagonism in the Nineteenth Century* (Dekalb: Univ. of Illinois Press, 1996). See also a recent special issue of *ESQ* (43:1-4 [1997]), edited by Lopez, dedicated entirely to the Emerson/Nietzsche connection.

3. Sir Karl Popper, *Of Clouds and Clocks*, quoted in Max H. Fisch, Max H. *Peirce, Semeiotic, and Pragmatism: Essays by Max H. Fisch*, eds. Kenneth Laine Ketner and Christian J.W. Kloesel (Bloomington: Indiana Univ. Press, 1986), 426.

4. Charles Sanders Peirce, *Values in a Universe of Chance: Selected Writings of Charles Sanders Peirce* (Garden City, NY: Doublday, 1958), 148.

5. Peirce, "The Doctrine of Necessity," quoted in Ilya Prigogine and Isabelle Stengers, *Order Out of Chaos: Man's New Dialogue with Nature* (New York: Bantam, 1984), 302-3.

6. Peirce, *Values in a Universe of Chance*, 149; 156-9; Gregory Bateson, *Mind and Nature: A Necessary Unity* (New York: E. P. Dutton, 1979), 64, 127, 145-86.

7. William James, *The Principles of Psychology* (New York: Dover, 1950), 254.

8. William Joseph Gavin, *William James and the Reinstatement of the Vague* (Philadelphia: Temple Univ. Press, 1992), 1.

9. James, *The Principles of Psychology*, 239-64.

10. James, *A Pluralistic Universe* (Cambridge, Mass., and London: Harvard Univ. Press, 1977), 212-3.

11. Richard Poirier, *Poetry and Pragmatism* (Cambridge, Mass., and London: Harvard Univ. Press, 1992), 129-68.

12. Poirier, 11.

Index

BAKER & TAYLOR